AA

D0540598

Leab

IRI

Invoice

Title: Battling for peace No

Class: 941.6094

Dublin City Libraries
Withdrawn From Stock

BATTLING
FOR PEACE

BATTLING FOR PEACE

RICHARD NEEDHAM

Northern Ireland's
longest-serving British Minister

THE
BLACKSTAFF
PRESS

BELFAST

To the people

of

Northern Ireland

First published in 1998 by
The Blackstaff Press Limited
3 Galway Park, Dundonald, Belfast BT16 2AN, Northern Ireland

© Richard Needham, 1998
All rights reserved

The right of Richard Needham to be identified
as the author of this Work has been asserted
by him in accordance with the
Copyright, Designs & Patents Act 1988.

Typeset by Techniset Typesetters, Newton-le-Willows, Merseyside

Printed in England by Biddles Limited

A CIP catalogue record for this book
is available from the British Library

ISBN 0-85640-637-6

CONTENTS

ACKNOWLEDGEMENTS

Only one person has the patience and the ability to read my handwriting and turn it into passable English. Without the uncomplaining devotion of Sissy, my wife, the manuscript would never have made the publisher. I am indebted to the editorial team, who dealt with the manuscript in a deft and economical way, and which I am sure has made the book both more readable and more understandable. Everyone at Blackstaff Press has been encouraging and supportive and have put up (stoically) with my literary demands. I also thank Mike Shaw, my agent, who found me a publisher and encouraged me to write this book when I had doubts about my style and the interest of my story.

Most of those whom I worked with or came across appear in the following pages. They are all remarkable in one way or another and for every bad egg there was a basketful of good ones. They stayed behind when many left in despair.

Particularly I would mention my four private secretaries, Aileen Porter, Catrione Garrett, Norma Sinclair and Stephen Graham – they are all exceptional. Jim Beckett reminded me of the issues surrounding the councillors' boycotts. Dan Barry cleared my memory on many of the events in the early years of my time at the Department of the Environment. Billy Pinkerton gave me much background on the Belfast and Derry initiatives. Chris Ryder made available to me his background papers and articles and I have drawn on them heavily for the chapter dealing with racketeering.

I did not keep a diary so I apologise for any minor inaccuracies on dates or places. I have also not been able to include many who deserve recognition and who made my six and a half years as a minister in Northern Ireland the most influential, demanding and exciting time of my life.

War makes rattling good history;
but Peace is poor reading.

THOMAS HARDY

PROLOGUE

THIS BOOK IS ABOUT THE THIRD ARM of the British government's strategy to resolve the Northern Ireland conflict, the little-known story of the economic and social war against violence and those who waged it on all sides. There will be no apology, justification or bogus rationalisation for the behaviour of those who murdered hope for twenty-five years in Northern Ireland.

On Thursday, 30 November 1995, I stood opposite the podium to which was pinned the seal of the President of the United States of America. I was in the Mackies factory on the Springfield Road in west Belfast. About six months earlier I had had a call telling me that President Clinton's team had picked Mackies as a possible point from which he would make his appeal to the people of the North. If that was to happen, the directors and staff would like me to be there.

Sissy, my wife, and I had spent the previous night at Forte's Posthouse Hotel in Dunmurry, near Belfast. The Northern Ireland Tourist Board had given it a three-star rating which, with its tawdry interior, its 1970s decor and its paper-thin walls, the hotel hardly deserved. In its defence, the hotel had been gutted by the Irish Republican Army (IRA) on a number of occasions. So indeed had most 'economic' targets in Dunmurry, such as Locksley's furniture store and the Black Swan pub, no doubt because the owners had jibbed at the demands of paramilitary extortionists. Dunmurry is over the

1

motorway from Andersonstown, a 'Provo' stronghold, and it had suffered. A once-prosperous suburb of Belfast, Dunmurry had become run-down, its main street lined with fast-food take-aways, shuttered shops and gap sites filled only by fading 'For Sale' signs.

We arrived at Mackies at seven o'clock in the morning. We had passed the King's Hall, Northern Ireland's Earls Court and also a terrorist target, crossed under the M1 and driven up Kennedy Way. In my years as a minister I had only once been allowed up Kennedy Way, and then with a battalion of troops and three inches of armour protecting me. Now Billy, the Mackies driver, pointed out in a matter-of-fact sort of way, the familiar landmarks of horror: a Royal Ulster Constabulary (RUC) constable had been shot dead on that corner, an army patrol had been ambushed at that spot over there. We drove up the Glen Road under the Black Mountain where an encampment of itinerant people, known as the Travellers, huddled in miserable squalor. For six and half years I had tried to find them an alternative site. They had the highest incidence of infant mortality in Ireland and the lowest life expectancy. It was a failure of mine, and on this bleak, cold morning it was the first time I could see their plight for myself.

We arrived at Mackies to find a dense queue already forming in the half-light. The police were searching the buses, but not in the determined way I had been accustomed to. There were some waves from the crowd. We went through the foyer, past the plaque with my name on it commemorating the opening of the factory, and headed for the boardroom. The glass panes that had been scarred by the stones fired by children with catapults from the neighbouring estates had been replaced. Guests were gathered round a faltering television set, awaiting the news of the landing of 'Air Force One'.

I walked back down to the main gates to watch who was coming in. On the way I ran into the chief political correspondent of the BBC, who asked me to do an interview on the *Today* programme with one of the Shankill Road community workers. Her intervention was wonderful: sparkly and coherent, she made her point about this being a very special day for all of us, perfectly.

The world and his wife were filing through the gates: Father Myles Kavanagh and Sister Mary Turley from the Flax Trust; Father Matt Wallace, another extraordinary west Belfast priest, who must by then have puffed through his first ten cigarettes of the day; Catrione Garrett, my former private secretary, who had been the force behind Belfast's Healthy City campaign; Elizabeth Bloomfield, wife of the former permanent secretary, Sir Kenneth Bloomfield, who had so nearly been murdered with all her family when her home was blown up; Jackie Redpath, an astute man who could have made a fortune anywhere but had dedicated his life to the people of the Shankill. I stayed a while wondering what thoughts were crossing their minds.

I turned and made my way to the factory floor. Everyone was working as if nothing was about. Two fitters, whom I had last seen installing a line of Linmak machines in Korea, hailed me over. Others beckoned, keen to show me what they were doing and what new equipment had come in since the factory had opened. An hour later, after we had watched the President's plane land in a cloud of Ulster spray, we went to the newly built finishing shop. It was packed. I was shown my place in the front row, one away from Hillary Clinton and two away from the only female engineering apprentice at the factory, whom the White House had insisted should sit next to Mrs Clinton.

All around me were the blue overalls of the Mackies workers. Placed in the wing to the right of the stage were the President's men – senators, congressmen and members of his Cabinet. The Secretary of State for Northern Ireland, Sir Patrick Mayhew, sitting near them, appeared surprised to see me and courteously added that if anyone from the past deserved an invitation perhaps it was me. I did not tell him that not everyone in the Northern Ireland Office (NIO) shared his view. Mo Mowlam, the impressive and feisty shadow Secretary of State for Northern Ireland, was busy making contacts. The two brave MPs for Belfast West and North, Joe Hendron and Cecil Walker, sat side by side, as did Protestants and Catholics throughout the assembly. It was an emotional moment as I looked on so many friends and acquaintances – and a few enemies too. All these people looking alike, sounding alike, often with names alike, worshipping the same God and yet divided by centuries of belonging to different masters. All believing the Almighty to be on their respective sides, yet coming together in this unlikely place to be told to put their past behind them.

Even two years previously, very few of those in the audience would have dared to come to the Springfield Road – indeed very few would even have seen the Springfield Road before. In front of me, large men in large suits to cover bulging guns were chewing gum and talking into tiny tie-pin microphones, their hands cupping their earpieces, while their searching eyes ensured that everyone was in their place. The journalists were all clustered in the gallery above the podium and there was a constant clicking of photographers' cameras. The Mackies workers lucky enough to draw tickets were watching the proceedings from the other side beyond the gallery; we could hear from the laughter that they were enjoying the crack as only the Irish can.

In swept the President's staffers, smart young men and young women who reminded me of the Downing Street 'garden girls' who work for our Prime Minister. Soon after came Hillary Clinton. I shook hands and welcomed her to Mackies, half drowned by the enormous roar which erupted at the entrance of the President. He was late; he had been up the Shankill and had stopped to buy a bag of apples!

Some of the RUC Special Protection Unit who came in with him and who had looked after me for so many years smiled at me before returning to stare icily across the sea of faces.

Two young children mounted the podium, a Protestant boy and a Catholic girl. They each read out a little message and then, holding hands aloft, invited the President to speak. More roars, more applause. The President began:

> Mackies plant is a symbol of Northern Ireland's rebirth. It has long been a symbol of world-class engineering. On this shop floor men and women of both traditions are working together to achieve common goals. Peace, once a distant dream, is now making a difference to everyday life in this land.

That the most powerful man on earth had come to Mackies was a justification of all that so many of us had long struggled for. Politics and security are the issues that grab the headlines, demand the time of the pundits, inflame the emotions and often perpetuate the divisions. But it is jobs that allow opportunity for self-respect and personal independence compared to life on the 'buroo'. It is jobs and the prospect of jobs that can do most to bring about the conditions for peace. If the President of the United States saw that, not many others had. I had spent some of the previous two hours frustratingly watching television's political sages examining and re-examining every aspect of the peace process without once remarking on the extraordinary success of the Northern

4

Ireland economy. Fatuous and offensive resemblance was made between the president of Sinn Féin, Gerry Adams, and the assassinated Israeli Prime Minister, Yitzak Rabin. Sinn Féin was compared to the African National Congress (ANC) as if President Nelson Mandela and the egregious Martin McGuinness might have something in common, or as if Sinn Féin's 10 per cent share of the Northern Ireland vote might provide them with a mandate similar to that of the ANC in South Africa.

That Mackies, a textiles machinery manufacturer, had survived at all was something of a marvel. The greatest movement of people in Western Europe since 1945 had taken place in Belfast in 1969, as communal violence swept the city. The Protestants to the west of the Mackies site were driven northwards and eastwards. The traditional routes for Mackies workers from the Shankill became more and more dangerous. Mackies was a Protestant plant run by a Protestant family. In 1969, the Catholic workforce constituted, at most, 10–15 per cent of the whole. They were mainly employed in dirty foundry jobs, where they were referred to as 'strong backs', implying little brains. Every July, the factory was festooned with flags and emblems as the beleaguered and ever-reducing number of workers paraded their loyalism around the plant. To the IRA, Mackies was an orange stain on an increasing carpet of green. Attack followed attack. In 1976, an explosion ruptured the oil tanks and fired the machine shop. In 1986, the IRA forced their way into the front hall and damaged the offices so much that they had to be sealed up. The site and its buildings became ever more scarred, ever more dilapidated. Men came to work in groups, arriving early and leaving early. The costs of securing the site were crippling the factory. By 1988, the game was up for Mackies. The last manufacturing employer of any consequence in west Belfast seemed doomed. When in 1985 I had become Minister of the Environment I had known of the growing crisis at Mackies, but the responsibility for its future was not mine.

The Department of the Environment in Northern Ireland had devised a set of strategic plans for the regeneration of Belfast. But zoning land for residential, industrial, commercial or recreational use was only of value if these sites could be developed, usually with a mixture of private and public money, with the support of the communities. A dry, remote plan covered with technical jargon and surrounded by legalistic, pompous caveats was not going to persuade deprived and desperate

5

people that government, especially the sensitively named Northern Ireland Office, could change life on the ground for the better. By 1989 we had crafted a design for the regeneration of west Belfast which hinged on a tongue of land running north to south across the sectarian divide. We called it the Springvale project. This was to be the government's offensive of hope for the people of west Belfast. Mackies was at its core – the survival of this company within Springvale was the only source of industrial employment possible.

Sinn Féin, the political front of the IRA, had long argued for a government-sponsored industrial complex. What this complex was to manufacture, they could not say. On whom might manage it, they were silent. How its products could be sold, they did not know. The Catholic Church argued that jobs should be brought to the people rather than the people taken to jobs. That the church-run education system in Catholic west Belfast had never produced pupils with a mechanical bent did not seem overly to concern them. Government was held to be responsible for providing work in the ghettos for desperate youngsters raised amongst squalor and violence, where unemployment on many estates ranged between 50 and 80 per cent. It was, of course, ridiculous to suppose that in a free-market economy the government could do other than provide infrastructure.

The Irish Catholic Church was, however, the sworn enemy of a godless Sinn Féin. It may have lacked vision in education and have been naive in demanding locally created, government-sponsored jobs, but it had some of the most determined entrepreneurial priests in the Church of Rome who understood what was possible and what was not. On its own, this was nothing like enough but it could be built into something with help from outside. But no outside investor would contemplate putting money into a decaying, Victorian, inner-city slum controlled by a Marxist terrorist clique who trumpeted their opposition to capitalism as much as they did their opposition to the British. The key that could open the door to the Springvale dream remained Mackies – and Mackies was in trouble.

In July 1989, Peter Viggers resigned from the Department of Economic Development. After a hiccup or two, I was made Minister of Economic Development as well as Environment. The future of Mackies became a top priority.

The Industrial Development Board (IDB), which is an integral part of the Department of Economic Development, had been locked into negotiations with the Mackies Trust for months trying to hammer out a package of support that would involve much-needed reinvestment and radical changes in management and ownership. As these negotiations dragged on, the company continued to bleed. The IDB had made a number of proposals to the Treasury for propping up the company but they had been rejected, which led to the alternative hunt for a white knight. Heading the IDB team was David Watkins, a bright young former private secretary to Tom King, the previous Secretary of State for Northern Ireland, who had been posted to the job to give him 'industrial' experience. The problem, which I was to confront during the whole of my ministerial career, was that the pressure put on civil servants was as much to avoid criticism for wasting public money as to save or change the situation. As the deLorean fiasco had occurred less than ten years earlier, such care was understandable. But fear of antagonising the Public Accounts Committee is a powerful motivation for caution.

Furthermore, as is generally the case in our system, the actual business experience of the government negotiators was minimal although they did have significant development experience and financial expertise. They thought that the Mackies trustees were crafty businessmen playing a Machiavellian poker game to squeeze as much money as was possible out of the government purse. On the other hand, the trustees, mostly local worthies, were confused by the questioning of their position and the apparent need for ever more information on facts, figures and performance. The way in which discussions seemed to hint at a hidden agenda bemused them. At every turn they resorted to lawyers and accountants to protect their backs. Any way forward seemed closed. The IDB had been unable to convince the Treasury that anyone in Northern Ireland had either the managerial skill or the resources to rebuild the business so they had been forced to identify a number of potential white knights. Of these, only the Howden Group became a bidder, together with Lummus Industries of Columbus, Georgia, which had been identified by Mackies. Howdens were initially preferred by the trustees but negotiations broke down in January 1989. Lummus was left as the only other bidder. While Lummus was already a textiles machinery maker in the cotton industry and the IDB was initially impressed with its American 'hands-on', 'no-nonsense' management style, Lummus's problem was that it had just gone through a highly leveraged management buy-out, and so both money and time were scarce commodities.

In September 1989, I was told that deadlock had occurred. I told the IDB that I would take personal responsibility for Mackies and that it was to be saved at whatever cost. I would square the Secretary of State and the British Treasury, but Mackies' new factory was to be built and the company sold. I brought in the trustees and explained that I was determined to see Mackies survive. The tensions eased. I went to see Johnny Johnson, boss of Howdens, to keep him on-side in case Lummus's bid failed, and I then called on my friendship with Sir Terry Burns, the Treasury permanent secretary, whom I had invited to Northern Ireland two years previously. I told him that if his ministers blocked the £13 million required as a dowry for Mackies, the economic fight in west Belfast against the IRA would be lost. The Treasury stayed neutral. Peter Brooke, the new Secretary of State for Northern Ireland, supported me doggedly. We also had to secure American investment through million-dollar loans from the Overseas Private Investment Corporation (OPIC), which had been introduced to us by Lummus. The head of OPIC was a wonderfully helpful former American ambassador who, supported by his officials, backed me to the hilt.

In June 1990, Lummus took over and the company was restructured. But instead of success, failure loomed ever closer. Lummus's own problems had multiplied. The hands-on, no-nonsense management never materialised. The order book had vanished – promised new contracts turned out to be illusions. In the year to March 1990 the company had a turnover of £30 million. The following nine months' sales dropped to £14 million. In 1991 they were down to a catastrophic £6 million. The moneys from OPIC and IDB were haemorrhaging by the month. The shadow of deLorean stalked my office.

In 1990, Pat Dougan, a prominent Catholic businessman, had asked to come to see me. I was told that in his youth he had had republican sympathies. Since then, he had built up a very successful quarrying machinery business, Powerscreen, which had gone public only for him to fall out with some of his colleagues and to find himself out on his ear. He was abrasive and opinionated and I was not sure about him, but in September 1991 I was told that he might be our only chance. It was the last throw of the dice. So in November at our prompting Pat became chief executive of Mackies.

Pat is a brave if sometimes foolhardy man. He has enormous charm, is shrewd and is very tough. He is big, dark and impressive – the good, the bad and the ugly rolled into one. He was brought up by his grandparents. As a small boy, he claims, he used to steal hand-grenades from the back of British jeeps and would then lob these into the River Bann, scoop out the stunned salmon and sell them back to the officers' mess! He was a fine rugby forward. Chairman of the nationalist selection committee that chose Bernadette Devlin in the 1969 Mid-Ulster by-election, he is one of the new breed of self-confident, successful, well-travelled, rich Catholic businesspeople that have done so much to change economic fortunes in Northern Ireland over the last ten years.

In 1992 Lummus filed for Chapter 11 administration in the US. It was now vital to disentangle Mackies before they were sucked down the same plug, and this gave Pat his chance. He had already brought in several key new managers. He had won over the workforce through his charisma, cut out waste, restored morale and raised productivity. In February 1993, he persuaded Lummus to transfer all the ordinary shares to him, to be held in trust for the other directors and the employees. The Americans dropped out and the name Lummus disappeared. Pat appointed a City merchant banker as chairman. He expanded the foundry and opened up a water and sewerage treatment system division. In September 1994, OPIC and the banks agreed to write off a substantial proportion of their debt and the company was floated on the Unlisted Securities Market. Mackies was back in business.

In 1992, when the new Springvale factory was finished, Mackies asked me to perform the official opening. At the ceremony, I said:

> Mackies is a very remarkable company in a very remarkable city. It encapsulates both the very best and, in the past, the not so very best of Ulster's genius for making things and employing people.
>
> It is a symbol – the last symbol – of the great manufacturing tradition on which Belfast and particularly west Belfast was built. Its name is known on every continent and in every country of every continent. It remains one of the great textiles machinery companies of the world. Its survival and prospects have exercised every Secretary of State and every Minister of Trade and Industry in Northern Ireland for the last twenty years.
>
> But it is more than that. It still stands between the light and the darkness. If it succeeds it forms the core of a new base for industrial

expansion in the west of the city. It will be a monument to the determination of a company and its workforce to survive everything that modern terrorism can throw at it. It will change both the image and the reality of west Belfast. It will act as a magnet for new investment. It will show that two of Europe's most bitterly divided communities have learnt to work together for the prosperity of both. It will be a wonderful footing on which Springvale can build. It will be another nail in each of the coffins of the horrid men who peddle violence in our city.

It is you who work here who have seen the disappointments, seen the leaving of friends, lived through the doubts of closure, faced the possibility of redundancy and continued to come to work through communities convulsed by division. You have continued to produce the finest linen-making machines in the world. Belfast is proud of you, as is Ireland and Britain proud of you: you are a very remarkable people. It is a privilege to be given the honour of opening this factory but for me it is much more than that, it is coming back to the city and the people I love and where I have spent so many happy times. It is also a joy in a dark world to announce good news: the opening of Mackies new factory on the other side of the Springfield Road.

Three years later I was back in Mackies to hear the President of the United States endorse my sentiments. As we followed Clinton's cavalcade down the Falls Road, I saw Gerry Adams coming towards me. Some of his followers recognised me and waved. The RUC were standing around in small groups, some sitting, some chatting; a sergeant cheerily beckoned us on.

What a change! I read again the President's injunction: 'You must stand firm against terror. You must say to those who still would use violence for political objectives – you are the past, your day is over.' For the first time in my life I really believed he might be right.

1
A POLITICAL APPRENTICESHIP

M Y FIRST REALISATION OF AN IRISH connection was when my grandmother told me, when I was aged about twelve, that she would never become a countess. My grandfather had died before his brother, who was an Irish earl. In 1961 my great-uncle died. He was succeeded as earl of Kilmorey by my father, easily the nicest man I have ever met but entirely unsuited for a world after empire. He retired from the Grenadiers at the age of thirty-two and became a gentleman market gardener in Falmouth, from where he sent anemones in the winter, daffodils in the spring and hydrangeas in the summer to Covent Garden. He had no money, so we lived partly off my mother's inheritance from her father, which consisted mainly of lovely 'things' that quietly disappeared at regular intervals.

My father's pitiful earnings from anemones and daffodils were also supplemented by an allowance from my intimidating grandmother. She had a tight fist and a voice like a foghorn. Nevertheless, I had an idyllic upbringing in the far south-west of England. The only connection with Ireland was a Christmas card from our cousins and the odd exotic shrub which my parents would send to the County Down where the soil and climate were not too dissimilar to Cornwall.

As soon as I left school I decided on a career in business and politics. Looking back, I have no real idea why. I did not want to be a soldier, perhaps because my family is the longest-serving family in the

Grenadier Guards and I was a teenage rebel. My only military service was as the longest-serving private in the Eton corps. I had flat feet and given a chance I was a barrack-room lawyer. My uncle, John Sheffield, who was chairman of Portals and several public companies (as well as being the head of the family to whom every member turned for advice), said that if I wanted to go into politics I would have to make money and suggested I become a patent lawyer. I could see the connection between patent lawyers and money but not between patent lawyers and politics.

So when I left school, having tried but failed to generate any information on the world outside from my Eton housemaster, I went to South Africa with a school friend. There I criss-crossed the country, working for the Rembrandt Tobacco Corporation. Soon after I returned, I decided to give up the notion of doing law and went to work for Carreras Rothmans, the Rembrandt subsidiary in England. It was while I was at Carreras that I first travelled to Ulster. Carreras owned Murrays of Belfast. They made pipe and chewing tobacco and I, as the assistant product development manager, was responsible for producing their packaging. My only recollection of the visit is of poring over the twines of tobacco being rolled around stainless-steel forms to make the plugs from which chewing tobacco was cut. It tasted filthy.

In 1965 I married, left tobacco and joined an engineering company. Although I was set on politics, I had become absorbed by the ways the manufacturing industry sought to motivate and reward its workers. In Carreras I had joined the Tobacco Workers' Union, to the consternation of the directors. In 1967 I bought out, for a small amount, a silk-screen printer whose premises were sited above a Yeovil striptease club. At the time I was called Viscount Newry, but being without land or inherited money invited ridicule rather than reward. So on 1 January 1968, I announced in *The Times* that I wished to be known as plain Mr Richard Needham.

For the next ten years, I lost all contact with Ulster. I was raising my family, establishing my business and making a career for myself in politics, first at the local level and then as a parliamentary candidate. I contested without success the two general elections of 1974, the first at Pontefract and the second at marginal Gravesend. Six months later, I began work with Jim Prior, who had been allocated the shadow Employment portfolio by Margaret Thatcher following Ted Heath's defeat. The trade union movement soon nicknamed me the Tory Trot. My speciality was to reassure them that they would not be decimated by Mrs Thatcher. I had built my political reputation on my contacts with the union movement and my experience of bargaining with them. I hoped that one day that experience would stand me in good stead with my leader. It did not.

In 1976 I was chosen as candidate for the Conservative seat of Chippenham to replace the retiring sitting MP Dan Awdry. Nine months later my father died and I became the sixth earl of Kilmorey. Though I had no need to renounce my title, I decided politically it was best, with my background in industrial relations and industry, to continue as 'Mister'.

A month after my father's death, my great-aunt Norah Kilmorey, widow of the fourth earl, wrote to me saying that, while she quite understood my reasons for not using my titles, she thought it sad that I knew so little about my family and so little about its role in Irish affairs over the centuries. She invited me to our old family home at Mourne Park, which is set in the Mourne Mountains near the little fishing town of Kilkeel; here the Needhams had lived off and on for 180 years. I accepted the invitation, not least because I was, in a detached way, proud of my family's record of 'endeavour'. Nearly every generation of Needhams have served the Crown in one way or another and there have been Needhams in parliament since 1451, including one who had been Tory MP for Pontefract before the arrival of the miners. It was no coincidence that I had decided on a career in public life. My upbringing had instilled in me the belief that public duty was the natural role for someone from my background.

In August 1977 I flew with my wife and mother to Belfast's Aldergrove Airport. Kilkeel has four churches and six thousand parishioners. On Sundays, all six thousand are in their places. My first service was an instruction. The Church of Ireland has the smallest congregation in Kilkeel, but there was not a seat to be had as six hundred worshippers crammed the knave and transept. As is often the case with those from the mainland, to me the minister seemed closer to Presbyterianism than to Canterbury: his sermon was full of hell and damnation. The children wore signs begging for the forgiveness of their sins; it was a relief that forgiveness was soon at hand and was promptly rewarded by a Mars bar. The sermon was uncompromising on the Church of Rome. The singing was glorious, while the choir and congregation were in their Sunday best. God should have been pleased.

At the end of the service, as we waited to shake the minister's hand, one of the ushers asked me if I knew much of my family's history. I demurred. 'Your family first came to Ireland in the reign of the Great Queen to put down the Irish rebellion of 1595 and you were created viscounts in the Queen's County of Ireland. Your ancestors returned to put down the rebellion of 1798, for which you were created earls. Your family has protected the Union for hundreds of years and now you are back, I hope you won't forget it!' It was my second day in Ulster, and I had been given my instructions.

On the sectarian maps which the British army use to brief VIPs, Kilkeel is shown as a blob of orange in a sea of green. The farmers in the hinterland behind the town are mainly Catholic and the fishermen mainly Protestant. Fishing is the life-blood of Kilkeel. In the 1970s generous EEC grants had improved and replaced the old boats and their equipment. The most forceful proponent of European Community subsidies was the Community's most eloquent opponent, the local Ulster Unionist MP, Enoch Powell. Kilkeel had a doughty champion in the former member for Wolverhampton.

The final night of the first weekend was spent in the bar of the Mourne Park Golf Club. Just before closing time, two men who had drink taken accosted me. 'Tell her Ladyship in the big house that if the Brits ever get out of Ulster we'll be on the council estates in Newry within the hour!' To which the other one added: 'And tell her Ladyship we'll be in Cork by the weekend!' The two of them were fishermen. According to them, some of the guns run in by my grandfather sixty years before were still in their crates and awaiting the day of judgment. The earl of Kilmorey was back amongst his tribe.

If the humour was sometimes menacing, generally speaking the two communities in Kilkeel coexisted well enough. Nevertheless, terrorism was never far away. The local butcher, an RUC reservist, had been shot behind his counter. Someone local must have fingered him. One of the local builders had been gunned down for supplying materials to the army and the police. As the years passed, Kilkeel got tawdrier as the economic consequences of the terror took their toll. The brightest moved away and those that remained kept their politics to themselves and prayed that, in that most beautiful part of Ireland, the Troubles would pass.

In 1979 I became a member of parliament and each year we went back to visit my cousins. Ireland had entrapped me and I had come to believe that during my political career I could do something for the people my family had lived among for so long. Little did I realise that it would be Margaret Thatcher who would grant me my ambition.

PARLIAMENT

When I became the candidate for Chippenham in 1976 I fondly believed that I was moving into what would soon become a safe Tory seat which, although it would require considerable attention, would not need my all. I had inherited a majority of 1,900 votes over the Liberals, but in 1976 they were in a sorry state following the dreadful publicity they had suffered during the Scott trial and the resignation of Jeremy Thorpe. David Steele was personable enough, but a Scots son of the manse did not appear to pose much of a threat in the West Country.

How wrong I was. My opponent, Ronnie Banks, was a veteran campaigner who had done well in Chippenham at the October 1974 general election. He was an old-fashioned anti-European Community Liberal and in many respects to the right of me. In 1979 he argued that he rather than I was the natural successor to my predecessor, also a liberal Tory, Dan Awdry. He rather than I would stop a divisive right-wing Tory government led by a strident woman from fomenting revolution and returning us to darkness and a three-day week. Ronnie did not succeed but he gave me a fright. My majority of just over four thousand was half that of Chris Patten, my neighbour in Bath, and mine was still one of the most marginal seats in the country. Would my political career be stillborn?

During my first term as an MP I worked all hours to secure my base. Constituency work was spurred on by the split in the Labour Party, the formation of the SDP–Liberal Alliance and the attractions offered by the two Davids (Steel and Owen). I was also out of sympathy with much of the social security legislation introduced by the first Thatcher government. At one Downing Street cocktail party in the early eighties, the Prime Minister grabbed me by the arm as the division bell sounded and marched me to the door exclaiming, 'Come on Richard, we're going to vote with the government tonight, aren't we!' Of the 'wets' I was one of the wettest. About the trade union reforms, I was wrong.

15

About making the poor poorer while we were making the rich richer, I was right.

I wrote articles for the *Guardian*. Richard Gott, features editor, more or less pressed me into his service, although I don't think the KGB ever considered me a sleeper. I wrote a series of sketches for the BBC and a short book about the workings of parliament. I spent four weeks in America on the Junior World Leaders programme, which was a tour, apparently sponsored by the CIA, which allowed me to go where I liked and do what I liked.

I was nervous of the House of Commons, frightened of making a fool of myself, unsure of my debating skills when confronted by the best of the best, and desperately keen to win the plaudits of my peers. Too often I found myself speaking after Chris Patten or Julian Critchley, which left me feeling decidedly second division. I was offered a junior parliamentary private secretary (PPS) post to the Minister of Overseas Aid, but as the offer came a day or so before I had decided to vote against the government for the third time, the Chief Whip told me it was a job or the desert. I chose the desert.

I was not, however, without friends. As soon as parliament had convened I was asked to the first meeting of the Blue Chips, one of the most extraordinary political clubs of the century. Because I had worked for Jim Prior for so long, my reputation on industrial relations was known, and I was considered one of those who might do well if I was prepared to trim to the Thatcher winds. The core of the Blue Chips were Chris Patten, John Patten, Tristan Garel-Jones and William Waldegrave. I became the last member of the politburo when I was invited to share their office a year after the election. In fact I was the last to join the office, the last to become a PPS ('Thank goodness we've finally got you over the wire, Needham,' Garel-Jones barked at me), the last to become a parliamentary under-secretary of state, the last to become a minister of state and the last to become a privy counsellor.

In 1981 the Blue Chips published a pamphlet called *Changing Gear* which had a major impact on the debate in the party over policy. I wrote the chapter on industrial relations and co-authored the chapter on industry with John Watson. William Waldegrave did the editing and fell out with Chris Patten over some of the presentation and content. It was about the only political disagreement I recall between any of us, which, considering the pressures and the personalities, is extraordinary. The membership of the Blue Chips includes one Prime Minister, seven Cabinet members, five ministers of state and a Chief Whip. Only four out of the remaining seventeen have failed to make the break.

In 1983 Margaret Thatcher won her second term and I increased my majority to seven thousand. Robbie Gilbert, who had worked for Jim Prior with me in opposition, said it was time for me to stop playing the rebel and start up Disraeli's slippery pole. I went to see Fred Silvester who had been Jim Prior's PPS and asked him if he wanted to continue. He said he had had enough. So I presented my credentials. On 1 July 1983, I became parliamentary private secretary to the Secretary of State for Northern Ireland. I was going home.

2
THE RETURN

B
Y 1983 THE SHOCK OF THE HUNGER STRIKES of a few years earlier was fading. But the enormous surge of support for republicanism had still to ebb away, even though horrendous
bombings, such as the Droppin' Well Inn massacre at Ballykelly, Co.
Londonderry, in December 1982 had started to chip away at the mar-
tyrdom image of those who had starved to death.

The hunger strikes remain one of the darkest blots on the chronicle of
British rule. Both sides underestimated the will of the other. Perhaps the
murder of Airey Neave, the shadow Ulster secretary, in 1979 had
steeled Margaret Thatcher's already steely will. But whatever the reasons, the results were devastating. The NIO had never fully understood
the political impact the hunger strikes would have either in Boston and
Dublin or in Fermanagh and Tyrone. Before the hunger strikes the IRA
were demoralised and divided. After the hunger strikes they had reinforced their unity. The young Northerners had taken over. They con-
ceived a strategy of combining the bullet with the ballot box and gave
Sinn Féin/IRA a military and political coherence it had lacked. The
Social Democratic and Labour Party (SDLP), who were themselves
attempting to recover from splits and personality clashes and with an
untested, newly appointed leadership under John Hume, were left marginalised and insecure. The British response to the hunger strikers forti-
fied the IRA's prejudice that Britain would stay in Ireland come what

may because of some deep strategic interest. Together with the arms from Libya, the hunger strikes maintained the conflict for another decade. It reinstated the cycle of revenge and gave terrorism a respectability it never deserved because the men of violence had substantial political backing from a large proportion of Northern nationalists. Furthermore, the concessions granted to end the hunger strikes differed very little from what the prisoners would have accepted at the outset. If the NIO had thought through the consequences, and if the Secretary of State, Humphrey Atkins, had realised what was happening in the nationalist areas and convinced the Prime Minister of the need to be more sensitive, a dark passage in Britain's rule could have been avoided.

It was against this background that Jim Prior arrived in September 1981, determined, as he said, to succeed where others had failed. His entrance appeared to herald a new era of British awareness of Ulster's misery and place it at the top of the political agenda. But the reality was otherwise. Prior was posted to Ulster to rid the Prime Minister of a turbulent wet. He maintained his seat on the economic subcommittee of the Cabinet, but from Belfast he could exercise little influence or input. Mrs Thatcher had dealt him a hand where he had either to gamble on solving one of the Western world's most intractable problems or to face the prospect of being sidelined as a political 'has been'. As always, he was too decent a man not to accept a chalice he knew to be poisoned. Prior's judgement over timing was perhaps slightly flawed. He had been loath to take the Ulster secretaryship, a fact he had made clear to me immediately before the Cabinet reshuffle, and which I had then reflected on, on Radio 4's *The World at One* twenty-four hours before he accepted the post!

Prior realised as soon as he stepped off the plane that something would have to be done to change the fractious mood and regain the political initiative. He was hampered by what turned out to be too much historical baggage.

Prior's relations with the Prime Minister had never been easy. Moreover, her parliamentary private secretary, Ian Gow, was a passionate unionist who believed that the only solution was to integrate Ulster so firmly into the UK that the republican movement, Northern nationalists and the Dublin government would realise the futility of continuing their campaign for Irish unity.

Integration is a ridiculous position to hold at the best of times: 40 per

19

cent of the population of Northern Ireland have long-term aspirations to some form of Irish unification. No Irish government could quietly abandon its objectives in the North, and a campaign – at times peaceful and often bloody – that had been waged for three centuries was hardly likely to be resolved by the snap of the fingers of the Iron Lady. The Labour Party's policy was one of 'unification by consent', and even the most ardent Tory would have to accept that one day Labour could come to power with an agenda closer to nationalist aspirations than to unionism. However, to hold an integrationist position at the end of the hunger strikes was literally incredible. But that did not stop Ian and his friends from doing all they could to undermine Prior's plans for a rolling devolution of powers to a power-sharing Assembly.

Prior's scheme had enemies in other quarters. Enoch Powell was an intense integrationist, even if his leader, Jim Molyneaux, had views which were expressed slightly more pro- or more anti- depending on whether he was in Westminster or Belfast. The SDLP were desperate to avoid losing any further ground to Sinn Féin. While Sinn Féin/IRA opposed any new form of government that would institutionalise the Northern 'statelet', as they so patronisingly called it, the SDLP were scared of being tainted as 'Castle Catholics' and resolved not to take up their seats in an assembly at Stormont, seat of British power in Northern Ireland.

Out went the step-by-step approach Prior had so successfully adopted towards trade union reform and in came an 'action man' initiative which might have worked over time but which Jim felt needed to be bedded down before the next election. If he had succeeded, he no doubt calculated, he could return from Ireland in triumph. Few British governors have returned from Ireland in triumph, and the only one of note, the earl of Strafford, soon found himself with an army he could not pay, a master who abandoned him and his head in the basket at Tower Hill.

Jim Prior is a decent man. You get what you see and there is quite a lot to see. Jane has been to him the perfect politician's wife. Shrewd and sharp, she has been a mighty shield at his back and a wise counsellor. They both threw themselves into the Irish morass with determination and verve. Jim found Northern Ireland a difficult place and he recoiled not only from the violence of terrorism but from the violence of language so often employed by the province's political drum bangers. If there were any friends about, he did not discern them.

He was soon in a bog. He had announced his proposals for an assembly four days after Argentina had invaded the Falklands. We had been staying with the Priors at Hillsborough the weekend of the attack and I could sense Jim's isolation from real power as phone calls came from Willie Whitelaw and Francis Pym detailing the disastrous House of Commons debate that had been called for an unprecedented Saturday morning. Whitelaw was Prior's closest confidant and supporter, and had himself come close to reaching a settlement in Ulster at the end of 1972. Whitelaw told me that he had never wanted to leave Northern Ireland when he was on the edge of a breakthrough, to return to deal with the miners where he knew no breakthrough was possible.

It did not take Taoiseach Charlie Haughey long to recall the nationalist dictum that 'England's difficulty is Ireland's opportunity', and as the Republic swung behind the Argentinians, relationships between London and Dublin became poisoned. Haughey had always rejected plans for an assembly. He saw it as a spatchcock that would stand in the way of 'joint authority' and as a British attempt at an internal solution that would thwart his aspirations for a united Ireland.

Jim was also in a parliamentary bog, with the Tory right, led by Sir John Biggs-Davison, Julian Amery and Nicholas Budgen, running a filibuster night after night, furtively bolstered by the Prime Minister's parliamentary private secretary. Furthermore, he was in a nationalist bog – the SDLP refused to engage in the political process unless there was an all-Ireland dimension. (The Sunningdale Agreement had been crippled when anti-Sunningdale candidates had wiped out Brian Faulkner's pro-Agreement Ulster Unionist Party. Perhaps the most obnoxious element of Sunningdale to the majority of the unionists had been the SDLP and Dublin's insistence on an all-Ireland dimension.) Finally he was in a unionist bog, because loyalists wanted the powers of the old Stormont government returned without power-sharing.

Prior battled through. The legislation was passed and elections to a new assembly were held. The SDLP did slightly better than they had feared, Sinn Féin slightly worse than they had hoped. Both refused to attend. The Assembly's powers were limited to debate amongst its unionist members and occasional interrogations of British ministers. The nationalists started to develop their own agenda with the Dublin government and its Forum for a New Ireland.

Prior was right to try to introduce a new political initiative. But he lacked both the authority and the personal experience to succeed. It was known to all that he came to Ireland as a reluctant Brit. He had roots in neither the Catholic nor the Protestant community. To the unionists he was suspect because of his team's known 'green' sympathies, particularly the Irish earl of Gowrie, who too frequently egged him on when he should have slowed him down, and to the nationalists he was a decent sort of English farming type and the more acceptable face of Thatcherism, which in general they detested.

It was clear by the summer of 1983 that 'rolling devolution' was free-wheeling towards the pits and Prior's days in Ulster were numbered. I had watched Jim's Irish initiative from the sidelines. Since 1981 and my interview with Adam Raphael on *The World at One* we had hardly had an opportunity to talk. But I relished the chance to work again with my political mentor, and I was determined to do all I could from a limited position to ensure that Jim's reign in Ulster ended on as constructive a note as possible.

The reshuffle after the 1983 general election brought new faces to the ministerial team. Out went Gowrie the 'black earl', John Patten, Jim's political adviser Rob Shephard, and his parliamentary private secretary Fred Silvester. In came Lord Mansfield, Chris Patten, Edward Bickham and I. Nick Scott became responsible for Security and Education, Adam Butler, of whom we saw little, was concerned with Economic Development and Finance, Chris was charged with Environment and Health, and Mansfield had to keep the farmers happy. Prior had around him a circle of old and trusted colleagues; however, it was clear that his political momentum had run out of steam, and in Jim's final year the best we could hope for was to avoid too many traps and too much bloodshed. The next stage of political development would depend on Dublin and London, not Belfast.

Although there were two ministers of state, Mansfield and Butler, they had little influence over the issues that filled the daily diary. Scott and Patten were Prior's key confidants.

I have never been sure what motivates Nick Scott. He is a man of astonishing talents and contrasts. Mentioned as a likely future Prime Minister, he never attained the highest offices – but I was never certain he wanted them. At 2,000 revs he could produce as much horsepower as the rest of us at 5,000, but sometimes the engine was idling when it should have been in gear. He had trying posts throughout his ministerial life, usually because Mrs Thatcher wanted him to follow policies that he abhorred. But he carried on, ameliorating their worst aspects and defending them ably even when confronted by one of his own children publicly abusing him. He managed his work lightly and organised his life around a ministerial black box a week, whereas his successor, John Stanley, immediately seemed to have enough paper to fill a skip. (Ministers in Northern Ireland have black boxes not red ones.) Nick was on the 'green' wing, as Irish hospitality, Irish culture and Irish fun appealed to him far more than the rather glum, drink-free, earnest, humourless world of Ulster's Protestant levellers. He was definitely on the side of the King not the Roundheads.

I suspect Nick's biggest disappointment was over mixed education. If Northern Ireland's children would all attend the same schools, the divisions would be over in a generation. No British government has been able to unlock the educational divide. The Catholic Church is as keen to hold on to the teaching of its flock as the flock is to be taught under the rules of Roman Catholicism. However reasonable this may be in a pluralist society, it can do nothing to reduce divisions in a divided one. Nick's main effort was to try to bring teacher training under one roof so that at least those who taught would have found ways of implanting common themes and building personal friendships that would last throughout their careers. It was not to be. For the Catholic community, both clergy and laity, the step was too great, and the divisions that initiate in the nursery still continue to the grave. Nevertheless, he did give a big push to integrated schools. By October 1997 there were thirty-three such primary and secondary schools at which a growing number of mainly middle-class children were being educated free from ignorance and prejudices about each other's cultures and traditions. It is something, but it is not enough.

Northern Ireland was Chris Patten's first ministerial posting. Having started his working life with Lord Carrington, he was appointed director of the Conservative Research Department at a Pitt-the-Younger age of twenty-nine and immediately became indispensable to Margaret Thatcher, Geoffrey Howe and Jim Prior. He was secretary to the shadow Cabinet and author of the 1979 election manifesto. Whenever the pressure between shadow ministers rose, it was Patten who found a way through. If politics is about creating policies which appeal to ordinary folk and articulating complex ideas which can be grasped by the public, Chris is a most powerful inventor and advocate.

Between 1979 and 1983 he had disagreed with the harshest aspects of Thatcherism, in particular some of the more divisive aspects of the Prime Minister's social reforms. He also had not been well. Northern Ireland offered not only an opening back into the mainstream but the scope to cultivate his administrative and management skills. He was competent and careful, never abrasive, always analytical, dependable and loyal. It was small wonder his civil servants adored him.

This has continued as Chris's career has developed. He is not a hands-on management reformer or a marketing professional or a business number-cruncher. He prefers to work out the simplest solution to the most complicated of problems and plan its execution. He is happy to allow others to deal with the detail, although he always looks out for the traps and keeps on top of his brief. He could have been the Rab Butler of his generation. He is a man of principle who, when John Major became Prime Minister, knowingly sacrificed his political career to have his friend re-elected in 1992. It was the most selfless political self-immolation I have ever witnessed. The aftermath was that boring Bath got a boring Liberal and Hong Kong got a governor who one day should have been Prime Minister. He has, in lonely and embittering circumstances, retained Britain's reputation by standing up to China and fighting to maintain essential freedoms for the people of Hong Kong. Under any other governor the reverse would have been more likely. Whether his advocacy will have succeeded in enshrining Hong Kong's limited democracy is too early to predict.

Another member of Jim Prior's team was Edward Bickham. A Secretary of State's political adviser must pick up those topics the civil servants miss, usually because they are political or they involve interparty relationships that the 'office' would not know, or want to know, about. The political adviser needs to be a perfect protector, always looking for and advising his boss on the weak points of the latter's position, particularly with colleagues. He must be constantly counterattacking through well-disguised off-the-record briefings and he needs to write both articles and speeches well. The political adviser must be at the heart of the Whitehall machine; he must know the other political advisers and what 'trades' are on offer in exchange for support in Cabinet or in Cabinet committees. It is an esoteric profession which teaches little about the 'real world' and nothing about the loneliness of decision-taking or responsibility. But it does teach back-room apprentices the art of politics and it remains the most profitable ladder to political advancement.

Once on the ladder, the adviser moves with his master from department to department. The issues may be different and the personalities may alter, but the mechanics of government and its interrelationships remain the same whether it is Northern Ireland, Agriculture, Health or Defence. The biggest difficulty for an adviser is to infiltrate the Whitehall machine. Political advisers are paid as civil servants but at best are tolerated by the civil service. Generally, they are seen as interlopers and interferers who should be told and shown as little as possible. Edward Bickham was the perfect model of his class and we were to work very closely.

3

EARLY DAYS ON THE LADDER

THE YEAR I SPENT AS PARLIAMENTARY PRIVATE SECRETARY to Jim Prior was my first rub with real power and my first opportunity to see officialdom in action. The duties of a PPS are as broad or as narrow as the occupant wants to make them. It is the first necessary step up the ladder for every MP and gives an insight into how a department operates and how ministers and their civil servants interact. PPSs are tolerated as less of a threat to the smooth running of government than are political advisers. They can even be useful to senior officials as they can circulate feedback on the mood of MPs from all sides and provide an insight into parliamentary procedures which civil servants can find arcane and baffling. Nevertheless, they are not allowed any departmental facilities, are always called by their first name even by administrative assistants and are kept well away from anything sensitive.

During the passage of the Assembly legislation and because of his need to be in Northern Ireland, I felt that Jim had lost touch with the broad base of the Conservative Party. His contacts were chiefly with the back-bench Northern Ireland Committee, which tended to be monopolised by right-wing integrationists under the chairmanship of Sir John Biggs-Davison, supported by Nicholas Budgen, who was Enoch Powell's Wolverhampton successor and had in many ways become his clone. Then there were other, more tetchy characters, like Ivor Stanbrook and George Gardiner, who required recognition and humouring. The Northern Ireland Committee were important because, firstly, they represented those most interested in Northern Ireland affairs and therefore most likely to intervene in debates or at question time, and secondly, much of the media on both sides of the water took them as reflecting back-bench – and perhaps the Prime Minister's – views. (There is a bitter fight every autumn between 'wets' and 'drys' to elect the officers of the committee; during Prior's time, the right-wing usually controlled key positions.)

It was a constant battle to keep them in order. I used to attend the meetings, make notes on the discussion and then arrange for Jim Prior, Nick Scott or Chris Patten to see them and revisit their grumbles and prejudices. Frequently, the discussion used to voyage round and round the same old buoys.

One of my most crucial tasks as a PPS was to listen to, cajole and charm where possible all shades of Northern Ireland's political opinion.

Unionism had been criticised as bereft of leadership and the complaint was that too few unionists of real stature and intelligence would enter politics. The two brightest young stars in the Ulster Unionist ranks in 1983, two men who promised to contribute much to the future of unionism were Frank Millar, the party secretary, and Edgar Graham, a lawyer and lecturer in law at Queen's University Belfast. I spent a lot of time with both, and both became my friends. If Prior's Assembly had one merit, it was to give Ulster's young politicians their spurs.

On 1 December 1983, Edgar Graham wrote to tell me that 'since our discussions the situation in Ulster and the Assembly has taken a turn for the worse. . . . I hope to fly over on the first shuttle on Thursday, 8th, and if we had an opportunity to talk things over, I know that I would find it most useful.' On Wednesday, the 7th, Edgar was sitting on a wall outside the law faculty at Queen's when two young men walked up behind him. One of them pulled out a gun and shot him in the back of the head. He died instantly. He was an only son. With him died the aspirations of moderate young unionism. His killers have never been found. Frank Millar left politics and is now the London correspondent of the *Irish Times*.

FINDING MY FEET

Jim Prior's office arranged my first trip to Northern Ireland in my new post for four days in the middle of September 1983. We took off from

Odiham, the nearest RAF base to the Priors' Hampshire farm, in a
Hawker Siddley 125 which the NIO leased from the RAF. It was fitted
out for senior officers and was comfortable if cramped. The early morning run had already collected senior civil servants from Northolt who
flew over to Belfast either for the day or for the week. This was before
the IRA acquired ground-to-air missiles and the plane was in the finest
RAF livery. I have always disliked flying and in fact for many years in
my twenties and thirties I refused to fly at all. However, aeroplanes were
now to become part of my life, although being crammed into the fuse-
lage of a small jet, buffeted by the air stream or Atlantic gales, remained
the least enjoyable element of my time in Northern Ireland.

The next two days passed in a whirl of meetings and briefings. What
I most recall from the first day are the army maps which divided every
part of every town or city by religious affiliation. The maps identified
the parts of the province under the control of various army brigades and
showed how they overlapped, or sometimes did not, with the RUC divisions. The army briefing was given by Colonel John Wilsey (who
later served as general officer commanding (GOC) in the early 1990s). It
was typically competent, well rehearsed and clear. It was also plain that
though the army might know who the terrorists were and where they
operated from, neither they nor the police could obtain enough evidence either to convict them or to find their arms. Both the RUC and
the army claimed their interrelationships worked well and their contacts
with the Garda in the Republic were close and friendly but pointed out
that it was impossible to patrol properly three hundred miles of frontier.
If everything was as well organised as they both maintained, it was hard
to see how the IRA could survive.

The reality was, of course, not so sanguine. Army battalions came
and went. New *roulement* detachments were parachuted in every three
months in the most dangerous areas. Some settled better than others but
none had time to win over the local population, which on the nationalist side had developed a deep distrust of some of the British army battalions and their methods. The RUC was – and remains – almost an exclu-
sively Protestant force and, although well disciplined and well
equipped, it kept itself to itself under the formidable leadership of Sir
Jack Hermon. As for cross-border security, its effectiveness was limited.
The Garda had long since lost influence over many border areas, which
had become fiefdoms for paramilitary chieftains and harboured their

arsenals for attacks in the North. I soon realised that along the border and in much of the province to the west of the Bann the Queen's writ ended after dark and could only be maintained in daylight at the end of the barrel of a gun.

On the second day I toured a training centre which taught mechanical and building skills but did not teach estimating or bookkeeping. So although the trainees could make almost anything, they could not run anything. I talked to the Chamber of Commerce, the Confederation of British Industry and one of Ulster's largest manufacturers. It was abundantly obvious that the economy relied very heavily on the public sector which accounted for 71 per cent of GDP in 1983/4. The private sector had shrunk as the inward investment of the early 1960s had come to the end of its useful life. It was clear that much of the young talent had also gone and that what was left depended on government grants and government orders. It was depressing, but it was also an opportunity.

The third day was my first trip to Londonderry. After Jim Prior had hired me, I had received a letter from a Malmesbury constituent named David Richardson. A bookbinder by trade, he had been enticed to go to Derry to work in youth and community workshops teaching the young unemployed the secrets of vellum. David was one of those extraordinary characters who appear only to quickly disappear again in the shadows of Ulster's difficulties. I don't know whether he had any knowledge of where he was going or who he would be teaching. A straight-forward moustached Englishman who enjoys his pint in the Rose and Crown, he now found himself teaching the children of republicanism how to rebind the books of Londonderry bequeathed by their former colonial masters. Anyway, after eighteen months David returned to Malmesbury, where he became a postman – bookbinding in Derry had taken its toll!

In his letter David invited me to visit Londonderry to see what he was doing and meet his boss, the famed Paddy Doherty – nicknamed Paddy 'Bogside' – who was one of the early leaders of the Civil Rights Movement. One of the challenges that faced me in my early days as a PPS was to find roots in the nationalist community which I could cultivate and call on when confronted with official briefings from the NIO. David Richardson presented me with my first exposure to Irish nationalism.

I joined up with Chris Patten at Aldergrove to drive across the

Sperrin Mountains. At that time ministers were supplied with four escorts, two in the front of the car and two in a back-up car. The minister always sat behind the passenger seat so that in an emergency he could be pulled out the non-driver's side. The escorts never wore seat-belts in order to give them freedom of movement. This was an exemption from the law insisted on by the RUC. I came to the conclusion that an injured bodyguard was of less use to me than one strapped in by a seat-belt and I half believed that there was an element of machismo in some of those who refused to belt up. Later when I became Transport Minister I tried to have the dispensation reviewed, as more police officers in Northern Ireland were injured by not wearing seat-belts than were wounded by the IRA. I failed. The RUC were a law unto themselves.

As we drove towards Londonderry, Chris pulled out of his papers the draft proposals for the forthcoming annual NIO expenditure round. They involved reductions in his budget and he was not quite sure how to lobby against them. Nor was he certain as a 'rookie' minister whether I, as a PPS, should be seeing confidential papers. I showed him my personal itinerary which was also marked 'confidential', so he relaxed and for the first time I was allowed a peep into the inner workings of government: the power and authority of the chief secretary of the Treasury and the alliances that had to be built up among the spending departments to try to thwart him. My own battles were to come.

Our initial call was to the social security offices. Overall unemployment was running at between 25 and 30 per cent and for young men in the north-west it could be as high as 80 per cent. The social security office was one of the city's major employers. We went to the manager's office. He was flustered by the arrival of two government representatives and to be on the safe side called us both 'Minister' at every opportunity. We were served with tea, biscuits, scones and butter, which was spread as thick as the scone. We were then taken through the organisation of the office, introduced to the senior staff and taken walkabout through the various benefit departments. Rows and rows of mainly young men and women laboriously checking claims and writing out giro cheques. Computerisation was still in the future.

The highlight was a chance to see the public area in the front offices where claimants either received their cheques or made their claims. Claimant and adjudicator were separated by thick glass panels because angry applicants, their claims rejected, often lunged despairingly at the clerks on the other side. A long queue was waiting at the pay-out counter. Here, we were told as we peeped round the door, Martin McGuinness, former local commander of the IRA, came every fortnight to collect his money. One of the most obscene aspects of terrorism in Northern Ireland is the way in which those who plot to murder and maim collect money from a government whose servants have no way of investigating their financial affairs or refusing their demands. It is humiliating for democracy when those who wish to destroy it year after year claim benefits which are themselves a pittance compared to the rewards of intimidation, blackmail and fraud that the IRA have become so adroit at perfecting. After this demoralising demonstration of the limits to parliament's jurisdiction we moved off for lunch at the Guildhall.

The main point of our coming to Londonderry was for Chris Patten to announce the city's new enterprise zone, a tax haven for inward investors which had already worked in London's Docklands, Liverpool, Glasgow and Belfast. Such occasions were and are treated with considerable formality. The mayor was berobed in his parlour to welcome the visiting dignitaries. Alongside him were the bishops, senior business-people and top local officials. There was a long, large top table and the remainder of the Guildhall was packed. A free lunch always encourages a crowd. There was a video presentation, introductory speeches, explanatory speeches, exhortatory speeches and finally grace. The food lacked nothing in bulk if something in variety. No one from outside would have realised we were in one of the most divided communities in Europe and fourteen years into a terrorist war.

Most of those in the room had suffered from violence, witnessed violence and been tarnished by its residue. Bishop Edward Daly, the local Catholic bishop, was sitting alongside his Church of Ireland counterpart, Bishop James Mehaffey, both completely united in their efforts for peace and employment. There was distrust of the government and dislike of the Prime Minister's style and some of her market-driven policies, but to Chris and myself there was no antagonism, only a wish to inform and welcome.

After lunch came the next paradox. The minister went back to Belfast with his escorts. The PPS was picked up by a driver from the Northern Ireland Office. Under the RUC security rule-book a minister is a target but a PPS, even though he is an MP and the Secretary of State's eyes and ears, is not.

I met Paddy Doherty and David Richardson in Paddy's half-built library on Shipquay Street. Paddy immediately poked my tie. 'It's nice to see you wearing the City tie,' he growled, 'with the City emblem of an Irish skeleton starved to death by the British occupiers.' So began an acquaintance that, in spite of the provocation we have hurled at each other, has lasted over fifteen years.

During the late seventies and early eighties, the IRA had waged an 'economic' war which included bombing the centres of cities and market towns. How blowing up greengrocers, butchers and estate agents would further their cause was not clear, but the damage done to some of the finest historical buildings of the province was devastating. Paddy was determined to rebuild his city within the walls to its former glory and through the Inner City Trust he raised money, cajoled the district council, threatened ministers and ploughed on. When I met him in 1983 his work had just begun and it was far from obvious whether every three or four months, even with his nationalist credentials, he would not have to start all over again. His assistant, Colm Cavanagh, was responsible for small company start-ups as well as bookbinding; there was a silk-screen poster enterprise, a young apprentice learning pewter work and an industrial sewing course. It was all very much hand-to-mouth and what was needed was practical, technical support rather than more public money. As I was a silk-screen printer, I decided to support Una Green's fledgling company and a link was built between Londonderry and my little factory in Yeovil. In all, Paddy had two hundred places for sixteen-year-olds whose education was rudimentary and whose attention was inclined to wander. Training them for jobs they knew did not exist was a difficult task that required a school-master's dedication. Thankfully, this came naturally to Paddy and the trainees respected him.

I was nervous that first day, and looking over the barbed-wire-festooned walls down into the Bogside, with its enormous flagpole flying the tricolour and the monument to those who had died for 'Free Derry', I became more nervous. The walled city with the army observation post glowering over the bleak council estates below had every semblance of a place under siege: the Apprentice Boys of Derry slamming the gates in the faces of the Jacobite army, the Rossville flats, scene of much of the rioting at the start of the Troubles, the Bogside Inn . . .

every cobblestone and every building had witnessed violence and division over the centuries.

Londonderry is a city of some 100,000 souls divided by the River Foyle. The last twenty years have seen the Protestants abandon the west bank for a variety of social and economic reasons, some of them IRA-inspired. Londonderry has always been a matriarchal city. The first shirt factory opened in the 1840s, and as the trade grew and Derry became the shirt centre of the Empire, the Catholic people flocked from the countryside of County Londonderry and County Donegal to find work, but there was only ever jobs for the women. The men brought up their families, bred greyhounds and cursed the unionists for gerrymandering the boundaries and discriminating against them in housing and jobs. Many left and joined the British army; they took the King's shilling and did the King's business, but when they returned some turned their trade to terror to kick the Brits out.

I very soon learnt that Derry was a place apart. It had largely achieved its independence from the rest of Ulster by the early eighties. The nationalist politicians of the north-west were tolerant of the Protestant minority, for it offered them no threat; however, they had little understanding of the art of the possible in Belfast, Antrim or the County Down.

When I returned to Stormont that evening, Chris Patten hosted a dinner for the consultants of the Belfast City Hospital. Little did he know that Northern Ireland was to be the training ground for his own posting as Britain's last colonial governor. As all power in Northern Ireland lay with ministers, every lunch and every supper across the province was marked by professional lobbying.

On the fourth and final day of my tour, Chris Patten paid his first visit to Northern Ireland Railways as minister. The board were on the platform to meet him, a brightly painted new train standing by. The minister was given a driver's cap, placed in the cab and off we went for a short trip. The new train was named, Chris was presented with a miniature name plaque and lunch followed in the boardroom. Years later, when my wife was asked to perform the same duty, I formed the suspicion that it might have been the same train with a new coat of paint!

The board of Northern Ireland Railways consisted of solid Northern Ireland businessmen who came from the pool of local talent – mainly Protestant – that Northern Ireland departments drew on when making appointments to public quangos. Half-way through the lunch, one of the board members remarked to me through the chairman, 'Are you one of the Kilkeel Needhams related to the Earls of Kilmore-y?' 'Yes,' I replied, 'but the name is Kilmurry.' 'Don't you come over here telling us how to pronounce your name!' came the chairman's nimble response.

That afternoon, surrounded by policemen, Chris and I toured Belfast city centre. Except for the vicinity of the City Hall where Marks and Spencer had held its ground, the streets were dirty and pock-marked with bombed-out gap sites. The great Victorian buildings were empty above ground level and masked in crumbling estate agents' 'To Let' signs. The fascias above the shops were ugly and gaudy, and every hundred yards or so there were checkpoints and gates at which every bus, car and delivery vehicle was scoured before it could pass. We were passed by an army patrol with unsmiling, helmeted, young soldiers gazing at the shoppers, their guns pointing at the pedestrians' knees. It did not look like a place to take your children to see Father Christmas.

I went home on the shuttle that night, my mind filled with the contradictions I had seen and heard during my four-day visit to Ulster. I had known the problems were labyrinthine in their intractability, but I had not fully understood the depths of the division or the narrow scope for compromise that existed in communities with such opposing national aspirations.

THERE IS NO ANSWER

Over the remainder of the autumn of 1983 I read the contemporary books on the Troubles, but found that, whatever perspective they were written from, they offered no new way out. Everything had been tried. Padraig O'Malley's book *The Uncivil Wars*, based on a series of interviews with the major protagonists, summed it up:

> Indeed, the story of Ireland today – North and South – is the story of endemic division, symptomatic of the larger illness, a creeping paralysis of will choking off political dialogue at every turn, its debilitating contagiousness more pervasive because of the seemingly irreconcilable divisions between the two parts of Ireland and within Northern Ireland ... Thus the opening months of 1983. For Ireland it was very definitely not the best of times.

I also attended two teach-in conferences which sought to analyse the challenges and debate the solutions to the situation in Northern Ireland. At every Anglo-Irish banquet, the United States is Banquo's ghost. No political initiative can be undertaken without sounding out both the US government and the Irish-American community, in particular the Kennedys. So the first of the two conferences was a weekend get-together at Airlie in Virginia. It was a gathering of the movers and shakers – business, politics, government, academics – all shades of opinion – American, Irish and British. Even the unionists, including Peter Robinson and Sammy Wilson of the Democratic Unionist Party (DUP), came. Most of the weekend passed unsurprisingly in an alcoholic fog but a few memories stand out. Labour MP Clare Short staunchly representing her Crossmaglen mother's outrage. Professor John A. Murphy of University College Cork battering Ken Maginnis about the head like a grey squirrel attacking a grizzly bear. (Afterwards Murphy became a sophisticated advocate of the unionist case in the South, so sometimes conferences do help alter perceptions.) The Irish ambassador playing the piano while Peter Robinson and John Hume sang 'We Shall Overcome', the hymn of the 1960s Civil Rights marchers. Seamus Mallon – bitter, ill and venomous about the police and the army. Chris Patten representing the authority and intelligence of government, which covered up for a lack of both in the NIO. Journalist Bruce Arnold giving a learned treatise on how the British Establishment needed Northern Ireland as a strategic flank from any attack to Britain's rear from across the Northern Atlantic. This was too much for me and I interrupted to say that, as a member of the British Establishment and a member of Pratts Club (aptly named) where the cream of the Establishment met nightly to discuss affairs of state, I had never once heard this argument addressed. As far as I was aware, there were only two proponents of such a view: Enoch Powell and Sinn Féin – one was no longer a member of the British Establishment, and the other unlikely to become one. It was another seven years before Peter Brooke was finally to put to rest the canard about Britain's 'selfish or strategic interest' in Northern Ireland.

The difficulty with such conferences is that everyone agrees about the problem but no one agrees about the solutions. So the solutions can never be discussed without causing a row, which ruins the conferences. John Hume has claimed over many years that a most important first step is for the people of Ireland to respect each other's cultures and traditions. The drawback is that neither side believes the other does, and both sides are right because they don't and they won't as long as violence or its threat is used to achieve the supremacy of one culture or defend the supremacy of the other.

Also that autumn I spent a weekend at a British-Irish Association conference at Oxford which was organised by Marigold Johnson (Paul Johnson's wife). Marigold was supported by a team of Irish well-wishers, some of them of high Anglo-Irish birth who felt slightly guilty about the role of their ancestors during the Famine of the 1840s. It was an annual 'encounter' addressed by the Secretary of State for Northern Ireland and an Irish minister, attended by politicians representing every hue in the British Isles and watched over by senior officials who transcribed every conversation to analyse whether any side had moved an inch in any direction. As after about ten o'clock most participants were incapable of remembering let alone moving, it made for a good party for those who enjoyed their drink and a disagreeable two days for tee-totallers. Chris Patten rather tactlessly called the conference organisers 'toffs against terrorism' but the occasion gave me the chance to mix, meet and drink with the leaders of the Irish and British political, official and media establishments. The unionists periodically abstained from these gatherings. Sinn Féin and the Protestant extremists were not invited.

Most of the argument at the 1983 conference concerned the debate going on in the New Ireland Forum. The Forum, which met in Dublin and which was in part a response to Jim Prior's Assembly which Northern nationalists boycotted, comprised all the main parties in the Republic, plus the SDLP and the Alliance Party from the North. The unionists stayed away, arguing that they were not going to discuss the future of their country in someone else's jurisdiction – a jurisdiction, moreover, whose constitution laid claim to sovereignty over the North. They had a point, but the result was a debate which only addressed one side of the equation. The neutrality of the Republic was never even mentioned. The participants started from a shared, though one-dimensional, historical understanding that the fault lay with every British government since Gladstone and the intransigence of bigoted unionists whose veto the British would do nothing to override.

The outcome of the Forum was of great importance to the NIO

because the British government had long since realised that defeating the IRA was impossible without the wholehearted commitment of the South and unless and until the Republic could be drawn into taking some responsibility for what was happening in the North.

4
NEEDHAM'S TOURS

T OO OFTEN THE TERRORISTS COULD MOUNT their attacks on Northern Ireland from the Republic and then flee back across the border to replenish their stocks. Even when they were caught in the Republic, the arcane rules and procedures covering extradition proceedings led to endless argument and delay, and often to refusal to extradite by the Dublin courts. The Irish government realised that their efforts to sustain the aspirations of Northern nationalists through the New Ireland Forum could only be successful if the mistrust felt on the Tory right and amongst unionists could be blunted. In an effort to reassure the Conservative die-hards they sent a brilliant young Irish diplomat, Richard Ryan, to London. He is a bon viveur, a poet and has a beautiful Korean wife who is a perfect hostess.

Ryan is a complex mixture of Irish charm and Irish obstinacy. His Falstaffian figure and Irish tweed suits hide a razor-sharp mind, deeply rooted in Irish culture and history. He likes the Brits as individuals but his soul is scarred by Irish history. He seemed to despise some unionists and to regard the Northern Ireland Office as humourless, regimented English bureaucrats whose objectives he distrusted; however, he cultivated the Foreign Office and those he wished to neutralise. Hardly a day passed without Richard being seen in the Garrick Club deep in conversation with some improbable Tory MP, the best claret in their glasses and a grouse or partridge on their plates.

It worked. When the Forum Report was finally published in May 1984, the opposition to it within the British government was surprisingly muted and the Ulster Unionists found their erstwhile allies less supportive than they had hoped. But the cost to the Irish exchequer had been high, as Richard was not one to tolerate the form-filling pedants in the accounts department of the Irish Department of Foreign Affairs.

On one occasion, I unintentionally ditched him and me into some particularly choppy waters. I was called into Jim Prior's office in London. Behind the Secretary of State stood the permanent secretary, Sir Robert Andrews. Why, I was asked, had I been discussing sensitive NIO views with Ryan? Did I not realise that in my position of trust I was not to hand over information or opinions which might allow the Irish government to divide departments of the British government and give the Irish an advantage? I was deeply embarrassed by this allegation and not a little surprised, as it was Prior himself who had told me to tell Ryan that there were certain predictable nationalist proposals in the draft Forum document which would be unacceptable to him. I asked how my comments had become known. There was a cough, a moment's silence, and then I was told the Irish government had complained to our ambassador in Dublin about a junior official, me, telling the Irish what was and was not to appear in their report. I was dismissed from the room. I phoned Ryan and asked him what on earth he thought he was playing at. 'Oh God,' he gasped. 'I was ill two days ago with food poisoning, so instead of writing up our conversation and putting it in the diplomatic bag as usual, I decided to send it over the cipher. I suppose we are still using one of the old army codes we inherited from you, and no doubt your people found out what I said.'

The saga would have ended there except that late one night at the British-Irish Association conference I was relating this tale to a group of friends and was overheard by the dreaded Tim Pat Coogan, an Irish journalist and historian with republican sympathies, who, breaking the Chatham House rules of the conference, then published a thinly-disguised version in the *Irish Press*. I do not believe it caused either Richard or I any lasting damage. Unfortunately, neither did it do any damage to the villain in the plot, Tim Pat Coogan.

There was no likelihood of further major legislative action during 1983/4 and so I decided to spend the summer recess firstly digging into how Northern Ireland worked and secondly developing a programme to encourage a wide spectrum of Tory back-benchers to tour Ulster and take an interest in the one part of the United Kingdom that most politicians considered a backwater they would rather not know about. In this way I expected both to change a few minds and to keep Jim and his team towards the front of back-benchers' attention, which was some ambition, given the officers of the Northern Ireland Committee. I was boosted in my aim by a change of parliamentary rules which allowed MPs to claim travel expenses to other parts of the United Kingdom provided their trip was in furtherance of their parliamentary duties.

In the autumn of 1983, I began conducting my back-bench tours of Northern Ireland. As time went by, I widened the invitation to include lobby correspondents and the occasional peer or interested businessman. The trips were also an invaluable apprenticeship for me, as we travelled the length and breadth of Northern Ireland and met political, church and business leaders wherever we went.

I always began the two-day tours with a political and security briefing from the NIO, the army and the police. We would then spend the rest of the first day in and around Belfast, touring the city in a minibus and stopping off at the 'peace line' in west Belfast. On one occasion Bill Benyon, MP for Milton Keynes, insisted on marching boldly towards two very large and sinister-looking men who were standing by a security gate in the 'peace wall' as the rest of us disappeared in the opposite direction. When he returned and we asked him what he was doing; he replied 'Canvassing, just canvassing'! In the evening there was dinner with some community leaders and a local MP, and then those who wanted were allowed to go out with an RUC patrol. Interestingly, those who were the most vociferous about the need for tighter security and executing terrorists were the ones most often early in their beds as the rest of us sped off in our armoured Land Rovers.

Some of the local RUC units showed astonishing resilience and bravery. An RUC sergeant took us around the Short Strand in a supposedly unmarked vehicle. The Short Strand is a small Catholic enclave in Protestant east Belfast at the bottom of the Newtownards Road. It has a population of around two thousand and a male unemployment rate of over 50 per cent, even though it borders both Harland & Wolff and Short Brothers, two of the biggest employers in Belfast. The sergeant pointed out some local members of the IRA as they came out of a republican club. They recognised him and waved – some nerve coming from terrorists who spent much of their time planning the murder of police officers just like this sergeant. He told us that he and his colleagues were trying to make progress in police–community relations by giving talks in the local schools. It was an uphill task, overshadowed by the constant threat of casual violence from a few who were supported – mainly unwillingly – by a cowed community. Of course, there is another side to the behaviour of some RUC and army personnel in Ulster, but too little is written about the unsung community work of many police officers who try to create normality in very abnormal conditions.

On another visit to the Short Strand we were shown mug shots of all the local republican activists and told of their alleged crimes. Lack of evidence made it impossible to arrest and convict them. On the way back to Stormont, the armoured Land Rover stopped by a piece of waste ground and we all got out so the divisions between the communities could be explained to us. There was a crack and the only figure left standing was the towering, twenty-stone bulk of David Lightbown, MP. The rest of us were lying on the ground behind him.

On the second day we would tour the province and then return to Westminster on a late-evening shuttle. The tours may not have changed many opinions and they certainly had no discernible effect on Ivor Stanbrook or George Gardiner, but they opened a few minds on both sides of the Irish Sea and provided a mine of memorable anecdotes.

The most demanding visit was an outing to Londonderry with Julian Amery and Sir John Biggs-Davison. I had been asked by Julian to pick him up and take him to the airport, but I did not realise this would require me to pack his 'smalls' into an old, battered, leather hold-all while he drank half a bottle of good claret with his breakfast.

I had warned Paddy Doherty that he would be receiving high-ranking Tory grandees, and he had grumbled. But before meeting Paddy's team, we had lunch with the Honourable the Irish Society. The society was founded by the City of London to raise the finance to plant settlers in the north-west of Ireland, hence the 'London' prefix to 'Derry'. By the 1980s most of its wealth and power had long since gone, but it still had a wonderful Georgian house next to the cathedral and right by the army barracks within the walls of Londonderry. Its secretary, Peter Campbell, brother-in-law to the duke of Abercorn, gave us a spectacular lunch, at which Julian, Sir John and others reminisced about the Empire.

After brandies and with large Havana cigars clamped between our teeth, we strolled down Shipquay Street to discover how the other half lived.

Paddy had arranged a slide presentation of the work he was doing with the unemployed. He had also brought along the unemployed, a considerable number of whom had pink Mohican haircuts, rings in their ears and high-laced Doc Martens. They looked in astonishment at the cigar-smoke-shrouded, astrakhan-coated grandees before them.

Paddy invited us guests to sit down while the punks lined the wall at the back of the room. The slide show started. Julian Amery decided that he would prefer to be facing the enemy rather than have his back to them. So he swivelled his chair and stared at the mob while sucking on his cigar, and the mob stared back. Paddy continued with his presentation, which grew progressively more anti-British as the slides moved from one bombed-out building to the next. Mercifully, both sides seemed so shocked by the appearance of the other that no words were spoken.

As soon as Paddy had finished I suggested we take a short tour of one or two of the sites themselves and visit the city walls. Paddy set off with Julian on one side and Sir John on the other. Julian, who had been parachuted in to help Tito's partisans in the Second World War, could recognise a fellow 'resistance' fighter when he saw one. He immediately started to question Paddy about his part in the Troubles in the early seventies. Paddy whispered to me that if he had known who I was bringing he would have organised a different sort of reception, and then explained to Julian how the Walker monument had been bombed. (Walker conducted himself heroically during the Siege of Derry in 1689 and his statue dominating the skyline over the Bogside had long been a source of irritation to the nationalist community.) 'There,' Paddy said as we got to the wall, 'Walker was blown up and he fell down the slope without dislodging a roof tile or breaking a window. It landed within six inches of where it was expected to. Who says Paddies can't do a proper job.' Julian, who had spent much time blowing up Germans in Serbia, looked on admiringly. Within minutes they were friends, swapping jokes and stories. On the way back Julian said, with a twinkle, 'We should have locked up Paddy years ago.' I said I was sure the Germans would have liked to have done the same, or worse, with him.

The remains of Walker's statue are still held in store by the Department of the Environment, and from time to time over the six and half years I was the minister, I received requests to put him back and rebuild his column. I always found reasons for delaying, as history in Ireland generally repeats itself.

On what I knew would be my last organised tour in the summer of 1984, I asked John Oaksey to come. John is a neighbour and a friend of mine, and I thought I was entitled to bring one 'guest' on tour before Jim Prior left Northern Ireland, taking me with him. He is also Britain's most respected racing commentator and a member of the House of Lords. What's more, John does have a connection, albeit a rather tenuous one, with Ulster. When the racehorse Shergar was kidnapped, Oaksey was given a tip that the IRA was involved and he might have a role as a go-between. He spent an abortive fortnight in a pub, and neither Shergar nor his captors were ever heard of again.

The tour turned out to be the most eventful of all my visits during my time as a PPS. After the political and security briefing at Stormont Castle I was stopped by the head of the Northern Ireland civil service, Sir Ewart Bell, who beckoned me into his office for a 'quick word'. The Secretary of State, he explained, had hoped to open a new Housing Association project in Strabane the following day, but unfortunately he had to cancel because of an important engagement at home. As I was going to Londonderry the next day, would I mind peeling off for an hour to do the honours for him? This version was not the same as the one I had heard in London the previous week. Jim Prior, who has a refreshing capacity for indiscretion when he is with friends, had asked me to apologise for him not being able to welcome my dignitaries; he explained that he had been told that his planned visit to Strabane had leaked to the IRA and it was their intention to blow him up when he arrived to open the Housing Association project!

Sir Ewart pushed the draft speech across the desk and told me it would only take a couple of minutes to memorise. I looked blankly at the papers, and he commented that it would be easier for me to digest them if they were not upside down. Everything was arranged to ferry me to Strabane and then back to Derry to meet up with the others, he concluded. The interview was over. I could hardly admit to knowing the truth without revealing Jim's involvement.

I sought out Oaksey. 'I am going on somewhere tomorrow and I will have to leave you in Derry. I probably won't be coming back,' I blurted. 'Don't be ridiculous,' he said. So I related my interview. 'I'll come with you,' he insisted. It was my turn to tell him not to be ridiculous. We sought out Jim Prior's private secretary, a bow-tied Englishman seconded from the Department of Health and Social Security. 'Could you check with the Boss if it's alright by him for me to take over his role in Strabane?' I asked him. 'Why, what's the problem?' he responded. 'Nothing, but I would like you to check with him urgently.' 'I can't,' he said, 'he is on his farm in Hampshire and there is no way of contacting him.'

I spent a miserable dinner and then went out on an RUC patrol. As we went around the courtyards under the Divis Flats, someone suddenly shouted 'slam' and the protective visor slid down across the windscreen. There was a loud bang on the roof and then another crash. A little RUC woman constable peered out of the gun slit at the back. 'It's only a fridge,' she said matter of factly. 'They must have thought we were collecting for the jumble sale!'

When we returned there was a message from the private secretary. The Secretary of State had rung in and confirmed that he would prefer the opening to go ahead without me and he would visit the homes at a later date. I slept easier that night.

The following day we toured Londonderry under the direction of the city council's chief executive, Colm Geary, a jovial, shrewd Southern Irishman. Oaksey was recognised wherever he went; his voice even drew instant recognition from a blind man in a social centre. Two things the Irish and the English have in common are racing and betting. But no one appeared to have ever had a winning tip from Lord Oaksey. We were shown neat, new public housing estates with magnificent leisure centres. At one swimming-pool Geary pointed out to us a group of tough-looking men, some playing with children, others endlessly swimming lengths. 'That looks like Martin McGuinness and his active service unit in training,' he whispered. It probably was, although we did not wait to find out.

As we hurried out to our car Oaksey was greeted by another fan. This one was sporting a Sinn Féin T-shirt and claimed to have known John's father (a judge at the Nuremberg war trials) and to have been his batman. Nick Budgen, who a day earlier had been giving rather grand legal advice in a loud, braying English accent to a dubious-looking character in the offices of the Progressive Unionist Party (PUP) above a butcher's shop on the Shankill Road, was for once in his life silent. We later had a lively and somewhat acrimonious debate about the British presence in the North with the city's mayor and councillors over lunch, and then left for Aldergrove and home, pondering on the contradictions of British–Irish relationships.

By the end of my year's parliamentary secretaryship, I had accompanied over thirty MPs, businesspeople and journalists on tours to Northern Ireland. These trips gave them a better feel for what might be done and some understanding of how, even at the bleakest of times, many people in the province had got on with their lives untouched by the Troubles.

5

THE EMPEROR HAS FEW CLOTHES

NORTHERN IRELAND APPROXIMATED IN A PECULIAR WAY to the books I had read about the last years of the Manchu Dynasty. In the Ulster of 1983 there were a number of semi-autonomous warlords and the writ of the Northern Ireland Office was strictly limited. There were the terrorists with their political front men: Sinn Féin/IRA on one side and the Ulster Defence Association (UDA)/ Ulster Freedom Fighters (UFF) on the other. There was the RUC under the iron fist of the chief constable. The chief constable was responsible for 'operational matters', which he defined. The influence of the Police Authority for Northern Ireland was limited and its membership, for security reasons, was secret. There was a Security Minister, but his role was one of 'advise and consent'; with the exception of Nick Scott, incumbents tended not to stay long. The army was responsible through the Ministry of Defence to the Secretary of State for Defence and was tasked by the RUC. What regiments were sent to Northern Ireland and where they were sent was not a matter for the Northern Ireland Secretary either to comment on or even necessarily to be informed about, although during his period at the NIO Douglas Hurd did draw a line on deploying Gurkhas when he discovered Ministry of Defence intentions.

Then there was the prison service. Following the break-out of Maze Prison by thirty-eight IRA prisoners in 1983 – the biggest escape in

British prison history – I recall discussing the situation with Nick Scott and David Gilliland, the NIO's shrewdest press secretary: how could we explain what had happened and what we were doing to stop a repetition? What we could not explain was that the prison officers were to a large extent autonomous, as indeed was the running of the prisons. What could we do if they walked out, worked to rule or decided to disregard government instructions? Send in the army? Call on the RUC? The logistics of either were impossible. Prison officers, who were predominantly Protestant, could be easily targeted at home by their prisoners' outside terrorist friends. They were therefore exceptionally careful how they dealt with their flock who as a result organised themselves pretty well as they wished. Reforms that were implemented later in Britain to curtail the powers of the Prison Officers' Association, reduce costs and raise efficiency were never introduced on the same scale in Northern Ireland for fear of antagonising the prison officers.

The powers of warlords tended to cancel one another out, and so every warlord had a veto over whatever he felt challenged him or his warriors. Some warlords had agendas that were clear. Sinn Féin/IRA's was the bullet and the ballot box, while the UDA/UFF's was to counter this with the bullet. Each group of terrorists was also determined to maintain 'military' control over its own territory and to exercise political and judicial control within that territory by excluding as far as possible constitutional politicians, the RUC and the army. Justice was meted out through smashing elbows and driving nails through knees.

The RUC's agenda was to do what it could to stamp out terrorism while maintaining as much operational independence as possible and gaining as much of the NIO budget as it could to look after the welfare of its officers. This was a laudable aim in itself, but in the hierarchical, authoritarian, semi-military organisation that the RUC was, such an aim could lead to the police force becoming overmanaged and remote both from the communities it served and from the other arms of government whose objectives were more economic and social.

The British army's agenda was more difficult to fathom. Ulster was a quagmire which the army could not solve and which placed a great strain on its resources. On the other hand, it was a perfect training ground for the type of conflicts which, with the ending of the Cold War, the army was likely to confront in its peacekeeping roles around the world. In Ulster, the British army was self-contained and remained aloof from the aspirations of both communities. Both officers and men had too little social contact with either community, although some enterprising young officers of the top regiments often carried off the prettiest daughters of Ulster's dwindling gentry. This lack of contact probably contributed to occasional army misbehaviour. When they did it was generally in nationalist areas, where they tended to be more involved; however if they had been deployed into Protestant communities, they would have performed no differently.

While republicans continued to make the calamitous error of believing that unionism devoid of British support could be bombed into a united Ireland, the constitutional nationalists, supported by Dublin, were caught in a fork. If they were too critical of the republicans they would be tainted with being British puppets, and they also knew that inevitably there would be incidents where the heavy-handedness of the police or the army would infuriate Catholic sensitivities. But equally they understood that violence would achieve nothing. Their aspirations for a united Ireland remained undiminished, but their suggestions for achieving it while IRA violence continued were hopelessly compromised. Whether the Dublin government, knowing it might just possibly one day become responsible for governing Ulster, ever really believed at that time that unity was an option is less clear. They wished to influence events in the North without events in the North influencing them. Understandably, above all else they feared a spread of the Troubles southward. They had suffered enough in the past. If there was to be civil war, let it at all costs be north of the border rather than south of it.

It was for the NIO and the British government to make the best they could out of these glowering antagonisms and construct a strategy that would marginalise terrorism and produce sufficient wealth and social improvement to help both communities come to terms with their differing aspirations.

The NIO was led by a permanent secretary, supported by a second permanent secretary who was also head of the Northern Ireland civil service. The office was staffed on the security and political side by Whitehall secondees who had limited contact with the Northern Ireland civil service. As a consequence, policy operated in tunnels of responsibility. Because of unnecessary and suffocating security, there was little chance of co-ordinating a strategy that dealt with political, security, social and economic policy as a totality. As a result, a failure in one area immediately affected the others.

In Northern Ireland, history repeats itself in slightly varying ways: those who were senior enough in the NIO had usually been there for too short a period to recall what happened last time round, while those who did recall were usually too junior to have the ear of the Secretary of State.

In September 1984 Jim Prior resigned as Northern Ireland Secretary and was replaced by Douglas Hurd. I believed, in fact I had been told by the new Secretary of State's private secretary, that I would carry on, but after a couple of weeks Douglas Hurd phoned and told me he wanted to continue with Kenneth Carlisle, his existing PPS. I had anticipated that I might be promoted, but the reshuffle was small and the Prime Minister told Jim Prior that the only 'wet' in the frame was Peter Bottomley, who became a controversial junior minister at Transport. I was instructed to wait my turn, and barring unforeseen circumstances, it would come.

6

THE GAP YEAR

THE FAILURE TO GAIN PROMOTION in the mini-shuffle of 1984 was a disappointment. I was falling behind my equals in the race towards the top, and of the five of us who shared an office in 1981 – the politburo of the Blue Chips – mine was the last desk left: Chris Patten was a minister in Northern Ireland, Tristan Garel-Jones an ever more influential whip, John Patten a parliamentary under-secretary at the Department of Health and William Waldegrave a parliamentary under-secretary at the Department of the Environment, wrestling with local government tax reform. I had set myself high standards in racing amongst such a field and my prospects were not boosted by my ambivalence over some of the Prime Minister's instincts towards Europe and her apparent indifference to the poorer sections of society. Or perhaps there were other reasons. As Tristan used to ever so slightingly tell me: 'Us fellows with beta plus or alpha minus brains must always remember what we can and cannot do.'

My absent friends were a kaleidoscope of differing talents but similar convictions. Tristan once told me that it was a close-run thing whether he entered British or Spanish politics. He was persuaded, he claimed, by the fact that when you knock on an English door at tea-time to canvass a vote, the occupants invariably tell you to sod off, while in Spain if they answer at all it is because they think the Inquisition has appeared and they will disappear. I have no idea whether this story is true or not, but then there is an awful lot about Tristan that I don't know. For a public man, he is also a very private one. He is a wonderful husband and father in a Latin sort of way. Dedicated to the survival of a Tory government and anyone who leads it, he has intense likes and dislikes, has a tongue like a viper and is ruthless. But if you are his ally he will be your protector, adviser and supporter and he will fight like a tiger to keep you in play. At certain times in my career when he could have lifted a finger he didn't but at other times he backed me to the hilt. He is a friend in the truest sense in that he knows me as I am and he will stay my friend to the grave.

William Waldegrave was a golden boy: captain of the Eton Society, president of the Union at Oxford, fellow of All Souls, Lord Rothschild's right-hand man, Lord Weinstock's right-hand man, Ted Heath's right-hand man – all well before he was thirty. For one so successful so young, ambition is a cruel taskmaster, and William is driven by ambition. His failing, if it is such, is that he was born a 'wet bob' (at Eton a schoolboy could either row – a 'wet bob' – or play cricket – a 'dry bob'; wet bobs were always considered less extrovert and less slick than dry bobs), and no matter how he rearranges his hair, he looks like a don. He has not quite mastered the art of presentation and timing, and he never will. He will not be a Chris Patten or even a John Major when it comes to the television or the Dispatch Box, but he has a grit that will take him further yet. Intellectuals are often political misfits. George Walden and Robert Jackson who were both Ministers for Higher Education are examples of academic comets that whizzed off beyond the galaxy. But William is tough and successful. He knew what he wanted to do in the jobs that he has done. He can charm effortlessly, he manages well, his civil servants trust and like him, and he is cleverer than his permanent secretary. If I were a City man, I would still be buying shares in Waldegrave as a future Foreign Secretary.

The final member of the office was the other Patten. John was the first of our politburo to become a minister; indeed he was the first of the 1979 intake to gain his buttons, being made Minister of Health under Jim Prior in Northern Ireland in 1981. He is an intensely shy and deeply religious Catholic, behind whose suave façade burns a radical fire of determination to emasculate the trendy, lefty, socially undermining values of the Permissive Society. But this shyness and determination came across too often as arrogance and insensitivity. As Education

Secretary in the early 1990s, he despised the liberal education establishment's sloppy approach towards disciplined learning and the inculcation of moral standards. As the attacks on him grew worse, so did his insularity; finally his political touch deserted him. His ambition to have Britain's children brought up imbued with a sense of their history and their Christian values and capable of expressing themselves cogently in the Western world's most spoken and most beautiful language was not to be. He reminds me in character of my first political influence, Nigel Nicolson. In many ways, too good a man for politics. John writes elegantly and wisely. He is a shrewd judge of others. The advice he has given me has never been wrong. When matters took a turn for the worse, he was the first on the phone. Why did he not let us do for him what he has done for us?

From 1981 to 1997 there was always a Blue Chip minister in Ulster.

In September 1984 I was asked by the Hong Kong government to visit the colony as part of a group of parliamentarians. We would be briefed about the position of the colony and the discussions that were tentatively weaving their way towards agreement on the hand-over to China in 1997. It was a 'jolly' in that, because I could change my first-class ticket to two business class tickets and all bedrooms in the Mandarin Hotel were double rooms, it cost nothing to take my wife. Furthermore, there was little I was likely to be able to do to influence negotiations between the 'Iron Lady' and Communist Party chairman, Deng Xiaoping.

If there is any justification for such trips it is that they open eyes and create political opportunities for the future. In my case, by 1984 I had visited Japan several times, spent a month in the US and developed an irritable bowel touring Indonesia with my parents-in-law in 1977. Hong Kong was something else. I had long been fascinated by Japan and its extraordinary recovery. But the success of Hong Kong's people, the magnificence of the setting, and the impressiveness and splendour of its modern architecture both seduced and alarmed me. If this is what could be done with six million Chinese refugees on barren rock, what would happen to the West when the remaining 1.2 billion started down the road to the free market?

A young Chinese district officer, sporting an Oxford University Balliol tie, toured us around some of the new high-rise flats sprouting out of Sha Tin. We met an elderly Chinese journalist who had fled

China. I questioned him on how the residents seemed so tidy, quiet and respectable given surroundings that in some British cities would have been turned into a ghetto. The weather helped, he told me; three hundred days of the year the washing dried by hanging it out of the windows, which was hardly feasible for British housewives. It was, the journalist explained, a mixture of social and historical factors that made the difference. Chinese people respected the rights of neighbours and were respectful of their elders. They came from backgrounds far, far worse than the new, smart, high-rise flats they now squashed into. They all had jobs; they were all ambitious to move on and expected to do so. They were a community of hope, self-confidence, boundless energy and social cohesion. I recalled these wise words when I started out two years later on my six-and-a-half-year stint as Housing Minister for Northern Ireland.

I returned home clear in my mind that much of Britain's future prosperity and opportunity lay in Asia. Conversely, the plight of the miserable boat people living family by family in rows of four-storey metal shelving was a warning of what could happen if Asia's ancient communities became embroiled in 'Great Power' politics.

The party conference in 1984 was held in Brighton. The politburo of the Blue Chips, together with Richard Ryder, later John Major's Chief Whip, used to hold a joint party for our constituency workers. We liked to think that the six of us represented a future force of some significance in the Tory Party and we would compete amongst ourselves to see who could give the more effective morale-rousing address to our mainly elderly workers. After the party most of us went home, unless we had to be on the platform for some reason or were helping one of our bosses to hone his peroration. On the Wednesday night, I had dinner in the Grand Hotel. The government Chief Whip, John Wakeham, and his wife Roberta were at the next table, and we all joined up and laughed the evening away. At about 11 p.m. I took the lift to the top floor where Alistair McAlpine was having his annual treasurer's party, consisting of lobster and champagne. By the time I arrived the lobster had been replaced by vegetable salad and the champagne by the 'house' white. I seem to remember Sir Robin Day weaving his way out with a pretty girl on his arm and wheezingly greeting me with a characteristic 'Dear boy!', which revealed he had not the faintest idea who I was. McAlpine's party invitation was the one to have. Even at that hour

most of the most senior ministers were gossiping with the lobby correspondents – each keen to gain something from the other without giving
anything away. At midnight I met up with the political secretary from
the French embassy, took the lift down and drove back to London, unaware that minutes later the IRA bomb went off.

My phone rang the next morning. There were few details available
but people had been killed and injured. Members of the government
were still missing. The Prime Minister was safe. I found Chris Patten,
who told me all our friends were unharmed. He had been told that the
Prime Minister had been in bed and Dennis brushing his teeth, or vice
versa, and that they had been entirely isolated as pandemonium broke
out around them. Seemingly, lessons were learnt, because when mor-
tars exploded in the garden of No. 10 seven years later, I was told, John
Major was promptly hustled into a basement broom-cupboard.

The bomb in the Grand had been planted two months earlier. If it
had exploded two hours earlier, the Tory Party's leadership – past, present and future – would have been decimated. As it was, four people lost
their lives and dozens more were injured. The IRA had gained its revenge for those who had died in the hunger strikes. The bombing left
a legacy of pain which has not passed. It destroyed Norman Tebbit's
career and crippled his wife.

Some weeks before the party conference I had been told that I had
been picked to second the Queen's Speech on the opening day of the
new parliamentary session. This was an opportunity indeed. Previous
seconders had included Jim Prior, Kenneth Clarke and Kenneth Baker.
It was a form of consolation for missing out on promotion and a test to
see whether I was deserving of it next time round. It was an important
speech – the first I would have to address to a full House. By tradition it
covered the virtues of the member's constituency and why the legislative contents proposed in the Queen's Speech would be so beneficial to
the lives of his voters. The seconder's character needed to shine through,
as the packed House had come to listen not to him but to the Prime
Minister and the leader of the opposition. It required wit, not flippancy,
and a final flourish that would still be remembered in the tea-room after
the big guns had fallen silent. In other words, it needed a great deal of
preparation. It was my first, maybe my only, chance of playing on the
big stage.

The night before the Queen's Speech there was always a dinner in

Downing Street where the Prime Minister would address her ministers and the chief secretary to the Cabinet would read out the speech with about as much gusto as the Queen herself would muster on the morrow. By tradition the proposer and seconder of the speech, in both the Lords and the Commons, sat with the Prime Minister, while each Cabinet minister hosted a separate table. We all paid for our dinners in advance. I had sent a copy of my speech to No. 10 so that the Prime Minister would be briefed. Alistair Goodlad, a Blue Chip Whip, told me to take out my best joke because Sir Paul Bryan, the proposer, was going to speak first and he needed the joke more. The Prime Minister remarked that my views on Enoch Powell were as biting as any she could recall. I could not make out whether this indicated approval or otherwise. For once in my life, I ate little and drank even less.

At 2.45 p.m. the following day, 6 November, I was in my place on the distant back benches, knowing that on this occasion I would catch the Speaker's eye. I had hoped to deliver without notes, but my nerves overcame me and it was wiser to feel comfortable and perform confidently than to be too clever and forget some of the best lines, or, worse still, dry up completely. Chris Patten had helped me draft parts, although any speech, if it is to be effective, has to be stamped with the author's own character, style and humour. Afterwards, John Patten whispered it was the best contribution from any member of the politburo, which was not true but nice nonetheless:

> For the past week I have been scratching my head as to why I should have been asked to second the Gracious Speech. After all, as has been pointed out, I am the only disfranchised Irish earl on these Back Benches. When I heard the Gracious Speech – particularly the bit proposing legislation for the better protection of the environment – it became clear to me that I had been chosen as a spokesman for one endangered species. Three members of my family have occupied these Benches. They all represented that beautiful part of the United Kingdom – South Down. Unfortunately, there is no evidence that they ever occupied the columns of Hansard. They did not, as Brian Johnston might have put it, much trouble the scorers. That may have been because their sixth sense told them that the current right hon. Member for South Down (Mr Powell) would make up for their long pregnant pauses with his own loquacity.
>
> We all know that the invitation to second the Gracious Speech

comes from the Prime Minister on the advice of the Patronage Secretary (Mr Wakeham). Neither he nor my right hon. Friend the Member for Chingford (Mr Tebbit), the Secretary of State for Trade and Industry, can be in their seats today. I, as much as anyone, welcome their recovery. I look forward, as does the whole House, to seeing the Patronage Secretary back in his place in the not too distant future, with that deceptive smile, which we rebellious Back Benchers know means 'Watch it'. I am also sure that none of us can even contemplate what they have been through. We know only that we want them back here where they belong. − [Hon Members: 'Hear, hear.']

I am also conscious that I speak today from among the junior ranks of Back Benchers. In such circumstances, many of us feel like nervous amateurs compared with the professionalism of Front Benchers. However, we can comfort ourselves with the knowledge that the ark was built by amateurs, but professionals built the Titanic.

I came into the House with several friends who at that point became honourable . . . Most of those colleagues have gone up in the world and done well for themselves, despite a helping hand from me. All of them − let me practise a little Christian charity, which the whole House will know is 18 carat − deserve the buckles on their coats. Nowadays I know a Parliamentary Secretary in almost every Department, so I can at least put a face to the people who sign the letters to my constituents . . . In the last year I have been Parliamentary Private Secretary to my right hon. Friend the Member for Waveney (Mr Prior). For a good few years before that he had been a friend of mine. I learnt not only to respect his balance and 'bottom', but to be grateful to him. After all, he gave me the opportunity to know the country of my ancestry rather better than my ancestors knew it. My right hon. Friend also taught me the need for politicians to be as good listeners as they are talkers and, when the going gets rough, to mix courage and determination with compassion and compromise.

Three-and-a-half weeks ago the British people saw how their Government behaved when members and their wives were bombed. They were rightly proud of what they saw. A few days later they heard the reactions in the House of Commons. They heard the right hon. Member for Manchester, Gorton (Mr Kaufman) say that the gap between one side of the House and the other was as a hair's breadth compared with the chasm between terrorism and democracy. They were rightly proud of what they heard. In a few moments the debate on the Queen's Speech resumes along familiar lines. It is through this House via the ballot box, that the government of Britain is conducted. Neither violence from outside, bomb or bullet will alter that. We know that, the British people know that, and every one of us will fight to the last to ensure that it stays that way.

Jim Prior took me off to the tea-room and showed me off as a proud housemaster would his star pupil at the end of the school play. Sometimes the House has its rewards. The approbation of one's colleagues is the greatest reward the Commons has to offer. Then Chris brought me back to earth by suggesting that it would be another ten years before I again caught the attention of a full House. He was right.

One of the disagreeable aspects of a political career is that, in order to get on, clever men and women have to dissemble over what they know to be right in order to placate the emotional and often irrational prejudices of their supporters inside and outside parliament. In 1984 Leon Brittan, who was Home Secretary, and the Prime Minister, who was a 'hanger' by instinct, had agreed to allow the House a debate, followed by a free vote on capital punishment as promised in our manifesto. Leon, whose Jewish background had sometimes counted against him amongst the worst, nether regions of the Tory Party, had, however, stood in his constituency on a platform of only hanging terrorists. Now in late 1984 as Home Secretary, he had to introduce the debate on the floor of the House, define his own position and explain why that position was total anathema to the Secretary of State for Northern Ireland, who would be confronted in Northern Ireland with the consequences of executing teenage puppets of IRA godfathers. The Home Secretary found himself in a maze of his own making, the only exit from which was signposted humiliation. He had a terrible day in the House and it made me wonder whether perhaps it was preferable to remain on the back benches and stick to what you believed in rather than be forced to compromise on the way up.

When I went into Prior's office the next morning, Joyce Wheeler, his diary secretary, and Edward Bickham, his political adviser, were imploring him to ring Brittan and bathe his wounds. Jim grudgingly obliged. What was doubly unfortunate was that Leon's utterly undeserved reputation for shiftiness was reinforced in the eyes of those he was hoping to placate on the right of the party. Many pragmatic Tory MPs had long since learnt that they could support the death penalty for one particular type of crime which they knew would never win support in the Commons but would satisfy their bloodthirsty constituents. Long may that continue.

Early in November William Waldegrave asked me whether I would be Patrick Jenkin's parliamentary private secretary at the Department of the Environment. Jenkin had been under a lot of pressure in the previous session when he had been responsible for abolishing the Greater London Council. He had been duffed up by Jack Cunningham and Jack Straw in the House and by Ken Livingstone outside it. It had been suggested by sources 'close to Downing Street' that he would be out in the next reshuffle, and William felt that I might help him through what was likely to be his last year in the Cabinet. I knew that after the Queen's Speech my chances of promotion were now quite good, provided I kept my nose clean, and that the most likely position with my record would be to replace a promoted Patten in Ulster. Working for Patrick Jenkin would give me experience of another department and an excuse for not revolting, so I joined up.

There were two 'big' issues facing the Department of the Environment: the introduction of the Poll Tax and the never ending battle with the local authorities to control their spending. The Treasury under Nigel Lawson were in formidable mood and determined to cut as hard as they could, particularly in housing. With his reputation already dented, the Secretary of State was between a rock and a hard place. Patrick is a considerate, civilised man who had spent a political lifetime serving the government and doing whatever he was told with enormous application and determination. He is sensitive and musical but he is not a political jungle cat.

With the abolition of the Greater London Council Bill out of the way, his self-confidence started to return and by the summer of 1985 he had some justification for hoping he might still be kept on. However, Kenneth Baker, then Minister of State at the Department of the Environment, had been promised and Patrick's head remained on the block. Baker was on his long march from left to right and rehabilitation, although at the time not many of us noticed what was happening. He was nominally in charge of the preparations for introducing the Poll Tax but the details were left to William Waldegrave, who was parliamentary under-secretary at the department. As so often is the case, the devil lay in the detail, and it was the detail of how to collect the charge that was never properly addressed. I spent hours sitting in on meetings discussing what classes of people should be exempt or not. William's line was to keep it simple: there should be few if any exemptions; if necessary, take the money off them and then give it back to them. The real problem lay in an unthought-through manifesto promise which now could not be abandoned. The Prime Minister had been sold on the principle by a slick presentation from William and Kenneth that did not dwell on the mechanics.

The other bugbear was, as always, the Treasury. They had never believed in the politics of the charge and they were determined to reduce further the Treasury subvention to local government. The result was a controversial new tax which was inadequately funded by central government; the outcome, political disaster, followed by a U-turn which in the end cost the Treasury twice as much as they would have paid had they not cut the government contribution. So the tax turned out to be financially uncollectable and politically unacceptable. I learnt enough never to introduce it into Northern Ireland when I became Minister for the Environment there.

Patrick Jenkin, following the Toxteth riots and Michael Heseltine's intervention, had been responsible for Liverpool's regeneration and I flew with him whenever he went there. It was my introduction to the management of inner-city deprivation. The lack of co-operation between central government and the 'ultra-left' Derek Hatton-controlled city council had led to two different administrations attempting to alleviate the hardships and promote a new image for themselves rather than the city. I learnt a lot about what not to do when it came to my turn to run Belfast and Londonderry. I helped Patrick to write his speeches and prepare answers to parliamentary questions and I organised backbenchers to support him in debates and at 'statements', but I spoke little on the floor of the House. I had one devastating setback when I forgot a supplementary question I intended to ask following the murder of nine policemen in Newry and was left sinking to my seat in total confusion. It shattered my self-confidence for several months, and no reminding me of the fact that Churchill had once 'dried up' in a major debate could console me. I was not Churchill.

At the end of November 1984 I took the train to Brighton to see John Wakeham, who was still recovering in hospital. After the bomb

Roberta had slipped away to her death lying alongside him, crushed by the falling masonry. He had been terribly injured in the legs and it was far from certain at the time I saw him whether he would ever walk again. He survived, he told me chillingly, because he had always drunk a tremendous amount of water. His consultant instructed him shortly after arrival in hospital that if he was to live he had to consume huge amounts of liquid day after day. He did and recovered; others did not. The Prime Minister had allocated one of her most charming, long-serving and dedicated private secretaries to oversee his painful recovery. A year or so later, to everyone's delight, they married. I left his bedside sure that it would not be long before I would be back in Northern Ireland. John Wakeham has proved a good friend to me throughout my political career, and I really don't know why, as I have never socialised or worked closely with him.

The following summer my family and I went on holiday to Brittany with the Pattens where my efforts to teach Chris to water-ski resembled pulling a tethered seal at high speed just below the surface. After two sea-water enemas, he decided to try another sport. We all knew a government reshuffle was due early in September and what the moves for us were likely to be. What we did not know was that Chris had left the wrong telephone number with his private office. After two weeks in Brittany, we left to spend the final week of our holiday in Cornwall while the Pattens remained in France.

Sure enough, while we were in Cornwall, the reshuffle was announced on the afternoon of Monday, 3 September. I huddled with my family round the phone, waiting for a call from Downing Street that never came. The first call that did come was at seven o'clock the next morning; it was the BBC asking me to comment on the announcement that Tom King was to be Secretary of State for Northern Ireland. As Tom was a neighbour of mine and had started his political career in Chippenham, I was able to give him glowing references although disappointment was by then etching at the lining of my stomach.

The next caller was Patrick Jenkin to tell me that he had been sacked and how nicely the Prime Minister had fired him. He now had no idea what he was going to do. I asked him if he had been able to put in a word for me. There was a pause, then 'I'm terribly sorry,' he said, 'I was so keen to stop her getting rid of George Young, I completely forgot about you.'

The third call was from Chris Patten's private office in Belfast. No. 10 had been trying to get hold of him but no one could find out where he was. Maurice Hayes, one of his permanent secretaries, had heard my interview with the BBC on Tom King and had cleverly construed that I would probably have the right number. I had, but I had also been trying to phone him and there had been no reply. It was not until later that I discovered a similar family drama to mine had played itself out on the other side of the Channel. Chris could not understand why he had not heard from No. 10, and in the end had decided to take the family out for the day. It was later that evening that No. 10 finally tracked him down.

Late that afternoon I phoned Jim Prior, who in turn phoned the Chief Whip. The Chief Whip told him that it would be alright, the middle tier of the reshuffle had been sorted. After another anxious night, the call I had been waiting for arrived. I was to phone the Prime Minister at noon. From a call-box in Manaccan overlooking the Helford River where I had been brought up, I telephoned No. 10. Unfortunately, the Prime Minister had had to leave for Birmingham, but her principal private secretary informed me that I was to succeed my best friend as minister in the Northern Ireland Office. I went to have my hair cut and we set off for home.

7
SETTLING IN

A DAY LATER, ANOTHER CALL. 'Minister, this is your private secretary, Aileen Porter. I wish to make arrangements for you to
come over to the province as quickly as possible.' It did not
take long for the family to start accusing me of 'ministerialitis' at the
first hint of any pomposity. As my eight-year-old daughter remarked,
parliamentary under-secretary in Northern Ireland was hardly the
Cabinet.

Having Tom King as boss had one immense advantage. Because
his home was so close to mine, I could cadge a lift with him from
Lyneham, our nearest RAF airfield, whenever he flew to Belfast at the
start of each week. Travel is the curse of a British minister in Ulster.

The following Monday, 10 September, I was on my way. It never
occurred to me that it would be six and half years later before I would
take my last plane back to Lyneham. As soon as we touched down at
Shorts' private airport in Belfast, Tom and I sped off in different directions. Aileen and I sat in the back of my car with two escorts in the front
and a further two escorts in a back-up car behind us. Security was now
to become a mantra that dominated and occasionally haunted the lives
of my family and me.

The first two days passed in a blur. There is a semi-convention in the
British government that predecessors spend very little time briefing suc-
cessors. There are several inadequate excuses for this. Firstly, the

minister may have been sacked (though formally, of course, no minister is ever sacked; he resigns), and the last thing a disgraced and often embittered politician may wish to do is spend time explaining the joys of his past post to the delighted new owner. Secondly, the former minister may have been promoted to a more important ministry and will have all his time absorbed in grappling with his exciting new department. Thirdly, senior civil servants are protective and are keen to influence the new man about the detail, the programmes, the priorities and the personalities over which he will have final responsibility.

In my case, Chris Patten was straight into the cauldron of Education under Keith Joseph. He came over to Northern Ireland for a valedictory lunch and made a charming speech about his previous two years in Ulster and his delight in his friend replacing him. His two permanent secretaries responded with nice speeches and the gift of two books. (One book would have been an almost unheard of honour for a departing British minister!) Then he was off, with a cryptic aside to me that the key to Belfast was the River Lagan.

I spent the remainder of my second day meeting the staff of my private office and some of the most senior under-secretaries, and then I jetted home to tidy up. I had to clear my desk of all the constituency cases which had accumulated over the holidays. I held an advice centre. I called an emergency board meeting to resign from the chairmanship of the small printing and design business I had founded with three friends some twenty years earlier and which I had to give up once I became a minister, and then I started replying individually to the one hundred and fifty or so congratulatory letters that friends had showered me with.

Two days later, Sissy and I flew back to Belfast as I had drawn the short straw as the weekend 'duty minister'. The need for a duty minister to be present at all times in the province is mysterious. For the first four years until I had won my spurs any incident of any significance was dealt with by the duty officer at the Northern Ireland Office ringing the senior duty civil servant, usually a Home Office Brit, who would ring the Secretary of State's private secretary, who would then decide with the Boss and the press office how the 'event' should be handled. The first the duty minister would know of such an 'incident' would be when he turned on the television in the Hillsborough flat.

The flat was an annex which had been built alongside the main house, quite unnecessarily as there was plenty of space inside. The design and furnishings were typical 1970s Property Services Agency – 'bloody'. It was choreographed to the standard of an East Midlands three-star hotel. The lights were too bright, the beds were too narrow and the curtains had no lining. However, it was to become home for one weekend a month over the next six years and my family became rather fond of it. At least the phone did not ring with anxious constituents pouring out their problems. Moreover, the fridge and the drinks cupboard were well stocked at government expense.

Hillsborough Castle is quite a fine Anglo-Irish pile. It is certainly not Baronscourt or Castle Coole, but it has some well-proportioned, well-lit, high-ceilinged reception rooms which can be grand enough or cosy enough depending on the occasion. At least, unlike most other aristocratic Anglo-Irish houses, the roof only leaks occasionally. The gardens have become slightly too formal as every prince, princess and princeling has planted a shrub in memory of some long-forgotten garden party, which is commemorated by a plaque giving the date and the name of planter and plant. There are some fine rhododendrons, some even finer Wellingtonias and a spring walk along a little stream which is truly enchanting. The Queen has her own bedroom and Prince Philip an adjoining duplicate, each with its own bedside potty cupboard in which nests a royal-crested potty. I used to show the potties to visitors until the security guards split on me and the Secretary of State rather grandly disapproved. There is a Throne Room complete with throne, which many Ulstermen and women have tried to sit on while their giggling relatives snap furtively away.

That first weekend when I toured the house, entering by the side-door, by-passing the police control post and in through the pantry, I was dismayed by the gaucheness of the paintwork. The lack of any style or taste was relieved only by Sir John Lavery's two wonderful portraits in the small dining-room. The first and most famous is of the greatest of all Ulstermen, Edward Carson, who was a Dubliner, and the second is of Charles, marquess of Londonderry, wonderfully arrogant, slightly effeminate and beautifully formed. No wonder he had Ribbentrop to stay for the weekend and his Lordship would have looked irresistibly romantic wearing one of Marshal Goering's uniforms.

To unionists, Hillsborough represents their link with royalty and the mainland. It is where one day they hope to be invited to a garden party, where they will wait patiently to be presented and then take tea with their monarch. To nationalists it is at best a throwback to a long-past English domination and at worst a continuing reminder of the power that has ruled them and riled them for centuries.

One of Tom King's most memorable legacies to Northern Ireland is the way in which he transformed Hillsborough's state rooms in complete keeping with their eighteenth-century origin. Even the garden lost some of its formal pretentiousness. In this project, he relied on a small group of that nearly extinct tribe, the Anglo-Irish gentry. For once it proved the exception to the rule that committees create only compromises or camels.

From dawn to dusk on that first Saturday and Sunday, I absorbed the first-day briefs that are given to every new minister. Voluminous and boring, they deal with every aspect of a department's work and organisation. Tom King had asked me to take on Chris Patten's responsibilities. So I was Minister of Health and Social Services and Minister of the Environment.

Because the powers of local councils had been so emasculated, the Department of the Environment's remit was all-inclusive. I covered housing, planning, roads, urban renewal, transport and water; only refuse collection remained in the hands of the councillors. At my other department, social services had been amalgamated with the health boards, and the resulting hotchpotch of responsibilities included some unlikely candidates such as licensing of clubs, drink laws and gambling laws. These last three were fall-outs from the Home Office functions of the abolished Stormont government. They were contentious issues and some, such as club licensing, had much more to do with security than with health. This strange transfer of responsibility was to have dire consequences for Northern Ireland.

Most of the local councils' duties had been delegated to appointed boards, such as education and library boards, and the Housing Executive, health and social services boards, which were carefully balanced between sexes and communities. The authority remained with the departments and, depending on the determination of the minister, with him. The combined budgets of the two ministries including social security amounted to £2.6 billion in 1985/86, which was over 60 per cent of Northern Ireland's public expenditure. Most of the spending was on non-discretionary payments for supplementary benefits, including sickness, invalidity, pensions, unemployment and housing. Nevertheless, there was still quite a pot left over for me to allocate. The Department of Health and Social Services (DHSS) with a staff of 5,600 in 1986 and the Department of the Environment with its 10,000 were among the largest employers in Ulster. It took the whole weekend to absorb the structures and tasks, and I still hadn't come to grips with the management systems or their masters. If this was going to be a three-day job, the other four being spent travelling, voting in parliament or working in the constituency, it was going to take some doing.

On the Sunday evening, after Sissy had flown home having spent two days learning the life of a ministerial widow, Maurice Hayes came round to fill me in on the bits I had missed from the four-hundred-page brief. He was the only civil servant at any level during my ten years as a minister whose speeches I could deliver without changing a word or inserting a comma. Unfortunately, most of the best speeches he wrote he delivered himself, which was a mistake. He is a dishevelled sort of fellow, who tends to mumble and chuckle a great deal before he makes a joke. The jokes are very good, but you have to listen very carefully to catch them. He knows as much about Ireland, North and South, as anyone alive. His early years were spent as the town clerk in Downpatrick, and so he was very close to what was happening on the ground in both communities – what was possible and what was not. As my permanent secretary in the DHSS he fought our corner with great success at every annual public expenditure review, although even Maurice, Catholic outsider that he was among so many Protestant permanent secretaries, was not entirely immune to a compromise that would leave those in the room happier than the public outside.

His advice was matchless. His foresight prevented me from falling into many a trap, and I looked to him in my early years as the lodestar to follow. If he has a fault, it is his generosity. He is a man of consensus. In an era of exploding health costs matched by exploding demand, change is not only vital but inevitable. Maurice was ambivalent about the management of change. He wanted things to settle down and left people with many of their prejudices unchallenged – the health service is full of such. As a result we did not achieve as much as we might have done in cutting out waste, implementing new methods and challenging conventional wisdom. Maurice was at home in the socialism of the sixties even though he now works for Ireland's most successful capitalist, Tony O'Reilly. The market bothers him, but I could not have done without him.

At eight o'clock the next morning we sped to my offices at the Department of the Environment; in fact I had two private offices, one at each of my new departments, to which I was transported, always by a different route and always at speeds which confounded both terrorists and terror. I was lucky enough to be able to read in a car, even when travelling the bumpiest and bendiest of roads; since on average we drove forty to fifty thousand miles a year around the province, I read a tremendous amount. At that time, we had not been issued with mobile phones.

The two offices mirrored each other: two departmental private secretaries, two diary secretaries, eight administrative assistants, and one press officer, travelling private secretary, my Praetorian Guard. Everyone in the private offices, except the press officers, were in their twenties or early thirties.

Travelling private secretaries have a particularly demanding occupation. It is stressful and political, and requires immense patience and tact even when exhaustion loosens the tongue and heightens the nervous tension. A private secretary is the point of contact between the public, the departmental officials and their minister. All private secretaries must always be polite, knowledgeable and amenable. It matters not whether the caller be a furious MP, an opinionated businessman or Mrs O'Hara complaining about the drains. Each of them deserves immediate answers and demands immediate access to the minister. Indeed, private secretaries find civil servants, particularly those in senior grades, the hardest to handle. They are already lords of most of what they survey, and they expect these junior, youthful subordinates to do their bidding, and to ensure the minister also does their bidding. If not, the senior official can subtly imply that he will still be there long after the minister has departed. He can mark their promotion papers and appraise the annual performance review of those who have ignored his advice.

Private secretaries are the only public servants whose absolute loyalty is not to their service but to their minister. They are the only ones he can truly depend on to do what he asks, tell him what is happening, and assist him in avoiding the pitfalls while grabbing the opportunities. Only once did I ever have to question any of the private secretaries who worked for me. They were all different, all immensely talented, all attractive, and I adored them all. Sometimes the pot boiled over. Aileen, small and decisive, once slammed the door when she got really cross with me, and after two years turned grey. Catrione, tall, thin and sensitive, lost over half a stone from somewhere. Norma, utterly trustworthy and dependable, developed a rash, and Stephen, dark and determined, just went on answering back or handed in his notice.

My DHSS office was in the drab 1960s Dundonald House, although the room itself was bright enough. The other at the Department of the Environment was a room with a view, a view from one window down Stormont's great one-mile avenue of limes, and from the other out over the borders awash with colour in the spring, to 'Samson and Goliath', the distant cranes of Harland and Wolff which are Belfast's most dominating features. On the walls of both rooms I hung pictures by my favourite Irish painters, William Conor and James Humbert Craig, borrowed from the storerooms of the local museums. In Stormont I had one wall covered with maps of Belfast and Ulster. I was a Major General at last, or was I?

The range of work and its intensity required all my effort and very soon I lost all interest in what was happening at Westminster or indeed in the affairs of my other Northern Ireland Office colleagues. We lived separate lives except that once a week I would attend the Secretary of State's morning 'prayers' which were held in his room – the Prime Minister's old office in Stormont's Castle Buildings. Around his desk would gather each day the same cast: the NIO's permanent undersecretary, seconded from either the Home Office or the Ministry of Defence; the head of the Northern Ireland civil service, always an Irishman and up to now always a Protestant; the security adviser, a deputy secretary on detachment from the Ministry of Defence or the Home Office; the head of the political department, usually a Foreign Office implant; the NIO's head of information, usually British, sometimes an Ulsterman; the Secretary of State's political adviser; the Security and Political Ministers and occasionally other junior ministers interested in the latest security 'incident' or keen to keep abreast of the political gossip. I scarcely remember the discussions having any relevance to economic or social issues.

The early-morning meeting analysed the agenda for the day, discussed 'lines to take' if the Secretary of State was 'door-stepped' by reporters, dissected reports of the comments or speeches of local politicians, and tried to ensure that its harassed chief would avoid the embarrassing holes with which the outside 'real' world daily confronted him. Endless analysis was followed by differing, often conflicting, advice, offered by men, and occasionally women, who themselves would never have to either utter the words they were suggesting or answer the questions they were posing. The most impressive advice often came from the locals. The unrivalled local feel of Kenneth Bloomfield, head of the Northern Ireland civil service, was always quiet and persuasive. David Gilliland, coming to the end of his career as head of information at the NIO, was shrewd and not so quiet.

That such meetings served a purpose and avoided obvious disasters, I have no doubt. However, the obsessions with tactics, nuance and departmental sensitivities did nothing to set a broader framework for resolving Ulster's conflicts. Such a strategic forum may have existed in Whitehall but I was never part of it.

One of the nonsenses of Northern Ireland is that direct rule has brought with it some of the least attractive elements of former colonial rule. The locals cannot be trusted, and so there is always an Englishman who is permanent under-secretary to the Secretary of State, another Englishman. The Scottish Office is allowed its own locally bred permanent secretary, and so is the Welsh Office. Why not in Northern Ireland? Is it because Her Majesty's Government might one day want to hand Ulster to Dublin and an Ulsterman could not be trusted to do the Queen's bidding? Or is it that one day a Catholic might rise to fill the post and he would instinctively do Dublin's not London's bidding? The mystery remains. The result, as will be seen later, is consensus advice from clever people who have no real feel for what is happening on the ground and which in some cases, such as at Drumcree in 1996, can lead to tragedy.

The first act of any new government should be to give every Northern Ireland civil servant the opportunity to carry a marshal's baton in his rucksack. Should a successful candidate to Northern Ireland's permanent under-secretaryship have a background that was not steeped in the complicated contortions of security and politics, it would be nothing but a benefit.

The morning meeting apart, the daily round started between half past eight and nine o'clock. Of the three and a half to four days a week I was in Northern Ireland, I strove to be out of the office for 50 per cent of the time. To give an impression of how I'd spend my day, I include my diary entry for a typical office day in 1989 when I was parliamentary under-secretary of state in the NIO:

TUESDAY 9/5/89

8.00 ETD	RAF Northolt
9.00 ETA	Shorts
9.00 ETD for	Stormont Castle
9.15	Secretary of State's morning meeting – Video Conference Room, Stormont Castle
10.00–11.30	Meeting with Secretary of State re Laganside – Harbour Commissioner's Office
11.30 ETD for	Drumkeen Hotel
11.45–12.30	Meeting with National Confederation of Registered Residential Care Home Associations – Drumkeen Hotel (DHSS)
12.30 ETD for	Clifton House
12.45 for	Visit to Clifton House (to include lunch) – 2 North Queen
13.00–15.00	Street (DHSS)
15.00 ETD for	Donegall Pass
15.15–16.15	Visit to James Butcher Helpline – Elm Court, Donegall Pass – (DOE)
16.15 ETD for	Queen's University
16.30–17.00	Launch of book on Road Traffic Law by David Lavery – Canada Room, Queen's University (DOE)
17.00 ETD for	Stormont House
17.15–18.00	Stormont House: Interviewing Private Secretaries
18.00–18.45	Stormont House: Meeting with Mr Tim McNeill re UK–Japan 2000
19.30 for 20.00	Dinner for foreign journalists – Old Schoolhouse, Ballyrobin Road, Muckamore
	OVERNIGHT – STORMONT HOUSE

Avoiding Mr Blobby's waistline was a trial. I played squash once a week, always climbed four flights of stairs to the office and walked wherever I could. Golf, which is one of Northern Ireland's best-catered-for attractions, took too long. In ten years I have played at most ten times (my handicap or lack of it was another drawback!). Although Northern Ireland is surrounded by fish and shellfish, 95 per cent of the

catch is exported. Northern Ireland people – men and women, Protestant and Catholic – like meals of multiple courses, of which the common theme is overcooked quantity, garnished with saturated fats and
cholesterol-enhancers.

One of the five-star banquet providers of such menus was Stormont
House where junior ministers slept and dined. The cooks were Stephen
and Frank, the major-domo was Michael and the housekeepers, who
doubled as waitresses, consisted of the formidable Liz and her formidable daughters, Jane and Laris. They were all wonderful and they put up
with hell. They had to deal with ministers of all sorts and sizes, most of
whom were polite, and some not. There was a constant stream of senior
civil servants, often with assumed names, who would come for a night
and sleep either on the second floor or in one of the three ministerial
suites on the first floor. The British permanent under-secretary had a
smart flat of his own through a security door, to which I was summoned only twice. The entertaining rooms had three purposes. They
could be used for small receptions, used for dinner and luncheons or
divided into sitting-rooms with sofas, chairs and a television. As with
so many British government buildings, they were bright and ugly.
Michael and his team had to cart drinks and food all over the house at
every hour of the day and night.

Once a year I used to go on a fishing expedition in Larne Harbour
and come back with baskets of mackerel and herrings. We would then
have a feast. It was when gutting the herrings and baking the mackerel
that I discovered it was not Frank or Stephen's culinary skills that were
to blame for our sodden vegetables and leathery steaks but government
spending freezes which had delayed replacements to the elderly cookers
and the tired-out Kenwoods as well as denying them basic utensils. I
was later to discover much the same was true on a far greater scale in
Shorts and in Harland and Wolff.

New arrivals at the level of parliamentary under-secretary began life
on the second floor with a shared bathroom. Wives very soon gave up
visiting their husbands for a mid-week engagement. A mixture of well-
used mattresses and security floodlighting made sleep unlikely unless, as
the Ulsterman has it, 'drink had been taken'! Everyone in the house,
from the police on the door to the disabled boy who cleaned the shoes,
became friends. After so many years they knew all my personal
habits and they looked after me as if I were a king. The cook, Frank

McIllmurray, even claimed that he was a relative of mine. 'You may be Lord Kilmorey,' he boomed on my first day, 'but I am your Fenian cousin!' I hope he is.

During the day the paperwork built up in the office. It consisted of submissions from officials that needed ministerial endorsement, correspondence that I had to sign, and briefings for meetings and speeches. An enormous amount of other interdepartmental paper was weeded out by the principal private secretary before it reached me. What to show me and what to shred was a crucial part of the private secretary's job which all new occupants had to relearn to their discomfort. I could not stand being overburdened. The hand-overs from one private secretary to whom I had become attached to the next were easily the most traumatic experiences I had in a decade of ministership.

After a few weeks I introduced a traffic-light system: 'red' required my personal and total attention, 'orange' I glanced at and 'green' I signed mostly unread. Every evening there would be two full canvas fishing-bags and each one would take an hour or two to get through. Generally, I ploughed through one after supper and one in bed before breakfast. There is always a temptation to scrawl a comment or an instruction on a file to show the submitting branch that you have at least studied what they have proposed. The effect of this is to increase the workload all round; then the file winds its way back with reasons why the instruction cannot be fulfilled, and the minister's reputation for conscientiousness will have been won at the loss of his reputation for rational analysis. Any minister can, and many do, become enthralled and consumed by the detail of departmental administration. I always responded personally to anyone I had met and to MPs, and councillors, and anyone else who was important or thought they were, although I did not always read or remember what I had written!

I tried, if I could, to finish the work as I travelled to and fro and in Northern Ireland. I wanted to avoid having too much sent home at weekends because Friday nights and Saturdays were when I earned my MP's pay. When I first became a minister my salary as an MP was halved and my total remuneration rose from £26,000 to £38,000. I therefore was rewarded on the basis of spending one third of my time on my constituents and two thirds as a minister, which is, of course, nonsense. I probably worried too much about my majority, which had increased to just over seven thousand two years after I went to Northern Ireland, but Chippenham had been a Liberal marginal for twenty years and I was keen to make it safe. I was anxious that constituents, many of whom knew of my Irish roots, would not feel that I had abandoned them to become their MP in Ulster. So I delegated the day-to-day running of my constituency work to the most capable hands of my wife and then spent every weekend that I was not on duty in Northern Ireland working like a dervish – attending advice centres, visiting factories, farms and markets, addressing Lions, Rotaries and Round Tables, appearing in the newspapers and commenting on the local radio.

I need not have feared. Although hardly a Wiltshire soul knew what my ministerial responsibilities were, they were convinced that it was dangerous and important; moreover they rather enjoyed having as an MP a minister who they could still reach at home on his private number. I was further obliged by some local Liberal councillors complaining about the cost to the ratepayer of protecting me, and by some DUP supporters sticking 'Ulster Says No' stickers on road signs in my constituency in the 1987 election. Wiltshire people had no idea what the slogan signalled but they knew it was an attack on me and they did not like it. By the time I left Ulster my majority was over 16,000, but there was a personal cost. My children had been brought up and grown up for the most part without me.

A day or so most weeks, mainly on a Thursday and occasionally on a Wednesday, I would have to be in the NIO's London office, which at the time was housed in the Old Admiralty Building. The Secretary of State's panelled room was where Winston Churchill returned to power in 1940, when the First Sea Lord triumphantly signalled his fleets 'Winston is back'. Behind the desk was the map cupboard which Churchill found in 1940 to have been unopened since he had left in disgrace in 1915. Inside were the maps of the Dardanelles, showing the positions of the struggling empire armies and the surrounding Turks. Churchill's successor as first lord had been Edward Carson.

My office up the corridor was a humbler affair, furnished and costed to the criteria approved by the Treasury for a civil service under-secretary. Terence Conran's designs were not encouraged. There was one part-time administrative assistant who sat in the outside office manning the phones but with little or no knowledge of the names or the issues which suddenly poured down on her as soon as I passed through the door. The regional accents usually led to misunderstandings on both sides.

The building was filled with security and political advisers, most of whom, as far as I could make out, spent their time passing each other minutes marked 'secret' which I therefore never saw but which seemed to lead to argument and confusion rather than transparency and certainty. The only advantage of the London office was it faced out onto Horse Guards Parade and every summer we could invite friends, relatives and important political and business contacts to watch the Beating of the Retreat and the Trooping of the Colour. I worked hard on the invitations to reward those at every level – personal, constituency and ministerial – who deserved a treat for past services or who could be helpful in achieving some of my future political or ministerial objectives. We filled them full of champagne and smoked salmon. Even when it poured, they went away entranced at the spectacle and the professionalism of Britain's past imperial grandeur.

The travelling private secretaries disliked London days and tried to minimise them. They were showered with work. Their minister was either in parliament or preparing for a parliamentary committee, a debate or question time, all of which led to him being tetchier than normal. Furthermore, London involved party politics. Nearly all NIO civil servants disliked the intrusion of politics into their minister's life. They are non-partisan and therefore instinctively wanted nothing to do with the rough and tumble of Westminster life. It involved angles, deals, compromises and negotiations which they often found distasteful. They had little understanding or training in Westminster's conventions and procedures, and could never fathom a minister's relationship with the whips – his fear of them, the need to placate them or their importance to his prospects for promotion.

I also had a poky, windowless office on the lower ministerial corridor in the House of Commons which would have failed any Shop Act; my wife used this office when she was in town for constituency work, and I used to sleep in it if there were all-night divisions. I also went there before and after a debate to finalise my speech and sometimes waited there while the private secretary checked my contribution in Hansard for split infinitives, oxymorons and other linguistic blunders. As the years went by, the private secretaries weaned me away from the delights of parliament.

Domestic arrangements were tolerable, although living in three places at once led to a dearth of shavers in one bathroom and a surfeit of toothpaste in another. Family nerves, however, were sometimes stretched to breaking-point by arbitrary changes in duty allocations which involved cancelling at no notice a long-arranged family outing or missing one of the children's birthday parties. Cancelling a constituency engagement is not easy when your name is printed on the invitation.

There was a stream of niggles over money. Ministers earned less than many of their senior civil servants. What could or could not be paid towards a minister and his family's expenses was decided by senior public servants. This often created controversy. One ridiculous example was when Sir Jack Hermon withdrew ministers' back-up cars on the ground that security no longer justified their use, although there had been no obvious reduction in the level of IRA threat. Personally, I think it had more to do with reductions in the RUC budget. One of the side benefits of a back-up car was that the family could travel in it at weekends. Ministers were encouraged to bring their families to the province and to ensure that at weekends they got out and about so that Ulster's political masters could be seen by the populace. With the back-up car withdrawn, the NIO proposed that ministers should hire one of the office's duty cars. Then, while the minister sat lording it in the back seat of an unmarked police car, his family would follow in this hired car, with his wife driving (that is, presuming she could drive!). To add insult to injury, we were to be charged 40p a mile for this privilege. Compromise was finally reached when I insisted on driving my own family behind the police car and the NIO filled up the tank with petrol. (It was around this time I developed high blood pressure.)

There were many other such petty, infuriating instances which ministers liked to moan to each other about and which did little to improve morale or comradeship. For instance, offspring over twenty-one had to pay for themselves to come for a weekend and the NIO would then send the parents a bill for the cost of the room. The Public Accounts Committee must at all times be respected, but some British officials in the NIO had an almost savage desire to ensure the integrity of the public purse regardless of humanity or family feeling. After a year or two, my family, private office, police escorts and the staff at Stormont and Hillsborough found ways of beating the 'system' and we quietly exulted when we had succeeded.

8

THE PLAN UNFOLDS

FOR THE FIRST TWO MONTHS AFTER I arrived I toured Ulster like a provincial colonial governor inspecting his dispositions. But I was an amateur in the art of polite but pointless conversation. My first visit to a hospital ended in a very public humiliation. I was introduced to the sports correspondent of the *Belfast Telegraph* who had just had a serious stomach operation and was wired up with a tube for every orifice. This limited conversation. I was surrounded by nurses, doctors, television lights and officials. My mind went blank. In a ludicrous blurt, I asked whether he was enjoying the food. Then silence, which was broken by a sister saying: 'Minister, he is on a drip.' Where was the Queen Mother's book on helpful hospital asides?

Overhanging my visits was the ever-growing likelihood of successful negotiations leading to an Anglo-Irish agreement. Unionists have been weaned on the trickery of wily Southern politicians seducing their simple English counterparts into selling out the Union for a united Ireland from which the unionists would feel culturally and politically excluded. The signing of the Anglo-Irish Agreement on 15 November 1985 appeared to be the first step down the path to British withdrawal. To unionists, it showed that nationalist politicians North and South would use IRA violence as a way of extorting constitutional advantage to the detriment of the Union. In protest, 250,000 people crammed the centre of Belfast on the following Saturday. The NIO claimed it was

30,000. It was not. It was the biggest rally of the Protestant people since the signing of the Edward Carson-inspired covenant in 1912.

The Anglo-Irish Agreement followed negotiations between the two governments, which themselves followed the New Ireland Forum report. It had been clear for several years that there would be no security solution to the conflict in Northern Ireland, even if the British security agencies co-ordinated their act and that appeared as far away as ever. (My own personal knowledge of such matters I culled entirely from news reports. I was excluded from seeing any government papers classified as 'secret', except in the most exceptional circumstances.) Equally, a political solution was ruled out unless it involved the support of the parties in the Republic. Northern nationalists naturally looked to the Southern government to support their stance and, equally naturally, the Southern government gave it. This, however, increased unionist distrust of the SDLP and whoever was in government in the South, whom they accused of riding on the backs of IRA violence to attain their ambition of a united Ireland, as enshrined in Articles 2 and 3 of the Republic's constitution.

The position in the Republic was more complex than most unionists realised. The two main parties – Fianna Fáil and Fine Gael – sprang from the two main factions which had fought a bloody and pointless civil war following the Anglo-Irish Treaty of 1921. This led them, with varying degrees of enthusiasm, to articulate aspirations towards unity. However, the prospect of a million Protestants together with half a million often embittered nationalists being folded into one of Europe's poorest and smallest states must have filled them with horror. It certainly filled the unionists with dread. How could they ever feel part of political parties that were founded to achieve their destruction and most of whose supporters gave allegiance to a different religion. Southern politicians were scared of upsetting the rural, green heartland of Ireland and of the Troubles spreading, but they wanted a say in the affairs of the North. In the Forum report they put forward three options: a thirty-two-county unitary state, a federal arrangement and joint authority in Northern Ireland to be exercised by the London and Dublin governments equally. All three were anathema to unionists and also, apparently, to the Prime Minister, Margaret Thatcher, who had cried 'out, out, out' when such suggestions had been made to her.

The Anglo-Irish Agreement was an extremely clever attempt to square these circles. Through the establishment of the Anglo-Irish Inter-governmental Conference, with its two chairmen, the Secretary of State for Northern Ireland and the Irish Foreign Minister, it allowed a series of issues, as defined in the agreement, to be raised for discussion. The presence of civil servants from the Republic in Maryfield, on the outskirts of Belfast, allowed the Irish government, for the first time, a foothold in the North; this gave an element of assurance to nationalists but, of course, was rejected by unionists.

The Irish right to discuss, complain and question was matched on the British side only by a corresponding right to discuss Irish efforts to contain terrorism south of the border. The Irish accepted that any change in the constitutional position of Northern Ireland needed the consent of the majority of the people of the North but ambiguously retained Articles 2 and 3 of their constitution laying claim to the North. The rights were not balanced. Irish ministers had to be very careful to avoid being seen always as surrogates for Northern nationalists and on occasion as advocates for Sinn Féin. They had to act responsibly because what they said or claimed would have immediate repercussions in the North but minimal impact on events in the South. But as they had no authority in Ulster they could never be held responsible for what they did or occasionally demanded. It required consummate political tact, with which not all politicians in the Republic (or anywhere else for that matter) were naturally endowed.

Both governments hoped that over time the Anglo-Irish Inter-governmental Conference could move on to discuss economic and social matters where close co-operation was vital to the growth of both parts of Ireland and in avoiding unnecessary duplication of expenditure. It was a fairly forlorn hope, as violence continued to bedevil every road to political, social or commercial co-operation. However, as time went by, the work of the conference did start to give Southern politicians and Southern policy makers a much better feel for the intractable division between the two communities in the North. They began to appreciate the limits to British power in either coercing the unionists or defeating the IRA. However much Southern ministers complained about the abuses of the security forces, they began to acknowledge in private the limits of control that could be exercised on the young men and women who were fighting terror in the hedgerows of south Armagh and in the alleyways of the Ardoyne.

On the British side, the Anglo-Irish Agreement led to the NIO taking greater account of Southern sensitivities and of the need for more consultation and discussion. It started a process of binding the two governments together, which in turn led to the peace process of John Major and Albert Reynolds, because the mechanics of working together in an atmosphere of some trust had been tried and tested. It also began the slow but vital squeeze on the IRA bosses in the Republic, as cooperation between the security forces on both sides of the border started to bite.

Was there more to it, as unionists claimed? I doubt if either the Irish or the British side saw the agreement as a step towards a united Ireland, for both sides knew that if that were to happen, it would only be by overwhelming consent within both communities, and that a generation of peace would be needed before the question could even be rationally debated within the unionist community. Part of the problem in debating the causes of Ulster's conflict is that too often inappropriate parallels are drawn from Britain's colonial past – the American Revolution, South Africa, India or even Cyprus. These are the poorest of analogies. The causes of Ireland's divisions can best be examined in the light of European history. It is in Europe that the real similarities exist and the lessons of what can and cannot be done should be garnered. It was a war between a Dutch king with German mercenaries and an English king with French soldiers that started the present troubles. As I developed my social and economic strategy for reviving confidence in Northern Ireland's towns and cities and creating havens for both communities to come together to work and play in, I undertook a study of Europe's minorities. I outlined my findings in a paper called 'Ethnic Divisions in Europe' which I gave in 1990 and which formed the core of my strategic thinking. It is clear now that I was too optimistic in my hopes for reconciliation in Ireland and that none of the lessons of Ireland had been learnt in the chancelleries of Europe. If Slovak split from Czech, the out-turn in former Yugoslavia was bound to be hideously more difficult.

From this study I drew two further lessons. Firstly, it is unwise to lay claim on someone else's house even if they stole it from you in the first place. And secondly, in dealing with the IRA we were confronted not by a group of idealistic freedom fighters but by dedicated terrorists who – knowingly or unknowingly – drew their inspiration, their ideology and their tactics from Mussolini's early fascists. The similarities were uncanny. When once told that communism was the opposite of fascism, Winston Churchill replied: 'Well, if you were blindfolded and placed on the ice at the South Pole you would not know the difference from the North Pole which is indeed its antithesis.'

By 1983 it was clear to Margaret Thatcher that an agreement was probable rather than possible. The groundwork had been laid between London and Dublin, principally in the persons of Sir Robert Armstrong, head of the civil service, and Dermot Nally, secretary to the Irish cabinet. Douglas Hurd and Chris Patten had signalled their approval from Ulster, only Jim Molyneaux still believed that he had a route to the PM that could derail the process. Both he and Enoch Powell misjudged the influence of Ian Gow and his friends. Gow took the honourable route and resigned from his ministerial position on a matter of principle over which he cared deeply. The tragedy about Ian's views on Ulster was that they were romantic and almost entirely second-hand.

Tom King must have seemed to be an ideal safe pair of hands to see the agreement bedded in, although there were those who often unfairly pointed to a few missed chances in the departments he had served in. Physically robust, tough in defence of any position he had been entrusted with, cautious in any utterance, opaque in any personal opinion, he was ambitious as much for his party as for himself. His background was similar to Jim Prior's: national service, farming and business; in farming and business he represented the best of the English squirearchy. The difference between them was that Jim soon saw Ulster as a last chance to do something and when that faded, realised he was on the way out, while Tom started off believing he was on the way out but by resolutely defending the Anglo-Irish Agreement, soon realised he could be on the way up.

Tom had what was to us an endearing but to the press an infuriating response when asked a particularly awkward question: 'I will make one thing absolutely clear,' he would begin, and then cleverly obfuscate his answer, refusing to allow for interjection or interruption. The Ulster people soon learnt that whatever the issue, the Secretary of State was absolutely clear in his response to it. He spent four years in Northern Ireland and, although he may not have been the most admired Secretary of State, by the end of his term he had achieved his main objective. He was grudgingly respected by both communities – people and politicians

– as a man of integrity who took no sides.

Those first two months were lonely and in some ways frightening. The nationalist community and its leaders were always civil but any minister knew they had a different agenda and their loyalty was hardly to the Crown, let alone a Tory government. Unionists, who were natural allies, were becoming increasingly angry and disturbed by the possibility of a deal with Dublin. In a way I privately hoped that some last-minute stumbling-block might appear to allow me to build on my growing range of unionist friends and sympathisers. I feared the consequences of facing an angry and disillusioned majority so soon after I had arrived. The night before the signing ceremony at Hillsborough we had dinner in Stormont House with representatives of the councils in the Belfast area. Hazel Bradford, then Mayor of North Down and now deceased, told me, supported by others, that if the rumours of what was in the agreement turned out to be true, relations with the government were finished. I more or less confirmed the agreement's contents. She said, 'Thank you for the dinner; we shall not be dining again.'

Supporting the Anglo-Irish Agreement was going to be no easy matter for British ministers in Northern Ireland. Our position was made harder by the pointless insult to the unionist people of having the signing at Hillsborough Castle, symbol of the union between people and monach in Ulster. Symbolism is important and such a slap in the face to unionism was silly and avoidable. The day the agreement was signed I was out visiting an old people's home, knowing nothing of what was happening and even unsure that it was going to happen. The television pictures showed a furious crowd battering at the gates of Hillsborough Castle while the two Prime Ministers were flown in and out by helicopter, surrounded by hundreds of troops and policemen, to sign the historic accord aimed at bringing reconciliation to the two communities! My police escorts sat dumbly in the car listening to the news bulletin, while one 98-year-old remarked to my wife that, now we had sold him and his people down the river, she would not be invited back to his 100th birthday.

As so often when secrecy pervades politics, the impact of decisions were never discussed with those whose job it was to sell them to the public. No marketing plan had been devised to explain to the Northern Ireland public why the Anglo-Irish Agreement was the only way forward in the view of the two governments and all the political parties both in the South and on the UK mainland. There was no broadcast from the Prime Minister to the Ulster people, no explanatory leaflets, no detailed plan for briefing key decision-making groups. Nothing except the usual press hand-outs and bleats that if only people read the agreement in full they would not be put off by it – to which the unionist leadership replied that they had read it and they were disgusted by it.

A week later I sat long into the night discussing this failure of presentation and coherence with Tom King. He made it clear that he was determined to have his own junior minister dedicated to political presentation and policy. It did not take too much ingenuity to work out that it was his parliamentary private secretary, Brian Mawhinney, that he wanted for the job.

The unionist parties immediately instituted a boycott of Northern Ireland ministers. Even in the tea-room at the House of Commons we were cold-shouldered by our erstwhile friends, the unionist MPs. Wherever we went in the North we were tracked by bands of shouting protesters who beat at us with their Union Jack-draped flagpoles, shouting 'Lundy' or worse. It was unpleasant and frightening because I knew that whatever happened I could not retaliate. Nor could my police escorts do much, as they could be accused of assaulting the protesters. On one occasion Charlie Lyell, the Agriculture Minister whose father had won a VC, was hounded by a particularly nasty group led by one of Ian Paisley's pastors, Ivan Foster. Charlie's temper broke and he seized the barking parson by the throat while whispering through clenched teeth that he still could not hear what he was saying. The frightened clergyman then demanded that Charlie's escorts arrest their minister for behaviour likely to lead to a breach of the peace.

It seemed I was becoming a prisoner in my own departments. Fortunately, the permanent secretary of the Department of the Environment, Dan Barry, told me after a trawl of his senior colleagues that I could take comfort from their continuing support for the Queen's ministers.

The main effect of the boycott was the immediate withdrawal by all unionist councillors from any contact with ministers and an active campaign to disrupt the running of local services. Though these services were limited, a failure to set the rate would still have serious consequences: it would mean no money for local government staff, the refuse uncollected, weight measure officers on the dole, leisure centres closed and a whole host of minor services to local people put in jeopardy. Almost all the quangos that had taken over county and district council powers had a quota of councillors. Here, too, there was disruption: either the withdrawal of these councillors made it difficult to form a quorum or their filibustering made it difficult for whoever chaired the meeting to complete the agenda. None of their actions were likely to bring the Department of the Environment elephant down, but they collectively constituted a series of nasty running sores.

The department at the forefront of handling the boycott was Environment and I was its minister. A considerable number of senior staff were former local government employees and some must have privately sympathised with the tactics of the unionist community from which they came. The permanent secretary was himself a former town clerk. Dan Barry is a large, straightforward, pipe-sucking Ulsterman. He was very helpful to me, as was his wife Florence to Sissy. He was practical, knew the men and women on both sides in the councils and was determined to see his department come through, with services to the public maintained and its reputation intact. He was a real Department of the Environment man and he cared more about those for whom he was responsible than anything else.

He had a powerful presence and walked in and out of my office without any ado. Most days we would have sandwiches and a few glasses of wine together. I had complete faith in his judgement. It was a surprise to me to learn that the forcefulness and clarity of opinion with which he persuaded me were apparently not so much in evidence in the company of his colleagues, the other permanent secretaries. This sometimes put him at a disadvantage when arguing his department's corner. It was his support and advice that laid the foundations for my future plans for regeneration.

9

CONFLICT IN THE COUNCILS

In the Spring elections of 1985 Sinn Féin councillors were elected for the first time in considerable numbers. The IRA High Command had announced via Danny Morrison at the 1981 Sinn Féin Ard Fheis their new strategy: 'Who really believes that we can win the war through the ballot box? But will anyone here object if with a ballot paper in this hand and an Armalite in this hand, we take power in Ireland?' [So much for Sinn Féin being independent of the IRA!] The by-elections during the hunger strike had proved Sinn Féin's pulling power in Nationalist areas and over the following years the party had added to its grass roots support through the opening of 30 advice centres, even though they cost £300,000 a year to run.

Patrick Bishop and Eamonn Mallie, *The Provisional IRA*

SINN FÉIN/IRA'S TWIN STRATEGY REAPED ITS political dividend with the election of fifty-nine councillors in the 1985 local elections. When these councillors took their seats, all hell broke out. In the mid-eighties those councils sharing power across the community divide were the glaring exceptions. In some nationalist areas in the west of the province, such as Strabane, Fermanagh and Omagh, the SDLP and Sinn Féin forged alliances to keep the unionists out. (The Enniskillen Remembrance Day outrage of November 1987 sundered these arrangements as Sinn Féin refused to condemn the atrocity. The SDLP turned towards the unionists and the practice of rotating chairmen and mayors, alternating between nationalist and unionist candidates, spread from Derry to Newry, Omagh and Dungannon.) In unionist areas, councillors banded together and attempts were made to run these councils without calling formal meetings through the tactic of perpetual adjournment. All meetings were called off each month and business was done through a committee comprising only the ruling unionist groups. The SDLP and the Alliance Party, who found themselves excluded from all such council business in unionist-controlled areas, demanded the introduction of commissioners to be appointed by the Department of the Environment to run the council affairs. The SDLP and Alliance parties won cases in the High Court fining councils, but by and large the unionists paid the fines and continued with the process.

Tom King delegated this interesting challenge to me and asked me to prepare options for a solution and report back to him. My first four weeks as Minister of the Environment were largely taken up in meetings with different sets of councillors who had diametrically opposed views about what needed to be done. After two months, life became easier as the unionists had begun their boycott of ministers following the Anglo-Irish Agreement which, of course, denied them the opportunity for making their case.

They had a case. It was privately known that many members of Sinn Féin were also automatically members of the IRA. Since the IRA maintained that council workers or councillors who were part-time members of the security forces were legitimate targets, those being targeted had little confidence in the reliability of Sinn Féin councillors. There was evidence that Sinn Féin councillors were on occasion reporting back to their IRA warlords on the routes that councillors took on the way home from council meetings. Some unionist councillors, such as Ken Maginnis and Willie McCrea, were also MPs. There was no doubt that they were very 'live' targets as far as the Provisionals were concerned.

The solutions to the problem from a unionist perspective fell under two headings. Some called for Sinn Féin to be proscribed alongside the IRA and UVF. The other, more attractive, suggestion – to me at any rate – was that all candidates should swear a declaration against violence prior to their election. None of this, of course, went nearly far enough for Ian Paisley and the DUP, who accused us of kowtowing to Dublin when we should have been stamping on almost anyone connected with Sinn Féin. On one occasion when I visited a council for lunch, the only

Sinn Féin councillor was pointedly ignored by all the others. He ended up at the same table as my RUC escorts, where they chatted away about how lonely he found life to be.

There were other suggestions, such as banning candidates with a criminal record from standing for council office for five to fifteen years from the end of their sentences. One dilemma the government faced was that all ministers were barred from any contact with Sinn Féin while the Northern Ireland Office was exhorting local councillors to do business with them several nights a week. The nationalist side argued that the arrival of Sinn Féin on the local government scene was a step towards politicising republicans and moving them away from the bomb. The SDLP claimed that the proposed declaration was in reality an oath and as Seamus Mallon put it, 'The SDLP are opposed to it and would resist any attempt to contrive artificially the electoral system. Such an attempt would not only be an assault on the democratic process [!] but would be utterly counterproductive and beneficial only to those who espouse and support violence.' The SDLP would refuse to sign it, he said.

One difficulty with proscribing Sinn Féin was that it would also require the extreme loyalist political parties to be banned. On balance, I believed it best to allow some conduit for the political voice of terrorism, not because I thought it would make Sinn Féin turn away from violence, but because their views would be constantly challenged by their political opponents. To proscribe them would allow them to claim oppression by their British colonial masters. It would strengthen their recruiting drive for volunteers and bolster their fund-raising efforts throughout Ireland and in the United States. There was also the practical problem that if proscribed, they could reorganise themselves and could stand for election under a slightly different name. We could end up chasing shadows and looking ridiculous.

While a declaration was in principle reasonable whatever the SDLP might say, the question was also one of enforceability. How would the courts interpret a breach of the declaration? Who would bring an action? Who would fund it? Better no declaration, officials in the NIO argued, than a declaration that was found to be flawed and unenforceable.

Putting the Anglo-Irish Agreement on one side, the foundation of the government's political strategy rested on the introduction of devolved powers acceptable to both communities. The first tier of political responsibility was the district councils. If we could not find a way of pulling councillors together to share power, we would have no chance of proceeding further up the ladder of political responsibility. The reality was that unionist politicians would not sit with Sinn Féin councillors who were promoting the IRA. Since 1969 four councillors had been shot, three fatally, and two council employees had also been murdered. Of the fifty-nine Sinn Féin councillors elected in 1985, eleven had been convicted of terrorist offences, three were still facing charges and a further six had been convicted of offences connected to terrorism.

By the end of 1985 I accepted that the unionists had justice on their side and I put my report to Tom King advocating the introduction of a Bill which would require a declaration against violence to be sworn by all candidates. Little did I realise it would take a further three years to see it enacted. Elements of the NIO supported by some in the Foreign Office were deeply alarmed at the reaction of the Irish government and east-coast Irish-Americans falling in behind the SDLP.

For most of 1986 it was easy enough to do nothing because most unionists were boycotting not only the government but also the council chambers. In the spring of that year I had to send commissioners into many district councils to strike the rate in order to ensure that services would continue and money would be collected. Those who suffered most were the voluntary organisations, such as the Citizens Advice Bureaux, who were much respected by the public, carried out vital work in the local communities and who suddenly found their funds drying up because of the council's refusal to strike a rate. As the year wore on it became increasingly clear that the unionists' abstentionist policy was doing as much damage to the unionists as it was to the government. Sitting at home is never a very rewarding role for a politician, even if his powers are limited by statute to leisure centres, refuse collection and cemeteries. In October the DUP-controlled Castlereagh Borough Council even went so far as to withdraw authority to purchase fuel for the bin lorries. If the DUP wanted rubbish to pile up in the streets of their constituents it was their affair, but it was my duty to appoint a commissioner to protect the public interest.

The Anglo-Irish Agreement was like a red rag to the unionists but the meetings between the two governments did not appear to herald any change in the colour of the RUC's uniform, as one councillor had suggested, or the arrival of the Garda to police the west bank of the Foyle.

Behind the scenes the position was more tangled. In the first flush of Irish enthusiasm, a number of proposals to promote the culture and identity of the nationalist community had been raised at the Anglo-Irish Intergovernmental Conference. One suggestion was that we should move towards using Gaelic as a second language in government. Another was that we should produce a map of the North using Irish place-names and that we should have street names in both languages. The first idea was ridiculous in that virtually no one in the public service in the North spoke Irish, and much the same could be said of the position in the South. Apart from the cost, the opportunities for misunderstanding, mistranslation and mischief were endless. As far as the map and street names were concerned, I was not too bothered. But as the Irish were being so unsympathetic about the declaration against violence, I did not see why I should further antagonise unionists without anything in return. The debate within government was leaked to the *News Letter* and a pointless and fruitless leak inquiry ensued. My stance gained me a few friends on one side without doing too much damage on the other. The Anglo-Irish Agreement would not work if it was not balanced.

Gradually, during 1986, unionist councillors began to drift back into having dealings with me. A remarkable Catholic political officer in the NIO, John McConnell, started the process by persuading councillors to come and see me privately about this and that. As I had so many purse-strings and they had so many pet projects, it was inevitable that the boycott would not hold forever, particularly as SDLP and Alliance councillors could claim credit out of any meeting they had with the minister, which I naturally encouraged. I was determined that I would work towards a position where, in a year or two, councils would be sharing power and working towards common goals. I would reward the good and ignore the bad. But it was clear that before the next local elections, which were due in 1989, I would have to do something about the declaration against violence. This was the touchstone by which unionist councillors would judge me – and they would be right.

In the summer of 1986 the Secretary of State for Northern Ireland called a conference in London on the way forward. I was alone in promoting the declaration. My own two admirable Department of the Environment officials had been told to stay behind. This was a meeting for 'UK eyes only'. (There was a story, long treated as gospel in the

Northern Ireland civil service, that when the British officials arrived to administer the Province after the introduction of direct rule, they brought with them the seal used in other UK colonies which stamped sensitive documents 'UK eyes only'.) There were about twenty faces around the conference table, almost all of them unrecognisable to me. They were all against the declaration. The argument batted back and forth over the well-worn ground, about upsetting the Irish, the Americans, the SDLP; about problems over the wording; about enforceability and the costs of any action. After an hour or so, my nerve snapped. Who were these unelected, and as far as I was aware, uninformed, uninvolved and largely unconcerned officials whose existence I had previously been unaware of? A long list of names and initials was attached to the agenda but this meant nothing to me. Luckily the Secretary of State and the head of the Northern Ireland civil service, Ken Bloomfield, were staunchly behind me. Finally the meeting agreed that we would publish a consultative paper in the autumn of 1987 in support of my position, with a view to legislating in the autumn of 1988.

It was at that London conference that I realised for the first time how incestuous and how out of touch so many in the NIO were from the real world of Ulster and its desperate divisions. At the conference I encountered a patronising view, often expressed in private, that Ulster politicians were somehow an inferior breed because the middle class had opted out of politics. It ignored the stark truth that those who entered politics from both communities were, for the most part, brave and dedicated men and women, who, the further they proceeded up the ladder, faced an increasing threat of violence and sometimes death.

We produced our consultative paper, and in the 1988 Queen's Speech the government announced the introduction of the Elected Authorities (Northern Ireland) Bill. The kernel of our arguments was that local government needed men and women who could start their political careers in the foothills of council work, and that it would be increasingly difficult to attract candidates while the shadow of the gun hung over the council chamber. We gave the authority to bring a court action dealing with a breach of the declaration to a council, councillors or their electors. We decided that a breach should not be a crime on the grounds that the Attorney General and the Director of Public Prosecutions should steer clear of 'political' arguments. The political impartiality of the law in Northern Ireland was already under question. In any event, the difficulties of proving a case under the civil law were less onerous than under the criminal law, and the real problem of obtaining justice lay in the intimidation of witnesses which would be impossible if a council brought the action.

The newspapers undertook a poll and, when the silent majority spoke, 84 per cent were in favour of the government's proposals. Astonishingly, the Labour Party – whose spokesman on Northern Ireland, Kevin McNamara, had earlier proclaimed his hope to be the last Northern Ireland Secretary before unification – opposed the declaration.

Many recalled that John Hume had spent much of 1988 trying to persuade Gerry Adams to abandon violence and failed. Yet Adams and his followers could scarcely muster more than 3 per cent of the votes cast in the island of Ireland. No wonder the public concluded that his only way to power was through his support for violence.

The House of Commons discriminated against Northern Ireland. After fifteen years of direct rule, Ulster politicians had very little say in the legislation that governed them. British civil servants and ministers were scared of American and Irish objections to Ulster coming to be governed as if it were Scotland or Wales. The NIO/Foreign Office axis could hide behind the excuse that, as the British were awaiting an agreement on a new, devolved, power-sharing administration, it was only right that, in their advice to British ministers, officials should state that it was ministers who should determine the province's governance. One of the most bizarre outcomes of this policy was that at the committee stage of the Elected Authorities Bill – where the real debates took place on the guts of the issue, line by line, comma by comma – there were only two Ulster MPs, one unionist and one nationalist, on a committee of twenty-four members.

I therefore largely conducted a debate by proxy with my opposite number, Kevin McNamara. In order to see the Bill progress quickly, Conservative members were invited by their whip to concentrate on their constituency mail rather than on the debate. Kevin encouraged Labour members to filibuster for as long as they wished within a timetable that had provisionally been agreed by both sides.

The rules agreed by the whips determined the tactics but the debate was nonetheless fierce because I believed deeply in what I was proposing and I believed Kevin and his colleagues to be equally adamantly opposed. Much of the argument ranged over the practicalities of how the Bill might operate once it became law. But there was a deeper division. At the time, the Labour Party and the SDLP wanted to attract Sinn Féin into the democratic process because they believed that once Sinn Féin were in they could be influenced by the argument of their peers and seduced by the prospect of power. Eddie McGrady, SDLP MP for South Down, elaborated: 'The Minister said twice that the paramilitary groups especially the PIRA were seeking to undermine and eradicate local government. I believe that their aims are the opposite of that and they wish to use local government for their political purposes alongside their military purposes.'

I thought slightly differently. My parents had lived in Italy for the last ten years of their lives and my brother had married an Italian. I knew Italy and I had studied Mussolini and his methods. I replied:

> The Bill says to the men of violence who cross the divide in Northern Ireland: This far and no further. The democratic system cannot survive the onslaught of fascist thugs unless it is prepared to take a stand. If we do nothing but say that it undermines the basic democratic principle that people can get elected and then advocate violence, we shall fall into the trap that many European countries fell into in the 1920s. I look at Northern Ireland from the historical perspective of Germany and Italy in the 20s when Giolitti, the great liberal leader of Italy, allowed Mussolini in on the basis that it was best to include him and convert him to democracy. Appeasement policies were adopted in the 1920s towards the fascists who used the same language and techniques that both terrorist organisations in Northern Ireland use. Those policies led to the murder of Matteotti, the leader of the Italian Socialist Party, on the steps of the Parliament Building in Rome.

So died Italian democracy.

It was reassuring to see the Republic's Taoiseach, John Bruton, eight years later confirming in the Dáil the fascist origins of the IRA. The methods of loyalist terror are no different if sometimes less sophisticated.

A funny thing happened when the Bill returned to the floor of the House. Kevin McNamara, who at second reading had said the measure 'is misconceived, unnecessary, does nothing to eradicate violence, is futile and will strengthen the paramilitary case', fell silent. The Labour Party, for reasons of its own, shrank away and abstained at third reading. I taunted McNamara: ' "You're old father Kevin," the young man said, "and your hair has grown very white. And yet you increasingly stand on your head, do you think at your age it is right?" "In my youth," father Kevin replied to his son, "I thought it might injure the brain, but now that I am perfectly sure I have none, why I do it again and again." ' I relished my joke, but it was one o'clock in the morning and everyone else wanted to go home.

The Bill was passed in November 1989 and the declaration has now been in place for nearly a decade. It has not ended the violence – how could it? – but its proposed introduction was the first step to achieving a return to normality in the council chambers; it assisted confidence and without it the growing agreement to share the chairmanships of council committees would have been further delayed. It forced those councillors on the sidelines of violence to watch their tongues. None of the dire consequences dreamed up by the NIO and the opposition came to pass. The declaration was a useful little step in the fight against tyranny. But even a little step can lead to larger ones later. There may have been an unforeseen twist to these events. Some of the ultra-hard Sinn Féin councillors dropped out of local government rather than sign their declaration. This led to their isolation within Sinn Féin/IRA and left the field open to those keener to follow the political path which led ultimately to the ceasefire.

There were a number of young NIO civil servants who worked with me during the passage of the Bill. As we went along they became ever more supportive, even enthusiastic, and they worked all hours to ensure I had a detailed answer to every aspect of every point raised by the opponents. The group leader was a slightly untidy, tousled-haired professional who started us laughing when we were close to crying and never misread a chance to enable me to score a point. He was sort of a younger, English version of Maurice Hayes. He had been travelling private secretary to one of my colleagues and was destined for the top. He had done his apprenticeship and he loved Ulster. He married a local girl and had one small boy. His name was Steve Rickards. He was thirty-five when he died in the wreckage of a Chinook helicopter on the side of a Scottish hill.

It was not until March 1991 that the unionist boycott was finally removed when I was invited to a committee meeting of Belfast City Council. But there is no doubt that the consultations and the Act had served to break down unionist antagonism to ministers and led to a resumption of normal service between us.

10
DOING THE ROUNDS

IN 1985 THE NATIONAL HEALTH SERVICE (NHS) in Northern Ireland was very much a branch of the English health service. It had 25 per cent more money but because of deprivation and poverty, morbidity rates were much higher. It was funded on the same footing as Scotland. There was a local branch of the British Medical Association (BMA), a Royal College of Nursing, and militant trade unions such as the National Union of Public Employees (NUPE), closely allied to their brothers and sisters in Scotland and the north-west of England. There was a fine teaching hospital, the Royal Victoria in west Belfast, and a world-class medical school at Queen's University.

Northern Ireland historically always trained more doctors and nurses than it required. Many went to England but as many more went to Africa, the old Commonwealth and the United States. The medical fraternity was proud, professional, by and large non-sectarian and rightly held in high esteem by the public and patients. Some of the work done on heart defibrillation by Dr Frank Pantridge, on renal care by Dr Molly McGeown, on multiple sclerosis by Dr Ingrid Allen and on prosthetics by Dr Rab Mollan was world renowned. The abilities of surgeons at the Royal Victoria Hospital to save those shot in the head or patch up those half beaten to death were peerless. Where the NHS in Ulster was not so innovative a decade or so ago was in the management of resources, in planning for future requirements or in speeding up the introduction of care in the community for the mentally handicapped and the mentally ill. The health service was supported by a large, vociferous and very effective group of voluntary organisations which were well organised, well led and well supported by the local media.

Soon after my appointment as Minister of Health and Social Services in September 1985 I was asked by a local charity to launch a competition called 'Play Back'. The idea was to encourage youngsters to sit down with their grandparents and their friends and then to jot down their reminiscences. The most interesting entries won prizes, and I was to present them. One of the winners was an old lady from Newry who had discovered with her granddaughter an article from the *Mourne Observer* of 1928 which had a two-page spread devoted to the Needhams. She had underlined one paragraph which read: 'The old Earl was one of the last of his type of courteous Anglo-Irish gentleman who spent his life on his estates and endured with stoicism the challenges that came with his title. Whenever he visited Newry whose name he bore with such pride for so many years (he was the viscount Newry while his grandfather was alive) he was greeted with stones and hoots of derision.' 'I am sure you would find nothing different today,' she scolded, as I handed over her cheque. She was nearly right! I had had my first encounter with care in the community.

Several months later I was invited to Newry by the district council to speak at their annual dinner. The boycotting unionists sat at the back of the hall. I decided to take them all head on. I was accompanied by my eldest son, Robert, and my brother, Christopher. 'This is the first time,' I told them, 'that the earl of Kilmorey, the viscount Newry and Mourne and the earl's brother have been in Newry since 1913 when my great-grandfather, my grandfather and my great-uncle lived here. We are here to collect the rent!' There was a moment's silence, followed, to my relief, by thunderous applause. That was all we took away with us at the end of the evening although Mr McCann, the baker, told me that part of his lease was to provide Mourne Park, our family home, with a specially baked currant cake every Hallowe'en. He apologised that he was forty years in arrears!

There are always rows going on in the health service. My first row was over an accusation by the Royal Victoria's paediatric cardiologist, Dr Connor Mulholland, that because of lack of top-slice funding from the department, he was not able to operate on all children born with congenital heart defects and that therefore some who had died might have lived had he been given an extra surgeon to assist him.

This 'row' went to the very nub of the increasing financial strains within the NHS. Northern Ireland had one of the highest incidences in the UK of babies born with Down's syndrome, spina bifida and other congenital handicaps. Two causes were likely: firstly, larger families than in the rest of the UK, with mothers having babies later in their childbearing lives; secondly, the poverty of the families themselves, with the father sometimes out of work and the mother perhaps smoking and having an unbalanced diet. In these circumstances, the arrival of a handicapped baby could often lead to disaster; the baby would require much more of the mother's attention than the other children, leading them to feel undercared for and the husband to feel increasingly sidelined.

The incidence of mental and family breakdown was very much higher in such families. Yet there was Dr Mulholland, with his expensive, highly sophisticated, new surgical technology, saving the lives of physically disabled children who until a very few years earlier would have died early in infancy. It was heart-rending to visit his ward filled with the cots of Down's syndrome babies, alongside each a fretting mother waiting anxiously to see her son or daughter recover, and oblivious to the trauma that lay in front of them. But what else could be done? The babies were themselves suffering enough through breathing difficulties caused by their heart defects and a surgical remedy was now at hand that could at last ease one of the major physical handicaps that beset them. The solutions were of course complex, difficult to explain and almost impossible to implement. Part of the answer lay in family planning and health education, together with testing of the foetus as new medical procedures became available. But the churches were hardly advocates of contraception and all were opposed to abortion as an article of faith.

But once the child had arrived families needed support and counselling until the child reached maturity and then another kind of support was required to see the handicapped adult through life. In the fight for funding, surgeons could 'shroud wave' much more effectively than could care workers from either state or voluntary organisations. The difficulties in funding were intensified by the public outcry at any proposal to remove existing acute services, particularly accident and emergency facilities. The responsible press were nearly the only ones who dared raise the real debate which should have been raging between health professionals, politicians, government and the voluntary sector. The *Belfast Telegraph* said it all in an editorial in October 1985: 'To the public the solution seems simple: Government should provide the money which Dr Mulholland says is necessary for his extra consultant. If it doesn't then the public will want a very good reason from Mr Needham. But, as another consultant pointed out recently, there is a finite limit to the Health Service budget and the public should realise that choices on expenditure have to be made. Keeping local hospitals open may divert funds away from specialist regional services. The public, doctors and health service officials all have their priorities and they can sometimes be conflicting.' No one listened.

A few weeks later another row erupted over proposals to close Downpatrick District Hospital and turn it into a centre for looking after the elderly infirm and for non-invasive treatments which could be better catered for locally at a lower cost.

District hospitals were originally located one day's walk from the furthest homestead and were run by a matron who was chief nurse and hospital manager rolled into one. Operations in whatever discipline and for whatever condition were performed by the local clinician. By the time I arrived, matrons had long since disappeared and only Dr John Robb at Ballymoney District Hospital remained as the last bastion of the old order. As well as covering every condition at his hospital, he found time to be a senator in the Southern parliament and was an outspoken Protestant advocate for a united Ireland. He remained a wonderfully good doctor.

But as operations became more expensive and more sophisticated, the two imperatives were to ensure we had enough surgeons of sufficient skills, and to keep them and their theatres working for as many hours of the day and night as we could. Every session without an operation was an expensive waste of resources. In small district hospitals it was impossible to find doctors to cover the ever-increasing range of disciplines that modern medicine encompassed and the public demanded. The best and brightest young doctors did not see their future in a country backwater while their colleagues in large, city hospitals worked with the most modern methods and gained both experience and promotion at their expense. In the case of Downpatrick, for instance, it made much more sense to have a patient rushed to Belfast in the care of a well-trained paramedic which might take at most an hour, rather than relying on whoever might be available locally with outdated equipment and ageing facilities.

However, local politicians and pressure groups did not see it that way. They demanded that their constituents be treated within a few miles of where they lived and where their families could cluster around them, awaiting recovery or relapse. But modern operations do not need long recuperation in a hospital ward. The sooner the bed becomes available for the next patient, the better for all. Thirteen years later the row still rages and Downpatrick Hospital staggers on.

By the end of 1985 it was clear that the health of the NHS in Northern Ireland was under threat. In comparison with England, the health service had more money, more staff, higher levels of provisions, higher rates of hospital admission, lower throughput of patients, similar waiting lists, lower rates of day-case work, higher rates of outpatient referral and a higher use of accident and emergency units. In sum, we spent more money treating fewer patients.

There were other worrying failings. Almost all our ambulance men were trained to be little more than uniformed taxi drivers. In population terms, we had the youngest age structure in the UK and fewer over 75s; therefore although Northern Ireland was poorer than the rest, so the Treasury argued, we should have been using the health service no more than the rest. Of the over 65s, 25 per cent more were in institutional care compared with England, twice as many in acute beds, 70 per cent more in geriatric beds, 60 per cent more in mental hospitals and 20 per cent more in state residential homes; the number of those in psychiatric hospitals was 50 per cent higher per 1,000 of the population. It was grim reading.

It was clear that for the foreseeable future there would be no extra funding and that we would have to live off our fat. The DHSS had already taken a long, hard look at our particular shortcomings and had prepared a new set of guidelines which, of course, had been approved by the Department of Finance – the Treasury's proxy. The permanent secretary at the department, Maurice Hayes, and some of his senior colleagues had been assiduous in preparing the ground in discussions and debates with the health boards and a large number of the consultants. The boards had been instructed to take the new financial guidelines into account in preparing their following year's strategic plans and we had decided to devote the early months of 1986 to selling the new plans to the public, plans that had in every material respect been decided in London not Belfast.

It was my first realisation of the limits to my position and my scope for manoeuvre. I had no say over the policy I had inherited. I could not set the budget. The best I would be allowed, it seemed, was to avoid any real cut. The overall direction of the health service was decided in Whitehall, where I had neither influence nor contacts. I never once discussed the Northern Ireland health service with the Secretary of State for Health during the four years I was minister. We were known condescendingly as 'the territorials'. My function was to be a regional marketing executive for head office's hand-me-downs! There was nothing to be done but to put the best gloss on what was proposed. At least the facts were incontrovertible. The present situation could not continue, even if the public did not see it that way. Unionist politicians were fortunately outside the discussions, deploying protesters rather than arguments. I had no bother with them. It was the local BMA, the doctors, the SDLP, the Alliance Party and the vociferous unions that were antagonists, always calling for more money and more manpower.

What we had to prove was that once the reforms had been introduced, we would have a faster responding, better equipped, more flexible service than the one we already had, but at the same cost. There were three props to our strategy. Firstly, we would shift patients out of hospital and back into the community, where we would fund the extra local services from the savings from the closed beds; we would also provide bridging finance while this happened. Secondly, we would move as many as we could from long-stay institutions into more appropriate local accommodation to assist mentally ill and handicapped people to live more normal lives. Where the money for support of these new facilities and their staff might be found was left unanswered. There would be some savings from shutting the Victorian 'lunatic asylums' but not enough. Thirdly, we would change the habits of a lifetime and start the Ulster people eating less and better, smoking less and drinking less. Ulster had the highest incidence of coronary heart disease in the Western world, and it was no surprise. Butter, milk and beef were the national products of a green and pleasant land. Even though the province was surrounded by water, Belfast could boast only one good fishmonger. Belfast was one of the centres of the world's tobacco indus-try; Gallaher and Murray had originated in Belfast and Rothmans had settled a few miles down the road. Northern Ireland had the largest per-centage of teetotallers in the UK but also boasted the largest percentage of alcoholics. This was some achievement.

11
CHANGE OF HEART

IT TOOK AN ENORMOUS AMOUNT OF TIME AND EFFORT to sell the new health strategy. I visited every hospital, met with consultants, GPs, nurses, unions, social workers and voluntary workers, and spent hours walking the wards. I tried my best with the ill, but with them I am not at my best. I was once ushered into the delivery ward at Daisy Hill Hospital in Newry where a young mother was intermittently groaning as the contractions gripped. Why I was there I had no idea. 'Is this your first?' I ventured. 'Mrs Smith is a regular,' the sister responded. 'This is her sixth delivery.' She looked stunningly youthful for such a family. 'I expect your husband will soon be with you.' 'He's got enough to do caring for the others,' she retorted. 'Well then, at least he will be able to wet the new baby's head,' I suggested. 'He doesn't drink,' came the response. As I shrank towards the door, I finished with 'Not long now before there will be some lovely little screams!' 'I don't scream,' came the final rebuttal.

Such visits always included a buffet lunch or tea and scones with doctors, nurses and administrators. There was a common thread at every meal: 'morale is at rock bottom'. Whatever the government did, morale was always at rock bottom. The extra money was never enough. The reforms only threatened to lower further their self-esteem, they claimed. The health service was made up of hierarchies and each one jealously protected its position against the one beneath it; any change might alter the status of one group in comparison with another. What was always made 'absolutely clear' to me was that as they were caring professionals who only strove for the improvement of their patients' well-being, I, as a politician, was the last person who should advise them on their future or propose any alteration to their practices.

There were four health boards who administered the funding provided by the DHSS. They prepared an annual expenditure programme in line with the department's strategic objectives and they were held responsible for the programme's successful out-turn. The department employed staff to check that the boards were doing as the department wished, while the boards employed staff to check on what the other boards were receiving and on how they might circumvent the department's guidelines when there was pressure on them to do so. Boards comprised two sorts of members: those who were the minister's appointees and those who under the legislation were there as representatives of councils, voluntary bodies and professional groups. In order to get any business through, it was necessary to ensure that the minister's men (and women) outnumbered the rest.

I felt most sorry for the chairman and appointed members. They were 'pigs in the middle' who could not squeal and were barely remunerated. They carried the can without having any control over what went into the container. They were often criticised by their public-representing board colleagues, and they were roundly abused at public meetings when they were called on to explain the government's plans. I never really understood why so many intelligent, decent men and women were prepared to put up with such vicissitudes. They were an important local buffer between the minister and the health service, but it might have been fairer to them and less wasteful of resources to have given the department direct access to those managing and providing services direct to the public.

Every year in each health board, weeks were taken up preparing for the following year's programme. A day was set aside for each board to present its proposals to the minister and the departmental permanent secretary. The pillars of authority within the boards were the chairmen and the general managers. The chairmen, a varied group, were all remarkable in their knowledge of their communities and their grasp of their responsibilities. At the time the four chairmen were two dairy farmers, a former post office general manager and an academic-cum-journalist. The general managers were for the most part as tough as they could be and I never saw any of them duck a fight or run away from controversy, however bitter the row. They were to my mind as articulate and as brave a group as any I met in Northern Ireland.

The Eastern Board, which included Belfast, always had the lion's share of resources, while the Western Board always complained it had been robbed. As the Royal Victoria Hospital was the centre for regional services and was located in west Belfast, the Western Board had a case about which I could do nothing. The other two boards were not quite so vociferous but generally believed they were under-resourced compared to the Eastern Board.

Belfast's two main acute hospitals were within half a mile of one another. One, Belfast City Hospital, was brand new, a hideous eyesore and hideously expensive to run; the other, the Royal Victoria Hospital, was old and dilapidated, straddled the 'peace line' and had levels of over-manning which because of its position were unlikely to be addressed. Pilfering, car theft and vandalism in the area were nearly impossible to police without the lives of RUC constables being put at risk. The Royal Victoria survived amongst some of the most difficult circumstances in Europe. Because of the intense dedication of its doctors and nurses, it was the centre of care and excellence for both communities in much of Belfast and beyond.

As if three layers of management – department, board and unit – were not enough, there was also a Supervisory Board consisting of Sir Peter Froggatt, former chancellor of Queen's University, Malachy McGrady, the accountant brother of SDLP MP, Eddie, and Maurice Hayes. I wrote some grandiose guidelines for this august group. But as the board was only advisory we could only influence each other, and so we started to meet less and less. Delayering of management was not then the vogue.

Any stay in hospital has its dangers, but in most the patients can and do answer back. This was not so often the case in the mental hospitals at Purdysburn, Muckamore or Fermanagh. Those who look after the mentally ill and handicapped are in a class apart, but even they occasionally must have been sorely tried by the rules of the system and the daunting daily incidents that confronted them. The institutions were regularly inspected to ensure patients were well cared for, but somehow the size of the buildings, their massive ugliness, the barred windows and the dungeon-like dormitories seemed to deny humanity and any form of individual personality to those who were locked up there. In the conditions it was extraordinary that so many who worked in these places never lost their love for those in their charge.

I shall never forget the soulless dormitories of Purdysburn. The lines of iron bedsteads, the shiny linoleum floors, the pictureless walls, the cells which used to hold straight-jacketed inmates not many years before, the smell of antiseptic, the white-coated nursing staff, the groups of listless inmates sitting in the day-room waiting for tea, medication and God alone knows what. Anyone who has witnessed that has to believe in a better way.

I talked to one of the internees of Muckamore who was preparing for life outside in a supervised flat of his own. He was in his fifties but there was no hiding the delight and excitement that he exuded at the prospect of being able to fend more for himself. Of course there are those who are a danger to others and themselves and who need institutional care, and of course there are others who slip through the net only to be abandoned by society and left to fend entirely for themselves, but that should not blind us to the opportunities presented by community care for so many who have lived incarcerated and meaningless lives.

It was the right policy but it was always a struggle to make it a lasting success. Managing patients in their own surroundings needed a very different style of management from the previous, almost prison-like regimes. To find people with the right balance of toughness and tenderness, to train and retain them, was a well-nigh impossible task against the backdrop of the savings we were required to make. We were, in too many cases, returning the burden of care to the families, without making sufficient provision either for when parents became old and infirm or for when the mentally ill or handicapped themselves reached old age.

Northern Ireland had a major problem with heart disease. The only place in the world we could find with a higher rate of heart attacks than the North was Karelia in Finland, where a diet of reindeer fat was clearly more lethal than the traditional Ulster breakfast. As Brian Parker, the DHSS's press officer, pointed out, the North was the worst and the best place to suffer from a coronary blockage: we were more likely to so suffer but also more likely to recover, because of the network of defibrillators and coronary units that criss-crossed the province.

Many argued that it was all the fault of parents as heart conditions were inherited, but we knew that this was only partly true and that diet and exercise could massively reduce the prevalence of the disease. We devised a plan to bring us at least into line with what was happening in England and called it the 'Change of Heart' campaign. A tough and talented press officer, Brian Parker had another natural talent: he was a very good marketing man. He and his team used a comic character, 'Sadie', who appeared on television, billboards, leaflets, T-shirts, balloons and plastic badges, exhorting people to make less use of the frying pan. We undertook research into how we might change eating and cooking habits. I had always been haunted by J.B. Priestley's account in *English Journey* of the fish rotting on a quayside in the North-East during the depression of the 1930s, not because fish was unaffordable but because the local people did not know how to cook it. We discovered most poor families paid more for their food than they should. It was the middle classes who had the money to buy in bulk and travel to find the best bargains. In deprived families, chips and fries were the rule, the cooking fat was hardly ever changed, and the diet was monotonous and unhealthy.

Hospital kitchens and their managers were among the worst offenders. The food was unappetising and unappealing. It was either fried to a frazzle or boiled to destruction. I once was accosted by a coronary patient, recently out of intensive care. 'It's all Edwina Currie's fault that I'm here,' he remonstrated. 'That damned woman has caused me such stress that I have had a heart attack.' 'What do you do?' I asked. 'I am a poultry farmer,' he replied. 'How many eggs do you eat?' 'As many as I can!' 'Perhaps it's the eggs that are the problem.' 'Don't be daft, it's Edwina!' I was defeated, not least because eggs were still on his hospital menu.

Too many people were overweight and malnourished. The launch of the campaign in Parliament Buildings raised a few media eyebrows as portly, middle-aged ministers and civil servants in extra-large 'Change of Heart' T-shirts puffed their way up the steps to participate in a series of publicly available tests to check their pulses and their cholesterol. I discovered that I was suffering from hypertension, which proved that the campaign was taking its toll at the top. It was more difficult to cascade solutions downwards. We had to engage families in their homes and to make use of doctors' surgeries, schools, community groups and voluntary organisations. It is not easy to measure the success of such campaigns but we certainly reached our target audience. Preventive medicine took on a much higher profile.

12
ON THE BUROO

FOR FAR TOO MANY PEOPLE IN NORTHERN IRELAND in the mid-eighties, social security was the only income. Some may have earned a little on the side but for the majority of families – increasingly single-parent families – on social security, the housing estates were hardly conducive to encouraging the latent entrepreneurial flair in either community.

Voluntary groups learnt all the rules and ruthlessly – and rightly – exploited any loopholes to extract what they could from the system. Single payments – one-off discretionary payments from the DHSS – were the major route to replacing bedding, furniture, cookers and fridges, but the government decided that washing-machines and televisions were not essentials which should be made available free of charge to the poor and unemployed. In Northern Ireland in the 1980s it was perfectly possible to get by and there was little incentive to find work. Too often the poverty trap caught those who in trying to benefit themselves only found that for every extra pound they earned in a part-time job, they lost a pound and more from their dole money.

Family income supplement was a top-up for low-paid working families, but for reasons that the DHSS could never solve, a large proportion of those entitled to it never claimed it. My experience as an MP made it easier to understand what the problems were for families, as I had many constituents coming to my advice centres in Wiltshire confused by the forms which became immensely complicated if their income fluctuated and which in turn led to them depending on their DHSS payments rather than trying to rise above them. One of the most absurd pieces of folk wisdom is that ministers become cut off from reality and fall foul of the arrogance of power once they have been in office for a long time. My weekly 'surgery' kept me much more closely in touch than any Fleet Street critic with what was happening on the street.

These savings may have pleased the Treasury, but what they saved on family income supplement they lost through the ever-escalating costs of single payments. Sinn Féin activists were masters at working the system. While their brothers and sisters in the IRA blew up hopes of new jobs coming to the province, they worked tirelessly to squeeze every penny out of the hated Brits on behalf of themselves and those they had done most to impoverish. In 1986 single payments in Northern Ireland amounted to £40 million, which was roughly 10 per cent of the total UK budget, although Northern Ireland had only 2.5 per cent of the total population. The staff in social security offices were given little discretion, but what little they had they used to try to help those most in need. The work was monotonous and routine, the offices were heavily unionised, and individual initiative was organised out. Many of the younger clerks were graduates whose talents were shamefully wasted.

When I first became a minister I asked the Industry Parliament Trust to second to me two senior executives from their commercial sponsors. (The Industry Parliament Trust was established by businesspeople concerned about politicians' ignorance of how their words and actions impinged, often unwittingly, on businesses' ability to invest and grow; I had persuaded the trust that this was a two-way shortcoming.) They agreed, and Nigel Colne, a main board director of Marks & Spencer, and Miller McLean, the company secretary of the Royal Bank of Scotland, were chosen to act in this capacity.

Nigel recently had also been made a member of the Social Security Advisory Committee and he was trying to instil in social security offices the same kind of customer service ethos that M & S staff were taught in dealing with their customers. But the differences between the two organisations were too often too great to bridge. The lack of discretion in assessing claims, the severity of the rules, the managers' fears of being accused of misplacing public funds, the rage of clients desperate for money, the paucity of modern information technology – all this did not make it easy to emulate Marks & Spencer in the DHSS offices of Strabane or Belfast.

There was still very much a social consensus that the safety net of social security should not entail the unemployed being forced to re-enter the world of work. It was up to government to find and create jobs for every community. Those who were most articulate in blaming the state were very often those whose left-wing sympathies led them to advocate a high minimum wage, draconian equal opportunities legislation and a high degree of unionisation. They never seemed to grasp that to oblige the state to find jobs for those who had not worked before, had little or no training, and were frightened of travelling outside their communities was a pipedream. Only in the field of fair employment, dealing with job discrimination between Catholics and Protestants, did I wholeheartedly agree with their demands.

As Minister of Social Security I used to have to meet regularly (too regularly for my taste) with the Equal Opportunities Commission (EOC) under the redoubtable chairmanship of Mary Clark-Glass. Along they would come, middle-class women with professional backgrounds, demanding large and immediate increases for women workers. What were the factory seamstresses in Londonderry to do if the EOC suddenly succeeded in gaining them a 30 per cent wage increase? In Londonderry the sewing-machine operators were paid a basic £60 a week plus bonus, quintuple the rate paid in Morocco and ten times more than that paid in Sri Lanka. The factories would close, since the advantages of nearness to market and being inside the tariff barriers of the European Union would be wiped out. The jobs would go. Then what would these thousands of breadwinners do? From earning £90 a week, their families would be reduced to £50 on the dole.

'Then we must find better paid, more interesting and rewarding professional work,' came the EOC response. 'They have solved the problems in Germany; why should we be any different from the Germans?' they demanded to know. It was always Germany that offered the solution. The EOC appeared oblivious to the plight of the migrant Turks, sent home every time there was a downturn in Germany's textiles industry. They also seemed to be unaware of the different economic and political realities in Derry compared with Frankfurt. What was even more depressing was that EOC delegations were usually supported by representatives from the SDLP and the Alliance Party. I am sure they did not later spell out the consequences of what they were proposing to those only too few constituents who still had jobs. The Commission also had a habit of jumping on those least able to defend themselves when they wished to establish a test case with which they could force others to comply.

As the years went by, I started to build strong ties between the health service, the Housing Executive, social services and the Department of Education in working with local voluntary groups and bringing everyone to a fuller appreciation of what it was possible for us to do, either collectively or individually. This was not the case with social security. Already tight rules grew even tighter, and an enormous budget of £1.3 billion a year was paid out without any thought as to how the money could be used as an incentive to people to use their income better – to improve their health, better their education, add to their qualifications or provide them with the confidence to find a job.

LONDON CALLING

As I struggled to have our health-care strategy accepted by the professionals and the public, the Department of Health in London suddenly announced its plans for wholesale reform. As always, there had been no consultation with the 'territorial' Health Ministers. The London officials would never have canvassed our opinions. Not only is there nothing in the civil service handbook requiring them to do so, but to do so could have increased the risk of leaks. As very junior ministers, what new thinking could we have brought to a debate being conducted by top mandarins and decisions being taken at Cabinet committee? Furthermore, I suspect there was precious little input from my senior civil servants. It is notoriously difficult to get the civil service to embrace radical change – reforms are inevitably a criticism of the status quo. So, too-close consultation by Whitehall with my staff could have met with strong local resistance, which might then have been supported by me and my Secretary of State. Much better that we did as we were told.

The introduction of an internal market in the NHS did bring the benefits of greater management control over budgets and did create opportunities for improving productivity and efficiency within the health service, but the language of capitalism was anathema to most of us working in health care. Instead of taking on greater management responsibility many recoiled from it and one result was a plethora of administration and a massive increase in bureaucracy.

Unsurprisingly, the lack of involvement inevitably led to a lack of commitment. I knew how the service worked in Northern Ireland, and had we been able to alter the proposals to fit better our particular circumstance, the changes would have been better received and more effective.

Early on in my time at Health I had asked the second of my business secondees, Miller McLean, to help us. He advised us on the senior management structure within the Royal Bank of Scotland which, he felt, could be fitted neatly into the organisational system we had devised for the Department of Health and the area boards. With his help, we were able to write much tighter job descriptions and to avoid overlap which, without his private sector experience, would have led to muddle and duplication. But the Whitehall-imposed reforms then came along and achieved precisely that which Miller had helped us avoid.

I attempted to open up a public forum for criticism and debate in the Northern Ireland health service by appointing advisory committees that shadowed the work of the health boards. I said that I saw these working in a similar vein to parliamentary select committees, but that was the last thing the Department of Health wanted to see happening in the rest of the UK: it could be a route back to influence for the unions and their surrogates. Dangerous ideas from Northern Ireland were not to be allowed to contaminate English plans and presumptions. I am convinced that much of the hostility to government actions in Scotland, Wales and Northern Ireland comes from the failure of central government to take into account local traditions and customs. If the UK does break up, it will have more do with the failure to manage change than opposition to the changes themselves.

Our job was to introduce and sell the London directives. I held a mass meeting of clinicians, GPs and administrators in the lecture theatre at the Royal Victoria Hospital. Shaped like a Roman amphitheatre rising into the night, it was packed to the ceiling. I entered the area, blinking into the spotlights, unable to see the crowd but sensing the hostility. If I failed to perform there would be no emperor's thumb to save me.

I explained the need to separate those providing care from those responsible for paying for it. I suggested that a lack of proper performance tables and a lack of managerial information, coupled with an ignorance of what anything cost, led to us being unable to determine where and how we might improve. I avoided talking about competition or markets, but they had all seen the government press releases and they exploded: we are not businessmen, we are not managers, we are not Sainsbury's, we have not got time to deal with all those new reporting systems, it will only lead to more paper and less patients being treated ... I tried to explain that new medicines, new treatments and new technologies made it crucial to prescribe generically, to use equipment efficiently and to question constantly the value for money we gained for each pound spent. You give us the money, we will do the job. I was sinking, but I knew that as long as I did not get cross or shout or be sarcastic, sooner or later they would start arguing amongst themselves – doctors, I have discovered, generally do!

'I should be one of your supporters,' shouted out a GP, 'I am a small businessman, I run my practice and still have time to manage two other companies.' He paused for breath. A voice interrupted: 'Then why don't you take over Harland and Wolff and Shorts!' Roars of laughter. The tension evaporated, the debate raged and my decision to ask to see them rather than await their summons paid off. Although I escaped politically, I am not sure confidence in the health service escaped as lightly.

We were entering upon years of contentious reform which did bring some considerable benefits through introducing an element of competition and choice to the health purchasers. But the reforms have since introduced layers of bureaucracy and do not sufficiently involve the clinicians or the managers of their departments and their hospitals. The boards of the trusts that now run hospitals are peppered with non-executive businesspeople who too often become supportive of whatever the administrators propose, their previous business experiences having little relevance to health care.

Finally, the reforms could never be a panacea. All citizens understandably want the best of whatever is available for their parents, their children and their spouses, and unless funding is to be limitless – which it cannot be – the NHS will continue to fail to meet the aspirations of the public.

In Northern Ireland there were two aspects of health policy which involved women and to which I felt personally committed: abortion and the right of mothers to have epidurals during childbirth on the NHS. I felt strongly enough about the first issue to resign if I had not been allowed to vote according to my conscience.

Abortion is perhaps the single topic which unites virtually all male politicians on the island of Ireland: they are opposed to legalisation that makes allowances for it whatever the circumstances. I have always held the view that it is up to the woman to decide what to do with her pregnancy once she has been properly counselled. I believe that in an increasingly secular society, it is for the state to prescribe what should happen only after the foetus becomes capable of an independent existence.

In the Republic abortion is a crime. In the North the British government, though happy to impose all its other social and health legislation there, has run scared on this issue and the law remains as it was before David Steel's 1967 Abortion Act. The consequence is thousands of frightened Irish women crossing the Irish Sea every year to have their pregnancies terminated in English hospitals.

In 1988 proposals were introduced into the House of Commons to change the law in the light of new medical evidence that babies could live at an earlier stage outside the womb. This allowed all sorts of amendments from the 'pro-life' lobby effectively to ban abortion altogether. As the Minister of Health I was expected to go along with Northern Ireland's existing consensus and keep the legislation as it was. But what was that consensus? I could hardly ask my two main advisers in the department, who were both Catholics. For all I knew they may have held my view – but I did not wish to find out. I would only get one response from any of the politicians. The women's voluntary groups felt themselves, I believed, to be isolated, vulnerable in the face of the 'Great Estabishment' coalition ranged against them. One of the most pernicious aspects of the Labour Party's refusal to organise in Northern Ireland was that it abandoned the women of Ulster to their fate. Their only defenders were a very small band of liberal conservatives.

The ever-increasing rush across the Irish Sea showed what was really happening. All available research indicated that once an unwanted pregnancy occurred, the decision by the family and the mother about whether to terminate was not affected by their religion. I told Tom King that I would continue to follow my beliefs and support only the minimum of change to the legislation. I also told him that in my opinion it was time to introduce the 1967 Act into Northern Ireland. Certainly any proposal to modify the abortion law in Northern Ireland would have raised a devil of a row, but in comparison with all the other rows it was, in my view, one worth having. Nothing, I am afraid, changed in Northern Ireland, though the proposals to tighten the position in Britain were for the most part, I am glad to say, defeated.

There was one other fight I was determined to have on behalf of mothers. I wanted to insist that all mothers who wished to have an epidural during delivery should have the right to have one on the NHS. The department was proposing to close all small maternity units as they claimed it was not economic to have a unit which catered for less than a thousand births a year. Furthermore, modern equipment could only be made available at larger facilities. All the more reason to take the pain out of childbirth, I claimed. I had not appreciated the strength of the lobby that advocated natural childbirth, not least a commanding group among the midwives, some of whom would have much less to do if mothers were all lined up to have their babies induced at times that suited the anaesthetists rather than nature. If I succeeded at all it was to raise the debate about the possibilities of having an epidural rather than to have it promoted as a first and necessary option to mitigate pain and reduce the exhaustion that long births cause some mothers.

Toward the end of my four years and after I had become the longest-serving Health Minister in the government, I suggested we held a three-quarterly meeting in Whitehall between the three territorial Health Ministers and the English junior Health Minister to swap ideas and discuss mutual problems. To my astonishment, everyone agreed. The first English minister was Edwina Currie until listeria led to hysteria and her demise. She was followed by Michael Portillo until my demise. We used to meet in a small conference room on the ministerial corridor under the chamber of the House of Commons. The agenda was dominated by the introduction of the NHS institutional reforms, changes in the training of nurses, care in the community and how we should best react to the criticism of the BMA and others to what we were proposing. Even if nothing much changed, we did at least feel involved.

EXPORTING DOCTORS AND NURSES

I was involved with one new scheme which combined friends, family, doctors, nurses, officials – and success. Northern Ireland's need for doctors and nurses was always less than its output, but we had never gained from those we had trained and nurtured and then exported. The developing world was peppered with the accents of Ulster aid workers who had no opportunities to come home and whose efforts brought no financial recompense to the North's health service.

After Chris Patten was appointed Minister for Overseas Development in 1985, I told him that our history of the best and the brightest from Northern Ireland working overseas should become part of his strategy for British aid. When we both had first visited Japan in the early eighties, the Japanese government told us that they were at a loss to know how best to spend the enormous budget which they had allocated to Africa. They knew very little of Africa: they had very few voluntary organisations and the volunteers they did have far preferred working in the jungles of Indonesia to the jungles of Nigeria. Chris put the Japanese overseas development agency (ODA) in touch with the Crown agents who had been the purchasing organisation for former British colonies in Africa, and so a partnership was born which has now succeeded in ever greater measure.

As I had been part of the original idea, I wanted a scheme of our own which we could build on elsewhere. There was a wonderfully entrepreneurial, determined doctor in the DHSS called Rab McQuiston, who was keen for a new challenge and so NICARE was established in February 1990. A small section under Rab's inspirational leadership initially chose Russia and Africa as the two places where we could find our niche.

In every generation of Needhams there is generally one saint. In the case of my generation, it is my cousin Robin, who has spent his life working in the most improbable places for CARE, a major British aid organisation. (He discovered a whole tribe of Needhams in Assam, the offspring of an earlier saint.) I went to see my cousin and he agreed to support a barefoot doctor programme in southern Africa. The idea was to send a small team who would teach a primitive community how to look after their basic hygiene and health needs. Once the programme was complete, the team could return to Northern Ireland and another team could be posted somewhere else. Just as Holman's compressors had followed the Cornish tin miners all over the world as the tin ran out in Cornwall, so Northern Ireland's health-care manufacturers, servicers and subcontractors could follow NICARE's initiatives. We even considered how we could introduce computerised social security systems in developing countries, which, as they grew richer, they could add to. Unfortunately, we had enough problems with our own computers without foisting them on others.

I travelled to Japan to see Vice-Minister for Overseas Development, Hanabusa. He agreed to find the finance, CARE agreed to take a team from Northern Ireland, Robin gave me some alternative schemes, Patten's ODA signed up and we were off. The only opposition came from the trade unions. As so often, jerking knees rather than reason clouded their judgement. They were frightened we were exporting jobs. Today NICARE has projects in Bosnia Herzegovina, Latvia, Ukraine, Russian Federation, Romania, Ascension Island, St Helena, Zimbabwe and Tristan da Cunha. NICARE's turnover is now around £2 million a year and Rab still directs its operations. The spirit of Irish adventure works on and at least some of the proceeds come home.

It was agreed that I should discuss our plans in this and other areas with my counterpart in the Republic, Barry Desmond. If there was one sphere where we should and could have agreed to combine our efforts it was in health care – at home and abroad. But even though our officials worked together at a senior level, the only real success we came up with was a lithotripter in Dublin that patients in the North could be referred to.

Before my meeting with Barry Desmond in Belfast at the end of 1986 we announced a full and detailed agenda ranging from radiation (though I dared not discuss Sellafield emissions) and disaster planning to immunisation and overseas care contracts. Barry Desmond was a delightful, old-style, Labour trade unionist turned politician who gave me his complete confidence, explaining how he and his permanent secretary had travelled the Middle East winning contracts to staff new Arabian hospitals. His only grumble was the heat and the difficulties of quenching an Irish thirst. Even though it was my first Health Ministers' meeting under the umbrella of the Anglo-Irish Agreement, we spent much of the time gossiping about what he would do if Garret FitzGerald lost the next election which was then imminent.

Sellafield and nuclear waste have been a long-running irritant in Anglo-Irish relations. It is very hard to see why. The prevailing winds would create far more devastation to the north-west and the north-east of England and the whole of Scotland, but it never seemed to be a major issue with their local politicians, even when the Kilroot and

Ballylumford power stations in County Antrim had been spewing acid rain over Ayrshire for a decade or more.

Sellafield, however, was a symbol of Britain's power and irresponsibility which nationalist Ireland could not resist resisting. Claims were made about cancer clusters which needed urgent investigation. Rumours abounded about safety lapses and British negligence which threatened catastrophe for Ireland. Facts and reassurances were never sufficient. It may well be that there is some truth in some of the claims of incompetence but when I enquired I was told by the British Ministry of Energy and Environment that Sellafield was no business of a Northern Ireland minister, even though Belfast is a lot closer to Sellafield than is Dublin. If the Irish had really wanted something done rather than making a noise for local consumption, they should have tried to join up with the local pressure groups who were in the firing line of the consequences of any leak or explosion. They didn't, and I didn't encourage them. But I appointed a distinguished Queen's University professor, Sydney Lowry, to investigate. He could find no evidence, but the row kept simmering.

At the meeting with Desmond we learned that the Republic's health problems were very different from ours. For them, the spread of drug-related AIDS was a real danger. We were given a terrifying prediction, over a liquid lunch, that the AIDS virus could mutate and we could catch it by sneezing at one another. In Northern Ireland, gruesome IRA knee-capping tactics kept drug-running to a minimum in nationalist areas and the RUC appeared to have a grasp on most loyalist drug gangs.

The Republic's health budget was being cut while ours was growing. I once boasted at the Dispatch Box that our budget had risen in four years from £690 million to £950 million while the Republic's had been severely pruned. I thought the record one to boast about. Afterwards I got a roasting from Tom King. The Prime Minister had arrived during my oration as she was next on for questions and Tom was terrified that if she heard the figures she would slash our budget. Luckily for me, she was more interested in polishing her answers than listening to me.

The island of Ireland has only five million inhabitants. The two governments could and should do more to integrate health care, particularly in expensive disciplines – otherwise the doctors, nurses and patients will go elsewhere. Unsuccessfully, I argued during my time in

117

Northern Ireland that the Anglo-Irish Agreement would be judged by the populace on how it improved their lot. But, as always, politics and security dominated Anglo-Irish relations; issues of health, jobs, transport, energy or tourism were marginalised.

Being Minister of Health and Social Services and of the Environment had led to some strange and sometimes helpful interdepartmental co-operation. As Minister of the Environment I was responsible for water. Northern Ireland's children had more bad teeth than English, Scottish or Welsh children. In the early 1980s, 78 per cent had some form of dental decay at the age of five, 100 per cent at the age of fifteen. It was the Department of the Environment who had to pass an order to grant itself powers to add fluoride to the water, but it could only do so on the advice of the health boards and with the support of the councils; I was nominally in charge of both. I was the keenest of proponents: fluoridation would improve children's teeth, it would save money and it was paternalism of exactly the right sort. It was precisely the sort of issue that Mrs Thatcher had sent me to Ulster to be paternalistic about. So I proposed the addition of fluoride to the North's water supply.

I soon found myself in an enormous pickle. The freedom freaks (including one of my oldest and best personal friends, Malcolm Pearson and coincidentally recently ennobled by Margaret Thatcher) combined with the health freaks to try to frustrate me. The father of one of my constituents turned out to be the co-ordinator of the 'freaks'. Protests came from all sorts of directions and even now I receive vituperative correspondence for my actions. I rejected their arguments and accepted the verdict of a Queen's University professor, who argued that fluoride strengthened granny's bones as well as hardening her grandson's molars. In any event, the order was debated late at night and passed in an almost empty House. It turned out to be practice for a much bigger row: a change in the licensing laws to allow drinking on Sunday – a matter which was known to drive the Reverend Ian Paisley to apoplexy.

13

NEVER ON A SUNDAY

As MINISTER OF HEALTH, I WAS IN CHARGE of the drink licensing regulations. They had become so sensitive a subject that most ministers had shied away from any change – sometimes because the opponents of change had the big Doctor at their head.

Ian Paisley had done great damage in Northern Ireland by his extravagant, exaggerated, inflammatory and sometimes seditious rants on the horrors about to befall the Protestant people. He had bashed and bullied his way to the top of unionist extremism by plucking on every nerve and every fear of the unionist people. The greatest ally he possessed in maintaining the prejudices of his flock was the IRA. Without violence, I suspect, he suspects that his war cries would soon appear irrelevant and arcane.

By the time I came to know him he was sure of his position and his strength in the unionist community. Yet, although he was more relaxed than he had been, he still had a formidable rage and a formidable presence. Privately charming and very funny, he undoubtedly is a wonderful husband, a doting father and a dedicated constituency MP who seeks solutions to local problems with real determination. He made me face up to the needs of the Rathlin Islanders through remorseless pressure, and there are very few of his congregation there. But he can be intolerant and, I suspect, occasionally frightening to those who rely on him for promotion or success. He has the zealot's conviction of his own righteousness. He also has a 'thing' about drink. He really believes it is the 'devil's buttermilk' which entices the weak down the road to damnation. By the time I had determined to change the law in late 1986, I was personally too far down that road to be saved by Ian's biblical threats of eternal damnation.

There were also some very strong practical grounds for change. The law favoured clubs and some clubs were known to be terrorist goldmines. The rule against Sunday opening, which did not affect clubs, was a major cause. In 1975 there were 376 clubs; by 1985 there were over 600. Their drink purchases had soared from £9 million in 1976 to £34 million in 1985. Some of the statistics were bizarre. One club registered returns showing each member spending on average £30 a week on drink, which equated to five bottles of whiskey or forty-five pints of Guinness each; the membership, for unexplained reasons, had drifted down to sixty-six hardened drinkers! Meanwhile pub numbers were dwindling.

Paisley had placed himself on shaky ground by agreeing earlier that he would not oppose guests in hotels drinking with their meals on a Sunday. This raised the awkward questions of when was a meal not a meal (when it was a burger but not a toasted sandwich, perhaps?), and if a hotel, why not a pub? I decided to consult widely and lengthily, which did not turn out to be such a wise move, because a massive petition against any liberalisation of the law was raised by Ian Paisley's Free Presbyterian Church and the Presbyterians. A public opinion survey showed 52 per cent against any change in the law. However, of the 26,000 individuals who took the trouble to respond by post to our questionnaires, 16,000 were in favour of relaxing the law.

At the same time we decided to introduce another order in the same debate that strengthened the law against the providers of drink. This made it harder for clubs to become registered to serve drink and allowed the police more powers to investigate their accounts. We also stopped clubs holding commercial functions or having youngsters in drinking areas after 7 p.m. Ian Paisley and his colleagues could hardly argue against the second order. They had already capitulated on some aspects of the first. The DUP were reduced to arguing that, because the orders were unamendable, the constitutional position denied them the same right as other UK MPs to oppose legislation in the House. Willie McCrea accused me of rushing through the legislation (after 14 years of direct rule, I thought he was exaggerating) and Ian Paisley, advancing across the green benches towards me wagging his finger, bellowed 'The Lord's Day should be special. The human body was so created that it needs a day of rest!' As I fled up the front bench towards the protection of the Speaker's Chair I wondered when Ian had last rested his lungs on a Sunday. The order on Sunday opening was approved by 179 votes to 22 (all the unionists voting against) and the clubs order by 134 to 8. As always, the law's effectiveness lay in its enforcement. Too often the RUC had other problems to deal with.

Kevin McNamara, who had just been appointed opposition front-bench spokesman on Northern Ireland, supported me. I often found it hard to agree with him, but I never found it hard to be in his company, except once. Just after the signing of the Anglo-Irish Agreement, Kevin and I were asked to speak in a sixth-form debate at Queen's University. It was not a wise debate to hold, and even less wise for us to be there. The hall was divided between smart, blazered, short-haired Protestant students on one side and the jeans, T-shirt and trainers of Catholicism on the other. Kevin came in for a ferocious personal battering for his nationalist beliefs until I was forced to defend him. We left hurriedly halfway through via a side-door after a frantic signal from one of my protection officers in the gallery.

Kevin was never one to compromise or back off when confronted with a row. His emotions sometimes got the better of him during the Elected Authorities Bill, but I never doubted his love for Ireland or his genuine commitment to the only solution he believed possible. Privately I never had a cross word with him. Nevertheless he was a strange choice for Neil Kinnock to put in charge. He did not empathise with unionism and it showed. The Labour Party's policy of a united Ireland by consent was deeply unsettling to unionists and would have been impossible to implement in government. I wondered whether Kinnock had ever applied his mind to the Irish question or whether the policy was a cynical move to keep the left wing quiet which he would reverse if he ever got to power. Either way it was not very fair on Kevin.

I had another problem. As Minister of Health I also had a duty to minimise drinking. Some time after the licensing changes a survey disclosed that some school-children were drinking the equivalent of ten pints of beer a week. There was also the anomaly that while some off-licences had to close by 9 p.m., those attached to pubs could continue trading until 11 p.m. Some town centres were blighted by booming lager louts, and local residents were not amused. So we forced all off-licences to close at nine o'clock and at the same time allowed pubs to have some extra low-stake gaming machines to try to further reduce the income of the clubs.

Northern Ireland ministers' posts are in the gift of the Prime Minister and the whips. As Northern Ireland has no Conservative Party to speak of and the Labour Party will not organise there, those ministers that go to Ulster go for either of two reasons: as a step on the way up or as a step on the way out. In either case, they do not stay long. I broke that rule of thumb. Had I not stayed as long as I did I suspect many of the changes I introduced, such as the drink licensing regulations, would have taken a great deal longer because of lack of continuity.

14

ROBBING THE BANK BY OTHER MEANS

The Supreme Council of the [Irish Republican Brotherhood] ...
refused to compromise their political faith by committing their
organisation to anything so sordid as improving the quality of life of
the Irish people.

> Joseph Lee, *The Modernisation of Irish Society 1848–1918*

THE NEVER-ENDING TORRENT OF ABUSE about Britain's past demeanours and present colonial ambitions still clouds in too many minds the really dreadful terrors that confronted the two communities in Northern Ireland. The failure of the British state to protect the innocent, and the failure of the Republic to disentangle its aspirations from the practical consequences that flow from such aspirations, led to unspeakable horror which neither government seemed capable of resolving.

There have been occasions when I have been ashamed to be Irish and others when I have been ashamed to be British, but three stand out. The first was in March 1988 when Michael Stone shot and grenaded mourners at the funeral in Milltown cemetery of the three IRA terrorists who had been shot by the SAS in Gibraltar. The second, a few days later, was when two newly arrived British corporals inadvertently and inexplicably drove into the cortège of one of those killed by Stone, only themselves to be obscenely beaten and finally shot to death. What incompetence could have allowed them to be there? The whole ghastly scene was caught on camera by the spy-in-the-sky helicopter hovering overhead. The third was the massacre at the cenotaph in Enniskillen on 8 November 1987.

In Ulster, the wearing of a poppy and attendance at a Remembrance Day service is very much a unionist occasion. Very few Catholics would openly commemorate the ending of the War, even though large numbers fought in the British army. De Valera did not approve.

Enniskillen is the home of both the Royal Inniskilling Dragoon Guards and the Royal Inniskilling Fusiliers, the 'skins'. It is a town full of military pride and tradition and these are two of the most distinguished regiments in the British army. The British won most of their battles with a large proportion of Irish and Scots regiments, and the Anglo-Irish produced the greatest of British field marshals: Wellington, Montgomery, Alexander, Alanbrooke and Templer, to name by no means all. In every great battle and every great war those that joined the Inniskilling regiments could be relied on to be at the front, too often, in the light of their casualty lists.

The IRA bomb had been placed against a wall inside a building that faced the cenotaph. Along the road were metal railings to keep pedestrians from stepping off the kerb. The unionist community remembering their dead included those leaning over the railings in front of the wall. The bomb blew the wall into the victims and the victims through the iron pipes capping the railings, cutting some of them in half and leaving others dying of dreadful internal injuries or horribly wounded. One of those who died was Marie Wilson. The following day Gordon Wilson described the death of his daughter in words which moved the world and should have haunted her murderers. His Christian bravery and his request for forbearance did more to calm the community than a thousand soldiers or any political or ecclesiastical exhortation could have done.

Three days afterwards it was decided that I should visit the hospital in Enniskillen to talk to the injured. Rightly and understandably, British ministers were not popular in Enniskillen. The buck stopped with us. Before going to the hospital, I spent the whole day in a desultory sort of way, undertaking a series of minor engagements in County Londonderry. Then we drove through a dreadful, pouring, blowing evening over terrible twisty roads to the hospital. Catrione Garrett, my private secretary was with me. Catrione was a friend of Marie Wilson's sister, Julie Anne, and had been at Enniskillen Collegiate School with her. I felt sick. I knew I had to think very carefully about what I was going to say, as the media were bound to be there in force and my arrival would be just before the main evening news. Whatever else, I had to speak calmly and suppress any emotion.

I arrived to a battery of spotlights and television crews. I told them that those who had been maimed and killed had been there to remember those maimed and killed in the war against Nazism. What had happened in Enniskillen was a fascist atrocity committed by fascists and it was a profanity to the dead.

The first patient I saw was a beautiful little blonde five-year-old girl who looked exactly like my daughter Christina a few years earlier. She had escaped with shock and a few cuts and bruises. Her mother said another yard and she would have been killed. I asked the girl what Santa was going to bring her, and the next day I had Santa deliver a month early.

The round became worse. The next victim was a young policeman who was a rugby player, a squash player and a keep-fit fanatic. No one could tell me whether he would ever play anything again. My final stop was by the bed of a young mother who had been leaning on the railings. She was heavily tranquillised but did all she could to chat and be cheerful. As I left her bedside her husband came through the door. 'You are responsible,' he said, 'for my wife never being able to bear any more children. You have done nothing to halt or solve the horror that has befallen us. All we get out of you is words and sympathy. That will do nothing for my wife. Get out before we throw you out!' He continued to shout as I went down the stairs.

We drove away through the pouring rain towards Belfast. I heard Catrione sobbing. We held hands for a bit. 'O Lord, what bastards could have done this?' 'I don't know.' I did and do know that the political leader of the perpetrators is Gerry Adams. Commentators tried to force him to condemn the massacre. He regretted what had happened but it was a consequence of the British presence, he replied. An argument as rational as Hitler murdering all Jews because of the money-lending tactics of some of them.

Gerry Adams was a bad man. He probably still is. I don't believe characters change much for the better over the age of fifteen. If he does not have blood on his hands, there is no shortage of it on his cuffs. He was once a senior IRA commander. The distance he tries to place between Sinn Féin and the IRA is disingenuous. No one can tell the difference, and membership lists are not available for public inspection. Adams is an intelligent man, sometimes witty in a bitter sort of way, but his mind is warped and his views ridiculous and dangerous. He claims a Marxist background. That would be bad enough, but in reality he is a fascist in the mould of an early Mussolini.

In Sinn Féin/IRA it is the military wing that determines. It is a racist organisation whose units in some areas have committed genocide, killing the sons of Protestant farmers to drive them out. Its methods of summary justice through kneecappings and beatings replicate the antics of the Arditti and the Squadristi in Italy of the 1920s. Its economic policies are Stalinist and collectivist. It has denied work and opportunity to the people in areas which it controls as a method of keeping them dependent. *An Phoblacht*, the weekly organ of Sinn Féin/IRA, expresses views that would have been a delight to Goebbels. The president of this mob is Gerry Adams. If Mr Adams was to walk unprotected down Royal Avenue in Belfast on a Saturday morning, he would be lucky to make the other end of it alive. His American admirers should reflect on that before showering him with praise and dollars.

Tim Pat Coogan, a republican sympathiser, writes in his recent book *The Troubles* of how he tried to persuade Charles Haughey to meet Adams in 1986. 'Haughey was fully aware through his intelligence sources of Adams's importance in the republican firmament. "He's the boss," he said simply.' Haughey wisely ignored Coogan's pleading. Recently Adams wished Jim Molyneaux a pleasant retirement!

Adams came to talk peace only because he and his movement were going nowhere. In the early nineties their vote in the Republic was always tiny, and in the North it was declining. Every time the IRA shot a policeman, the UVF shot twice as many Catholics in retaliation. In the numbers game of murder, Adams and his partners were losing. Adams needed a way out which would keep his organisation armed and intact while avoiding division and internal civil war. He had to show his followers that in some way the fight had been worthwhile and he had to prise his men and women out of the prisons.

His attempts to secure a united Ireland through violence have been a disastrous failure. The cause of a united Ireland has been put back perhaps for ever by his attempts to blast the unionist people into submission. In the history of Ireland no man has done so much damage for so little purpose. There are film libraries full of news agency footage of Gerry Adams carrying coffins or watching them pass by. Belatedly he seems to have realised that sooner rather than later he might end up in one himself. On balance the people of Northern Ireland should be thankful. Nevertheless history will judge him harshly and the Almighty will send him down.

While I was in Ulster, one of the overlapping responsibilities between the Department of the Environment and the DHSS which required most co-ordination and co-operation, and received little, was the containment of racketeering. Our job was to introduce controls to halt the massive flow of funds which kept both Sinn Féin/IRA and the UDA/UFF in the murdering business. It was like sending an unwilling elephant after a weasel. The Departments of the Environment and Health are service organisations, dispensing public moneys. It is not in their nature to control and police except at the margin. Furthermore, because of the excessive secrecy of the Northern Ireland Office, even the permanent secretaries knew little of the detail of racketeering, and in a place as dangerous as Northern Ireland, it was understandable that public servants not directly involved in the fight against terrorism would be concerned about pursuing matters which could put their colleagues and their families at potential risk.

Even though there had been a number of investigative articles by reporters, such as Chris Ryder, which bravely exposed the extent and the methods of fraud, the government agencies had done little over the years to co-ordinate their responses to the IRA's cleverly constructed strategy for raising money to control their communities. As Paddy Devlin, one of Northern Ireland's most remarkable political characters, had claimed, 'Belfast is the Chicago of the Eighties'. In the early eighties one of Chris Ryder's *Sunday Times* articles stated: 'The Provisional IRA is now so wealthy that if its income from bank raids and Irish-American donations dried up overnight it would scarcely notice the difference.'

After the destruction of about two hundred and fifty Belfast pubs in the violence of the seventies, the Provisionals ran drinking clubs which, unwittingly, were given credit and loans by some of the big brewers. They became the first pot of IRA gold. Scams on gaming machines could bring in up to £25,000 per year per machine. Why the punters

127

kept on punting for derisory jackpots was not clear.

Sometime in 1988 I had a phone call from the owner of an English supplier of gaming machines who was losing out to a competitor. We met in huddled confidence in a corner of the bar in the Dorchester Hotel in Park Lane. Apparently the Provos, and to a lesser extent the Irish National Liberation Army (INLA), ordered the competitor where to place his machines to the exclusion of the English company. Once a week the competitor sent round a collector, who would empty anything from £50 to £100 from a Space Invader video game and up to £500 from a well-placed gambling machine. The company and the terrorists then split the loot 80–20 in the terrorists' favour. I am afraid I sent my informer away empty-handed; the department had given me no solution in the 'line to take' briefing.

More money was made by the IRA from controlling the west Belfast taxi shuttle. Unlicensed, community-based taxis continue to operate in parts of Belfast and Londonderry, their patrons transferred from the buses. Annual revenue of these taxi operations has been speculatively estimated at approximately £2 million. There was systematic blackmailing of storekeepers to pay protection money, for example through contributions to prisoners' dependants. The Provos ran security companies on building sites to protect them from the Provos. Forged tax-exemption certificates forced main contractors to pay fictional subcontractors who were fronts for the IRA. Later in the eighties, the terrorists moved into video shops, pirate videos and bookmaking, and it was even rumoured they owned a smart hotel in County Down.

With all this money came political power. The money was put to evil uses. The men in the Maze Prison set about developing a political strategy to create an alternative form of local government. This would have been funded partly by the British government – a 1982 survey in one Belfast street showed householders on average £1,500 in arrears on their gas bills and £10,500 behind in their rent. There was summary justice for those who either dissented or disobeyed; between 1982 and 1987, a thousand victims were mauled and mutilated.

'Army men must be in control of all sections of the movement – in particular Provisional Sinn Féin should come under Army organisers at all levels and be radicalised to agitate about social and economic issues,' said one IRA document captured by the Garda in Dún Laoghaire. 'We see People's Assemblies as a "rubber stamping" of activity in local areas

– a merging of local social activity with the war effort. In this set-up the war, properly guided, will never be divorced from the people or the IRA will never be isolated from them,' another document chillingly reflected. The war effort included running housing associations, supporting squatters facing eviction, delaying the claw-back of rent or social security overpayments, protecting those doing the double, and paying for Sinn Féin advice centres.

The fraud investigators of the DHSS must have been the bravest men and women in Ireland. They had no protection other than their anonymity. They did all they could to catch the persistent offender. Then, even when they brought a successful prosecution, the levels of fines were often risible. The resident magistrates, before whom the cases came, were a breed unto themselves and any attempt to try to influence them towards consistent sentencing was likened to questioning the Stuarts over the Divine Right of Kings. We drew up a list of the different sentences passed by the different magistrates for the same offences. The failure of some of their number to punish was a disgrace to those brave people who brought the perpetrators to court.

The longer I was a minister, the more sinister anecdote after sinister anecdote crowded in on me. At the end of one lunch a director of one of Northern Ireland's largest contractors jumped up and, as he flew from the room, he whispered, 'My God, it's Friday, I haven't paid off the lads.' It certainly was not his own workers he had in mind. I was once asked to go fishing by a very powerful and successful businessman, along with a number of prominent public figures; I was told later that in future I should decline his invitations, as he was one of the UDA paymasters.

One day Chris Ryder brought a former publican to my office in the Department of the Environment. He had been told to make room in his bar for a coin-operated snooker table. Every week loyalist paramilitaries collected the proceeds. He offered to buy the table; 'It's not for sale,' came the reply. The other demands made on him were so extravagant that he faced bankruptcy. When he went to the RUC for protection, the terrorists discovered it; for his pains, they beat him up and then burnt him out. He described his final beating: ' "Don't kick him, f...ing shoot him," said the first voice. I felt the point of the gun against my head. It clicked. "The f...ing thing's jammed," said the second voice. It clicked once more. "F... the gun, kick him again," said the first voice. Both kicked me in the groin, ribs, back and head. I never thought I'd enjoy a kicking but I knew what the alternative was.'

At a meeting with chiefs of the RUC, where rackets often topped the agenda, I was told by the head of Special Branch that his son-in-law who ran a garage had had all the new cars on his forecourt scratched along both sides because he had refused to pay protection money. His father-in-law appeared to have no solution to the problem.

The RUC in action are impressive, big men immaculately turned out, well disciplined and well equipped. Yet for years they seemed unable to deal with the quicksilver terrorist machine. Why? The answer, I suspect, lay primarily in the narrow approach which the NIO and the RUC took to the issues. The NIO had become inward-looking and bureaucratic, staffed all too often by pedantic civil servants from the Home Office. The RUC, while they had made great strides from the disillusioned, discredited, sectarian force of the early 1970s, did not – with one or two notable exceptions – have the energy or the vision to think laterally about the causes of the terrorist violence and community tension that confronted them in a continual stream of security incidents. The main requirement to be a successful RUC chief constable is to combine political astuteness and authoritative, Machiavellian policing. I have always thought Jack Hermon was better at the former than at the latter.

By the late 1980s, the security situation had changed very considerably – as had the terrorists' tactics. Yet the response of the RUC (and the army in support) was all too often stuck in a time warp of patrolling and vehicle checkpoints which achieved very little and often served only to alienate further the communities whose help they desperately needed to starve the IRA of support and funds. The RUC is a remarkable police force with many brave men and women, but its management was top heavy, too often promoted on 'Buggins's turn', and its senior officers missed tricks which their university-trained, creative-thinking terrorist opponents took great advantage of. Dealing with racketeering required new thinking and the co-ordination of the forces of government beyond the capacity of the creaky and untrusting security machinery of the NIO, the RUC, the army and the intelligence agencies.

A British officer filed a report of the Austrian army fighting Napoleon in the Italian campaign of 1798. They were, the major wrote, an intimidating sight, as they drew up in line on the crest of a hill to oppose Napoleon's rag-bag army, crouching among the bushes in the valley below. But it was Napoleon's sharpshooters who dodged the bullets, who did all the killing and made all the running. For too long, RUC planners were left flat-footed by the IRA's university graduates plotting strategy in the Maze.

There was a constant stream of judicial criticism. At Belfast Crown Court in December 1985, Judge Pringle, commenting on a case involving five building workers accused of defrauding the Inland Revenue, said that a coach and horses had been driven through the tax laws and that the big construction companies – Laing's, H. & J. Martin and McQuillan's – had shut their eyes very tightly to what was going on. Senior counsel for the accused blamed the Inland Revenue for extraordinary laxity. In February 1987, Mr Justice Nicholson said that most of the housing estates that had gone up in Belfast and in other parts of Northern Ireland in recent years had been built under the control of terrorist organisations. At around the same time, the Lord Chief Justice, Lord Lowry, accusing the government of 'the grossest form of complacency', said, 'Everybody knows that absolutely nothing has been done to improve the system in order to try to stop or lessen this quite appalling racket, which the Government has known for years is going on and nothing can be done about it.'

In December 1987 the Foreign Office and the NIO produced the following general briefing programme:

Terrorists need money, and the main terrorist organisations on the republican side in Northern Ireland – the Provisional IRA and the much smaller Irish National Liberation Army (INLA) – have increasingly turned to organised crime to finance their operations. The illegal 'Loyalist' paramilitary organisations, which include the Ulster Volunteer Force (UVF) and the Ulster Freedom Fighters (UFF), have also resorted to crime in their search for finance. As a result of both sides' activities, gangster-style racketeering is now common in Northern Ireland. Such behaviour totally contradicts the image the Provisionals still try to portray of themselves as a 'national liberation movement', but none of its practitioners seem concerned at the way it discredits them. The methods which the terrorists employ include not only armed robberies, but also protection rackets, tax frauds that corrupt as well as defraud society. The financial proceeds of the terrorists' criminal activities are used to purchase arms and explosives from overseas. Often they also enable the terrorists to indulge in an extravagant lifestyle.

The Government is determined not only to deny the terrorist organisations the finances they badly need but above all to stamp out their use of corruption, fraud and violence to obtain money. Despite the legal and practical difficulties, such as the problem of persuading people to give evidence in court when faced by intimidation threats, the Government is also working out new legislative and administrative countermeasures.

In the mid-eighties the NIO estimated that $10 million was being siphoned into paramilitary coffers. Others thought the figure nearer to $50 million. Certainly Sinn Féin candidates in Britain's poorest and most desperate urban environment had no difficulty in topping the spending returns of local election candidates.

Tom King had to do something, and so 1988 was designated the 'year of the rackets'. Fifteen years after the first evidence of extortion had been exposed and three years after 150 tonnes of arms had been landed from Libya and disposed across Ireland, the elephant lumbered in pursuit of the weasel. An RUC anti-racketeering squad, C13, had been in existence since 1983. But the police lacked qualified accountants, and when they brought cases to court either intimidated witnesses refused to give evidence or the judges refused to accept their testimony. A co-ordinating unit was now appointed within the NIO to set out a legislative, administrative and security strategy which could answer the efforts of the myriad variety of sometimes conflicting interests and opinions. Because secrecy is so ingrained in the system, for most of the time the 'need to know' doctrine involved nobody knowing very much beyond their own narrow horizons. Everyone had a vested interest to conceal and a position to protect. I cannot comment on the co-ordination between the RUC, the army, MI6 and MI5 because I was never involved. But what I did find infuriating was the way in which the British Treasury tried to frustrate our plans to curb building frauds because to them deregulating the construction industry and breaking the power of the building unions was much more important than destroying terrorist-run rackets in Belfast housing estates.

The unit established by Tom King achieved an enormous amount with very slender resources; but, as a predominantly civilian unit, it did not always receive the whole-hearted support of the RUC, and the NIO ministers never found the strength of purpose to bang heads together enough to make it as effective a resource as it should have been. Nevertheless the new unit certainly made an impression and funds for paramilitaries became harder to come by. How much harder I do not know, as it does not appear that Mr Adams and Mr McGuinness, or their loyalist opposite numbers, are surviving on fees from broadcasting or their supplementary benefit entitlements.

15

HOME SWEET HOME

THE 1970S WAS A DECADE OF DESTRUCTION. In the values of the time there was £313 million of property damage. There were 27,102 shootings, 9,730 explosions and 1,991 violent deaths. For much of the time, a curfew was in place somewhere in Northern Ireland. The city of Belfast was ringed in steel, and migration to England, the Republic or America was at an all-time high. Between August 1969 and February 1973 up to 60,000 people were forced to leave their homes.

It was recognised by almost all that bad council housing combined with discrimination by gerrymandered, Protestant-controlled councils in granting tenancies to their own at the expense of Catholics was one root cause of nationalist alienation. Lack of houses was compounded by lack of quality and fitness. Direct rule had a great initial benefit in taking public housing out of politics and placing it in the hands of the Northern Ireland Housing Executive. Massive funds were injected, which reduced housing unfitness in Belfast from 25 per cent to 6 per cent between the mid-seventies and the mid-eighties. Additionally, while a minister at the NIO, Lord Melchett authorised the building of the best leisure centres in the UK. Motorways and trunk roads were expanded and improved to standards that were the envy of every other region in the British Isles.

One of the early chairmen of the Housing Executive was Charles

Brett, an Irishman who could trace his roots back to the Normans. He insisted on maintaining Parker Morris standards (the high quality regulations for council housing that had been abandoned in Great Britain in the 1970s) of house building. Whenever and wherever he could, he resisted the building of tower blocks. He believed in giving every family space and security. The people of Belfast should erect a statue to him, as he was the architect of Northern Ireland's housing revolution. He stood resolute against all the pressures of the 1970s modern architectural practices to cut corners and save pounds. As a result of his determination, Northern Ireland has some of the best public housing in Europe. He was backed by both Tory and Labour governments, who made housing the number one public spending priority.

Brett was followed by another remarkable chairman, Norman Ferguson, who comes from a long tradition of linen makers. He is a successful businessman and was a distinguished unionist politician. He was outraged by the Anglo-Irish Agreement, but having made up his mind to enter public service he was not to be deterred, either as chairman of the Housing Executive or later as head of the Eastern Health Board. He fought like a tiger to maintain his budgets as public spending was reined back. He backed his staff to the hilt and was always prepared to put himself at the front. He has not been adequately recognised by the NIO who found him prickly and difficult.

His successor at the Housing Executive, John McAvoy, was a different character. Large, jovial and broad brush compared to his angular, businesslike and occasionally pedantic predecessor, he was a formidable political operator who knew how to use the media to make his point. He was a Newry man and never let me forget that I was Lord Newry and had a Newry liver to go with my title. All of these people were supported by and gave support to the feisty chief executive, Victor Blease, who, after twenty-seven years, is now Northern Ireland's longest-serving, most senior public servant, which in itself is a tribute to his abilities.

By the time I came on the scene much of the work in housing had been done. However, there were still some terrible black spots that needed sorting. The policy in the seventies, though generally enlightened, had led to a few awful mistakes. Some tenants were moved out of Belfast to the fringes of county towns. Such developments in Antrim, Coalisland and Downpatrick soon became sump estates. As disastrous was the Northern Ireland effort to create a Milton Keynes at Craigavon. Row after row of soulless slabs of concrete without character, sense of community or job opportunities were inevitably breeding fields for terror and misery. District heating schemes that served a number of homes from one central boiler were said to be economical; that may have been so, because the one commodity that most did not produce was heat.

There were also a few appalling complexes of English invention, such as the Rossville flats in Derry, the Divis, Unity and Artillery complexes in west Belfast and Rathcoole in north Belfast. There was no discrimination between the communities in the dreadfulness or the inadequacy of the accommodation of these developments. Over many of the blocks flew the Irish tricolour, but that did not deter the landlords of the Artillery flats from calling them after famous British generals.

After 1979 the government introduced the sale of homes to tenants. It proved as popular in Ulster as anywhere in Great Britain. The discounts made a house almost as cheap to buy as to rent for those in work who could get a tax break on their mortgage. Of the 140,000 properties owned by the Housing Executive in 1979, some 29,000 had been sold by the time I arrived in 1985. By the end of March 1986, over £210 million had poured into the Executive's coffers. But by then sales were tailing off. It had become impossible to maintain housing as the top priority for public spending. Visiting British politicians and civil servants cast envious eyes over the scale and quality of the Housing Executive's efforts.

Every year I had to attend the Housing Executive's conference and explain to a disbelieving audience why their budget needed to be cut. I tried my best to butter them up, as they deserved their praise. Housing Executive property and Housing Executive staff, because of their high public profile, were easy targets whenever tensions rose. Some were murdered and others terribly wounded. Twice or three times a year I would attend meetings of the Executive's board to be given a briefing on what they were doing and what they could be doing if only the government were more generous. I also faced a stream of delegations from nationalist councils and housing associations (who had about 13 per cent of the total housing budget of £483 million in 1984/5) with complaints about our meanness and their penury. Nevertheless, progress continued. We agreed to demolish the Rossville flats immediately, the Unity flats over twelve years and most of the Divis over twenty.

Not everything in the garden was rosy. Intimidation and fraud in the construction and maintenance of housing were endemic and the management of such a vast undertaking sometimes was bureaucratic and remote. It was also occasionally incompetent.

The Housing Executive owned a horticultural nursery which was responsible for stocking the flower-beds on public housing estates. The nursery started with a stock of plants and shrubs with a specific written value in the accounts. Because of a serious systems error, the annual internal audits over a period of ten years allowed the value of the stock to appreciate, regardless of the absence of regular physical stock checks. This system made no allowance for the simple fact that items of nursery stock can and do die. By the time somebody decided it would be a good idea to physically check the stock of plants and shrubs, the book value had grown to £570,000 against an independent valuation of approximately £45,000. It was decided to privatise the nursery and sell the stock to garden centres, which would take over the task of maintaining the flower-beds.

When the matter came to the attention of the Public Accounts Committee, John Murray, the permanent secretary of the Department of the Environment, and Victor Blease, the chief executive of the Housing Executive, came to ask my advice on how they should handle themselves in front of the committee. 'How much do you hope to sell the remnants for?' I asked. '£45,000,' I was told. 'To whom will you sell?' 'To the garden centres we intend using, of course!' 'What will they then charge to sell the plants back to the Housing Executive?' I enquired. 'No idea,' came the reply. 'I doubt whether they will charge what they have paid,' I concluded, 'and I doubt whether the Public Accounts Committee will look lightly on you losing £570,000 only to repurchase the remainder at double the price you have sold it for.' Unfortunately all my tutoring failed to save them from a roasting by the committee.

The members of the Housing Executive's board were either councillors or ministerial appointees who had been vetted by the NIO's Central Appointments Unit. The great and the good of Northern Ireland were a small elite of professional men and women who on many occasions were married to one another. The advantage of the system was that everyone knew everyone else. There were two disadvantages: one was that selection was based on gender and religion rather than aptitude and experience, and the other was that most board members were little known to the tenants and only half the members were elected. They were, therefore, detached from the needs of individual tenants and hard to contact.

There was one exception. Paddy Devlin was remote from no one. He believed that the Housing Executive should be as transparent as possible but this openness sometimes led to problems with his more cautious colleagues. When it came to his reappointment most of the board were against him. I tried to wriggle every way to save him but his colleagues would not budge. I could never fault the advice he gave me. He told me how to keep the balance between communities, to be cautious in my tone on contentious tribal issues, to be careful with my language but to give people hope and leadership wherever possible. If he had half heeded the advice he gave me, he would have been Ulster's foremost and best-loved politician. He nearly was anyway.

Nevertheless, for the harassed families of Northern Ireland, the Housing Executive and all its staff were a beacon of fairness and support. The number of complaints I received about allocations, repairs and maintenance was very much less, pro rata, than I had to deal with in my own constituency. And its record speaks for itself. In 1988, for example, the executive started work on 2,061 houses, completed 1,712 new homes, completed improvement works on 28,458, paid improvement and repair grants to almost 10,000 owners and reduced the urgent waiting list by over 1,400 applicants.

16

PORTS, PLANES, BUSES AND TRAINS

THE GOVERNMENT OF NORTHERN IRELAND is a perfectly formed, miniature doll's house version of the Westminster model. It is precisely 2.5 per cent of the size. The important political difference is that one junior minister guides the fortunes of several departments, each of which on the mainland would have its own Secretary of State. As well as being responsible for health and social security and licensing and housing and local government and planning and water and urban renewal, I was Minister of Transport. We had trains, we had buses, we had airports and we had ports. Over each of these public undertakings sat a nominated board and over these boards sat the board of the Northern Ireland Transport Holding Company. Very often the people on the boards changed places like musical chairs.

As the transport holding company's directors had nothing better to do than look over the shoulders of their colleagues in the operating companies, they collected the generously subsidised profits from these subsidiaries and expanded the company into the property business. They took over all the land that became surplus to the requirements of the buses and the railways, parcelled it up and developed it. Soon they were the biggest 'players' in Belfast, building multi-storey car parks, supporting speculative commercial investments and letting space. They had fine offices and a fine chief executive.

Not unreasonably, the Department of Finance took the view that property development should be undertaken by property developers using private funds rather than by an underworked quango using public money. They instructed the Department of the Environment to wind up the transport holding company, liquidate the assets and have the boards of the railway, airport and bus companies report direct to the department. The appointed task fell to John Whitlaw, one of the DOE's most professional and dedicated civil servants. John was a devotee of German military history and as a result I unfairly nicknamed him 'Obergruppenführer'. Soon after he was given this new task, he strode into my office, explained his strategy and outlined his objectives. With my full support, he sent his DOE storm troopers into action but very quickly ran into a Maginot line that did not give and could not be by-passed.

A lot of time had been spent trying to persuade Derek Cheatley, the wily old chief executive of the holding company, of the wisdom of our plans, and I spent several evenings dining the board members. On the eve of their execution, neither fear, charm nor reason swayed them. They appointed expensive London lawyers, Slaughter & May, who told the board members that much as they might wish to do their minister's bidding, they could not. The company had been established under statute. The board had responsibilities and duties under the law which could not be discarded by order of the department or its minister. Members could be held personally liable in any action brought against them. In vain, we pleaded that their supervisory role duplicated that of the directors of their subsidiaries and that there was no point having a layer between the department and the government-owned operating companies.

As businessmen, we argued, surely they saw the need for efficiency and clear lines of control. Would they not accept that property development in a capitalist society should be done by capitalists? In any event, the large subsidies were government moneys which were to be spent as the department directed having listened to the advice of the relevant directors in the operating businesses. Yes, yes, yes, a thousand times yes, they replied, but the law is the law. When we asked them who would ever sue them, they responded that they did not know but they couldn't take the risk. So we retired the old chief executive and put in Jim Irvine, who we hoped would become a trustee. He did not.

We suggested slimming down the board to comprise the chairmen of the various transport companies, with the chairmanship of the holding company revolving between them. This at least had the advantage of saving the time of senior managers in the subsidiaries preparing ponderous reports on their investment proposals, which could then be rejected on the analysis of the holding company's chief executive supported by his directors, some of whom were unaccustomed to the day-to-day needs of the travelling public. This proposal also ran into the sand. The only solution was to change the law, which we could not do. Northern Ireland is given very little time in Westminster's legislative programme. As there are no votes of any consequence in Ulster for either the Conservatives or Labour, the whips will bend every sinew to keep Northern Ireland business to a minimum on the floor of the House. This allows time for other mainland departments to bring forward their electorally attractive pet projects. In the list of priorities, a Northern Ireland amending order would not appear in the Commons for years. The transport holding company lives on, as do its directors.

TRAINS

During my years as minister this organisational fiasco was made less damaging because the chairmen of the transport companies were remarkable and very different men who could stand up for themselves. Myles Humphreys, a large Ulsterman, liked his port and liked his fries. He was more concerned with the round than with the particular. But in his time at Northern Ireland Railways and on the board of the holding company it was the round that mattered.

The Department of Finance fought an annual guerrilla war to reduce the railway subsidy as a first step to closure. It was true that the railways lost a great deal of money, that fair employment did not appear to be a key management objective, that trains were often dirty and often late, and that productivity and efficiency fell far short of what was possible. The railway system also had a missing link. The north coast section from Belfast to Londonderry started on York Road and did not meet up with the southern section at Belfast Central Station. Anyone wishing to travel to Dublin from Londonderry would have to break their journey and take a cab or a bus across Belfast. There were also the usual problems of vandalism on trains, rubbish tipped on embankments and lack of investment in stations and rolling stock. But there was a bigger problem still.

For reasons that no one in Ireland could fathom, the IRA brigade in south Down and Armagh waged a ceaseless campaign to blow up any facility that might improve or add to cross-border co-operation. They blew up the electricity interconnector and they spent a decade either blowing up the railway or threatening to do so. An endless stream of hoax calls claiming bombs on the Newry viaduct, bombs in Newry station and bombs on trains or embankments was interspersed with real bombs. They were devilishly clever. On one occasion a massive mortar was dug fifteen feet into the bank of a cutting, with the iron rail being used as a command wire back across the border. It was luck that saved a passing patrol.

The line was shut for days, sometimes weeks. In 1988 – the worst year – the line was disrupted for 172 days. The immediate loss in revenue was significant, the permanent loss of frustrated travellers even greater (they had to be bussed between Newry and Dundalk at Northern Ireland Railways expense), and the harm done to economic integration on the island of Ireland unquantifiable. The Irish people North and South joined together in a fury against the IRA bombing campaign at Newry. A year later the Peace Train Organisation was formed, chaired by Sam McAughtry, the writer and broadcaster, and backed by Southern political leader, Proinsias De Rossa, the unionist McGimpsey brothers, Chris and Michael, and Paddy Devlin, who became president. They ran 'peace trains' up and down the line, which attracted international publicity and allowed ordinary citizens throughout Ireland to display their public revulsion of terror and its consequences. For once, the IRA appeared to listen.

Myles never lost faith in the railways; he argued their corner and never appeared dejected. He claimed, rightly, that with the roads to Dublin as diabolical as they were, a decent train was the only way to travel. He travelled regularly to the South, even though everyone knew that he was also chairman of the Police Authority. He demanded the link between his two lines in Belfast and he always promised that next year the performance would get better. I have no doubt he really believed it would. Usually it did not.

Once a railway line is closed, it is hardly ever reopened. In an all-Ireland economy that over time has to have an efficient, all-island transport network, to abandon our railways would have been shocking. Belfast roads were already clogged. The road network had had massive sums spent on it and was unlikely to receive much more. As incomes and car ownership rates rose, a province-wide railway network for freight and passengers had to become economically and environmentally more sustainable. Moreover, if we closed the railway we had no way of bringing Guinness business into Belfast. I supported Myles against the Department of Finance. We agreed to build a rail link across the Lagan to close the missing link between the stations at York Road and Belfast Central. We also opened a new station at Great Victoria Street to bring commuters into the centre of Belfast. Even though my budget was being squeezed as always by the ever-escalating drain of security, I had to rejig my priorities. Roads and housing were the two most obvious candidates for trimming in order to protect this investment in the railway infrastructure. Railway privatisation was never discussed. Perhaps it should have been, because service, punctuality and cleanliness still have a long way to travel.

BUSES

Ulster buses are best known for pictures of them burning or burnt out on TV newsreels of riots. Between 1968 and 1997, some 1,344 buses were torched. Yet Northern Ireland was fortunate in having a cobweb of bus routes that connected every townland throughout the province. Ulsterbus was in charge of this network, and for many years it was run by an extraordinary former German prisoner of war who had settled in the North in 1945. Werner Heubeck behaved as if every bus driver and conductor was one of his family and every bus belonged to him personally. At the first hint of a riot, he would be on the spot to protect his buses. On several occasions, and despite desperate pleas, he jumped into a bus to remove a bomb that had been left with a warning. His courage was legendary, his popularity enormous.

The busmen drew confidence and comfort from his lead. Most drivers were in the same genre as postmen, ambulance men and firemen: independent minded, keen to get on with their jobs, loyal to one another, fond of their passengers and as fond of their buses. Even though they faced intimidation, robbery and the ubiquitous and fraudulent competition of black taxis, they continued to provide a professional and respected service to their customers with buses which were mostly old and spartan.

When Werner retired as chairman, I had to find, with the help of the

Ulsterbus board, a successor. Because the pool of local talent available to fill top posts in the public sector is limited, common sense might suggest that bringing in committed outsiders would bring new horizons and new ideas. The pool of available local talent did not see it that way, and neither did many in the civil service who wished to make sure the quangos danced to their tunes. However, I stuck to my guns. Wherever and whenever possible, I introduced men and women who would use their free spirits to challenge the existing orthodoxy and find new and original solutions to our problems; whether they were local or not did not matter.

Chris Patten suggested Bill Bradshaw to me for the buses. On the downside, he was an ardent Liberal Democrat but everything else was in his favour. He was professor of transport at Salford University. He had been director of the British Rail policy unit and director of British Rail South-West, where Chris had come across him. He was in fact a big fish and we made a big catch. Although at first he appeared prickly (a brave man, he is in constant pain from a bad back), he brought a much broader dimension which rubbed off on his estimable managing director, Ted Hesketh. Since then, Ted has grown in stature and authority, and now runs both the buses and the trains with a lower percentage of subsidy and higher degrees of payment to the exchequer than on the mainland.

Bill and Ted improved the bus stations, refurbished the old buses and bought new ones. They introduced a 'Gold Line' network, started the process to qualify for ISO 9000 and 'Investors in People', the two foremost UK quality standards. They were both rightly proud that they had never paid a penny of compensation under the fair employment legislation.

Bill had another idea – a big one. The late eighties was a time of privatisation on the mainland, and after the original surge of competition and price cutting amongst the new bus companies had sorted out the sharks from the mackerel, some started to cast covetous eyes on Ulsterbus. Brian Souter of StageCoach came to see me; he and his sister were to become two of Britain's richest entrepreneurs from taking over public bus companies. Although I had no objection in principle to selling him the buses, I wondered whether a Scottish millionaire providing transport services in the Falls and the Creggan would lead to a boycott followed by an upsurge in the income of the black taxis and the number of fire-bombed buses.

Bill knew that when I had founded my own small businesses I had experimented with different types of worker participation and industrial democracy, and he suggested that we sell the buses to the busmen. It was a brilliant idea. Busmen are independent minded, used to working alone, running their buses like small businesses. Whereas across in Britain most management buy-outs had led to management having 80 per cent of shares and the workers 20 per cent, we proposed the opposite.

Everyone in the bus company was enthusiastic, and I was enthusiastic that my civil servants were enthusiastic. But the Brits in the NIO were not. It was a security matter. How could we ensure that the buses in west Belfast or the west bank of the Foyle did not end up in the hands of the IRA or those in east Belfast controlled by the UDA? From those who in countering rackets had made snails look electric, it was not a persuasive argument, but as always in Northern Ireland security 'advice' predominated. Requests for a debate were answered with arguments about security being paramount, although the reasons behind these arguments could not be divulged because they were secret. The reality, of course, was that caution and fear of a future finger being pointed at those who had taken a risk overcame a unique opportunity to bring wider share ownership to Northern Ireland and strengthen the buses in their fight with the unlicensed taxis. The fact that we were proposing to set up only two companies, one for Belfast and one for the rest of the province would have made it well-nigh impossible for the terrorists to infiltrate. The busmen, owning and profiting from their buses, could have become a cross-community bulwark against terrorist fraud. We lost. The buses still belong to the government and the unlicensed black taxis still fill the coffers of the paramilitaries.

PLANES

I was waiting for cocktails to be served at a Cambridge college at my first British-Irish Association conference when a vaguely familiar face approached and said through his nose: 'We were at school together, twice!' The face was considerably different from the one I had first seen as an eight-year-old. It was Hugh O'Neill. He was two years older than me and had been at Selwyn House in Broadstairs and then at Eton with me. Having seen little of their children during the Second World War, parents appeared keen to keep up the practice after the war by sending them at ridiculously young ages to places which, without crossing the Channel, were as far away and as difficult to visit as possible. Broadstairs in 1950 was not Deauville and, although the school was well run and friendly, my parents lived outside Falmouth in Cornwall and Hugh's outside Ballymena. Parental love came in the post.

I had not seen him since and indeed had not seen much of him at school, as two years in puberty is the difference between man and boy. He was to become my best friend in Northern Ireland. Hugh comes from perhaps the most distinguished of Anglo-Irish families. His grand-father, who became the first Lord Rathcavan, was the first Speaker of the Stormont parliament; his father, Phelim O'Neill, an irascible Stormont minister, once referred to his bullocks as having more collec-tive sense than his unionist colleagues; and his uncle, Sir Con O'Neill, was a famous diplomat. Hugh was at one time financial editor of the *Irish Times* and a feature writer on the *Financial Times*. He bought the Brompton Grill in Knightsbridge and turned it into St Quentin's Brasserie, opened a grill and a delicatessen under the same name and sold them to the Savoy. He later teamed up with Desmond Lorimer to put life back into Lamont's, Ulster's biggest textile business. He is a very good manager, a superb cook and the most generous host in Ireland.

By 1985 he was casting around for something else to do. His newly acquired French wife, Sylvie, was not sure whether they should con-tinue to live on their wonderful farm at the foot of Slemish amongst the Antrim hills or move permanently back across the water. He seemed the ideal choice to take on the chairmanship of Northern Ireland Airports. He was exactly the sort of man whose experience was vital if taste, quality and comfort were to replace mediocrity. It was in fact my permanent secretary at Environment, Dan Barry, who first thought of him for his job, and to my surprise, he accepted.

The managing director of Aldergrove, Jerry Willis, was a former pi-lot officer whom Hugh nicknamed Biggles. Biggles ran the airport like an RAF aerodrome and it showed. His only lapse into luxury was two enormous offices, one for him and one for the chairman. When Hugh was shown his new surroundings, he informed Biggles that they would rent out the chairman's office and that he, the chairman, would move in with the managing director. The relationship did not last very long.

Biggles's replacement as managing director, Jack McConnell, was an admirable former policeman who had originally been appointed to look after security, which at Aldergrove was important. He was also not likely to interfere with the chairman's broad brush for change.

The first upheaval involved putting the catering out to tender. The holders, Sports and Leisure Ltd, were not, in the minds of Hugh and his board, likely to win a Michelin rosette. After the most rigorous examination by a board committee based on quality and standards rather than the size of commission returned to the airport, the franchise went to Mount Charles Catering, a company run by Peter French, who had recently returned to Northern Ireland with his Irish wife after several years managing the Mandarin Hotel in Hong Kong.

Sports and Leisure Ltd was based in Macclesfield and its local MP, Nicholas Winterton, was an adviser to the company. Winterton immediately contacted his old national service colleague, Tom King, and accused me of giving the chairmanship to my supposedly old school chum who then gave the catering contract to his old chum. The Secretary of State took the matter very seriously and appointed the head of the Northern Ireland civil service to investigate this accusation of apparent sleaze. Kenneth Bloomfield, of course, found that there was nothing untoward, though that did not seem to placate Winterton.

Hugh brought new blood, professionals in the world of travel, into his team. One extraordinary character was a Londoner, Ian Sayer, who as a hobby wrote investigative books on such esoteric subjects as 'Nazi Gold' and had begun his career running lorries across the Irish Sea, at one time employing Mark Thatcher as a salesman. They came up with a plan to invest £7–8 million in a freight terminal. Everyone prophesied doom. It has been a triumph. Hugh then spent all his efforts trying to persuade British Airways to run a transatlantic freight/passenger night service with Belfast as a stopover. Even his friendship with Colin Marshall, then chief executive, and David Burnside (the Ulster PR director of British Airways) could not make up for the lack of available aircraft. He also badgered me, the Northern Ireland Secretary, the Transport Secretary and anyone else who would listen to force the British Airports Authority to improve the appalling conditions at Heathrow's Gate 49, where passengers were treated like lepers in comparison with the ever-increasing comforts that were being made available at Aldergrove.

There was no airport hotel at Aldergrove. At the time, hotels in Northern Ireland either, by and large, were a superior form of bed and breakfast accommodation with an extension for weddings and discos or belonged to Billy Hastings, who had established a near monopoly at three and four star level. There were no international chains operating in the province. Hugh decided to court Novotel and they set up shop. So after several years he succeeded in bringing quality at a price that had been denied Northern Ireland visitors at Aldergrove for decades. Unfortunately as soon as he went, so did Novotel when they fell out with the new airport management. But his work was not in vain. Everything in the airport improved. Ulster oysters and Ulster smoked salmon did a roaring trade, as did Irish whiskey, Irish linen, Irish porcelain and Irish crystal, and the profits reflected the growth in spending.

Meanwhile Bombardier had bought Shorts in Belfast and with it City Airport. Bombardier realised they had an asset they could exploit, which had not, of course, occurred to those running a 'publicly owned' business. They also had an advantage. Because they were a private airport they could entice airlines into City Airport without having to spend money on all the conditions that were laid down for a public user international airport by the Civil Aviation Authority. Soon airlines began switching or threatening to switch from Aldergrove. O'Neill's revenues remained static as the competition bit.

However, money was available from Europe for both airports, and once we were sure that the funds we received would not be clawed back by the British Treasury under the rules of 'additionality', we powered ahead with the new investment proposals on a £10 million freight terminal and upgrading the passenger facilities. If Bruce Millan, the former Labour Secretary of State for Scotland and then Brussels Transport Commissioner, had got wind of our privatisation proposals, he could have banned the investment programme on the grounds of public moneys finding their way into private pockets.

My behind-the-scenes instructions had been to prepare Aldergrove for privatisation. But, as with the buses, I did not want to see it swallowed into the maw of some multinational conglomerate such as the British Airports Authority, who would treat it no differently from any other regional airport. I wanted Northern Ireland's international airport to belong to the people of Northern Ireland through a public offering as we later achieved with the sale of Northern Ireland

Electricity. But how could we sell it if its prospects for growth were to be undermined by a private airport using different rules in the centre of Belfast? I suggested Hugh should discuss a merger with Bombardier's City Airport, but nothing came of it. I suggested using the planning system to control the number of movements at the harbour because of noise, but to do so apparently would have been a misuse of the system. The British Treasury kept pushing for action. In 1989 Peter Bottomley took over responsibility from me for the airport and he decided to push ahead with the trade sale as the only feasible option.

Within a few months of my leaving office, Aldergrove was sold by the government to a management buy-out. Within a few months of that, the management buy-out had sold out to an outside company. A few had made millions. The first efforts to bring wider share ownership to the people of Northern Ireland had failed.

PORTS

Belfast, Londonderry and Warrenpoint were trust ports established under statute, their duties and responsibilities laid down in law. I was responsible for appointing the chairman and the board of these ports. Beyond that, the harbour commissioners were masters unto themselves. Larne, the exception, was a commercial port with which I had little to do. However, I did help the owners bring in some EEC money. European rules discriminated against private ports. It was outrageous that the European Commission subsidised the often less tightly run nationalised companies to the detriment of efficiently run Larne, gateway between Ireland and Scotland.

Northern Ireland ports are a success compared with their Southern rivals. They carry over half the sea-borne trade between the island of Ireland and the mainland, and by the late eighties they had largely done away with the working practices that still bedevil the South and survived in Britain. Belfast is the richest port. In 1992 it had a turnover of £13.5 million, made profits of nearly £7 million and handled 11 million tonnes of cargo. Even allowing for dollops of Eurocash, its trade and its profits had almost doubled during the time I had been a minister. The success was no mean achievement.

The port also has a massive land-bank along the Lagan. Its chief executive, Gordon Irwin, is not a man of the sea. On one occasion, while giving us a guided tour of his facilities from the wheel-house of the harbour launch, he invited us to look to starboard as he pointed out a landmark to the left of us, although he claimed that we were looking forward while he was looking aft. He is a large, formidable, forthright man with a very clear idea of how he wanted to see his port and Belfast's riverfront prosper. He was to become an advocate for the Laganside development, which he did much to make successful.

The board was made up of local notables and local interests appointed since 1979 by the government. The port's profits had to be either reinvested or handed over to the Belfast Charitable Trust. As far as I am aware, the last cheque was in the last century.

I was keen to change the law and sell off the port operations while transferring the property assets to Laganside Corporation. Once again I was defeated by lack of parliamentary space and local conservatism. There is no justification for arrangements designed to solve Belfast's conflicting interests at the end of the nineteenth century still operating at the end of the twentieth.

I attempted to scare the harbour commissioners. I told them that if they did not co-operate with me I would sell the entire operation to a group of Liverpool businessmen, who would run down the port as a potential competitor and cancel the Liverpool boat. The Liverpool service did collapse – which, with the opening of the Belfast–Stranraer Seacat service, was more symbolic than real – but the ruse failed.

Earlier commissioners had shown little aptitude for developing the – increasingly large – derelict parts of their estate. Harland and Wolff had shrunk to a fraction of its former glory. Coal and scrap were piled high right in the city centre instead of being moved out onto derelict docks. Working arrangements, which had one stevedoring company employing only Catholics from the Irish Transport and General Workers' Union and another company employing only Protestants from the British Transport and General Workers' Union, were never challenged. The old excuse, 'if it works, leave it', hid a lack of transparency between port management and property management. An understandable complacency that comes from an unchallengeable monopoly and a panoply of inherited self-interest tended towards a 'no change' philosophy. As the chairman, Dawson Moreland, wrote in the 1990 annual report: 'Presently a Bill is passing through Parliament which will enable Trust Ports in Great Britain to be privatised and which makes provision for this legislation to apply in Northern Ireland in the near future. The Port of Belfast is of such vital importance to the Northern Ireland economy and has such close links with its City and hinterland that its position is unique among the major UK Trust Ports. For this reason it is the Board's view that any consequences arising from the restructuring of the Port authority should have no detrimental effect on the Northern Ireland community' (or on the businesses of some of the commissioners, he might have added).

The harbour commissioners' offices were wonderfully self-confident and Victorian, full of beautiful oils by McKelvey and Craig depicting the yards, the river and the docks in their heyday. An example of the decline in both confidence and taste was a vile 1960s four-storey flat-roof office block stuck on the back of the imperial core. I was determined to have the monstrosity refaced with the best of modern materials to show off our new self-belief. At least in that I was victorious. As the years passed, Gordon Irwin and the wily and shrewd Dawson Moreland, supported by his terrier-like deputy chairman, Robert Barnett, saw the plans for renewal in the rest of the city take shape, and they decided it was time they too moved with the times. They dismantled the Dock Labour Scheme and introduced licensed stevedores, with all dockers being employed by the stevedoring companies. The cost of buying out the past was minimal compared with the price paid in Great Britain.

The other trust ports were much smaller, although Londonderry sat on valuable land which offered interesting opportunities for redevelopment. They already had a new site nearer the mouth of the Foyle and they moved without fuss. At Warrenpoint there was a row. One of the board members there was Eddie Haughey, a volatile, irrepressible and imaginative south Armaghman who had built up an astonishingly profitable animal drugs company outside Newry. He can be amusing, generous and creative. He can also be obsessive and dictatorial. He likes getting results and getting his own way. He does not like corners and does not like officialdom. At Warrenpoint, where he smelt trouble, he was more inclined to blame conspiracy rather than cock-up.

Haughey decided that the board was inept in developing the land and opportunities at the port, and started a running battle with Ian O'Hagan, the chairman, and with the chief executive, which was disruptive. At the same time he was engaged in a fight with Newry and Mourne District Council over the location of his mobile home at Greenore in

County Louth, which must have sorely tested the chief executive of the council, Paddy O'Hagan. But as time passed, Warrenpoint (where my cousin Nicholas Needham Anley ran his stevedoring company) grew and grew, and by its own efforts and efficiency expanded to the detriment of ports in the South.

17
ROADS

THE ROADS MAY HAVE BEEN IMPROVED in the seventies, but the network extended to every farmhouse down every lane and the maintenance bills were enormous. When in the eighties the capital started to dry up, there was a constant cry from every town and every district for their by-pass or their improvement scheme to top a dwindling list. Even so, shortly after I arrived, the DOE managed to find £11 million to repair rural roads and rode roughshod over my objections that I would prefer to see the money spent on relieving congestion in town centres rather than on providing racetrack surfaces for milk lorries. There were limits to the powers of newly appointed ministers when confronted by civil servants who had their minds made up.

There were also complaints that earlier spending had been concentrated on the better-off, eastern (and therefore Protestant) end of the province. There was truth in the allegations because the criteria used by the Department of the Environment Transport division were based on road usage, and the wealthier areas simply had more cars and lorries. Taken to its logical conclusion, the policy would have led to better and better roads in the richer parts of the North, while the poorer, rural, remoter – and often Catholic – areas would have become even less accessible.

Road engineers were the most self-righteous of all the civil servants that I worked with. They had two simple rules: the needs of the road user were paramount and they never made a mistake. Unnecessary signs that littered and degraded many streets and pointed motorists in several directions at the same time were always necessary. Meanwhile, temporary signs, unless departmental signs, were opposed with fervour; every year I had a battle to allow the AA to mount directions to the Ideal Home Exhibition in the Ulster Hall. As the years rolled by, I managed to start integrating road networks into the planning system so that protecting the environment became a small if growing part of the agenda.

Every year for five years there was one battle that summed up the road engineers' view of the environment. At two-hundred-yard intervals down the side of every motorway there are painted posts slotted into the edge of the hard shoulder. Every year in early June the road engineers would go out and spray herbicide for two feet around every stick in case the growing grass made it difficult to locate the post. Whoever would want to find the posts should they be hidden I could never discover. These browning, bald patches, four foot in circumference, every two hundred yards were ugly, unnecessary and no doubt costly. Every year I gave instructions that the spraying should not be repeated. For five years out of seven my instructions were ignored. But as soon as I was out the door, the practice started again. Then, returning in 1997, I noticed the posts have been left alone. The money for the spray must have run out.

I was driven some forty to fifty thousand miles a year around Northern Ireland, so there was no road of any size (except along the border) which I did not know. What funds we had I concentrated on trying to make the west of the province more accessible. There was no point providing the highest level of incentive to encourage investment in Strabane, Londonderry or Omagh if the goods made there took as long to reach the shops as those from Morocco.

Then there was the Belfast to Dublin road, or the A I in Euro parlance. The road from Larne to Belfast was just about adequate, although there was a case for dualling its entire length. The road from Belfast to Newry was good and getting better. But from Newry to the border and from the border to Dublin it was diabolical. For years the first stage of the Newry by-pass ended in a roundabout that directed the traffic back through the centre of the town. No one wanted to stop in Newry, and so the town's development was blighted, as was the reputation of the Hereditary Abbot of the exempt jurisdiction of Newry and Mourne (a title that came with my earldom and allowed the Needhams to bury, marry and divorce their tenants as late as the 1860s). I was forever pressing to have whatever money was available spent on the road around Newry.

Tom King told me in early 1986 that the two governments had decided that improving the transport links between the two capital cities was to be top priority. It was of sufficient importance to warrant a special conference under the auspices of the Anglo-Irish Agreement, at which John Boland, the Irish Environment Minister, who was also the TD for Dublin North, and I were to seek a way forward.

It was a blowy winter day as I crawled into our Cessna hoping for a briefing on the way down, but for once Obergruppenführer Whitlaw let me down; he apparently hated small planes even more than I do and had taken the road south the previous evening. The venue was Malahide, County Dublin, a splendid but sadly isolated example of the Republic's remaining Anglo-Irish heritage. As soon as we landed we were surrounded by officials. No meeting of the Intergovernmental Conference could take place without both Foreign Ministries being invited. Press officers noted every word, security men with bulging armpits manned every door, secretaries occupied every desk. There was a cast of thousands. John Whitlaw tried to whisk me aside to tell me what to say. This was not to the liking of my Southern counterpart, who clearly believed that he being an Irish Cabinet minister and I being a junior British squirt allowed him under the auspices of the Anglo-Irish Agreement to instruct me on what was to be done.

Time was of the essence, Boland told me. EEC money could not wait. An election was coming. The rich Brits could surely help out with a few pounds north of the border which were a vital link for the suggested by-pass around Dundalk and which, in his opinion, would do so much to improve communications North and South. I told him we had already spent a fortune on our side while virtually nothing had been spent on his, and that I had other priorities, like a bridge over the Lagan and by-passes for Downpatrick, Magherafelt and other towns. Furthermore a planning inquiry would be required and the security forces were not sure that his proposed line would not endanger their lives. This was not what he wanted to hear. Surely there were ways of speeding up a public inquiry? Was not the Anglo-Irish Agreement supposed to benefit border communities and bring both sides closer together? Did we really need to take the advice of the security forces so literally? It was a fractious meeting, with the Irish moving close to suggesting that their demands should become our policy.

There was no meeting of minds and after sixty years apart there appeared little in common over the culture of political influence, or how to handle planning inquiries or what could and could not be done in the interests of constituents. After lunch I told Boland the Latin names for the shrubs in his government's garden. He was not amused. For the first time I was pleased to take the tiny plane northwards into the teeth of a gale. I told John Whitlaw that if there was another occasion, he would travel with me. To all our relief there was not, and the road continues to meander through Ravensdale Forest as it always has.

If there was always a shortage of capital, there was almost always an annual underspend on current expenditure. Treasury rules forbade funding being carried forward from one financial year to the next, so there was a frantic fortnight at the end of every March to dispose of the money. There were certain circumstances that did allow funds to be carried over, but no one seemed sure what these were. There were plans for prioritising the spending of the underspending, but come the crunch most contractors could not digest extra work in such a short and unpredictable time-scale. The consequence was that every spring the Stormont Estate was resurfaced until it became so perfect that sleeping policemen had to be introduced to slow down the traffic. The sleeping policemen were the newest and most expensive available. So well designed were they that any car passing over them at more than five miles an hour nearly catapulted the driver and any passenger through the sunroof. After a battle with John Whitlaw I persuaded him to remove most of them. The end of March was also the time for ministers to have their offices redecorated and refurnished.

CLUNK CLICK, BUT NOT EVERY TRIP

Northern Ireland has a poor record on traffic accidents, though not because of any lack of enthusiasm on behalf of Ronnie Troughton, head of road safety in the DOE, who for years has led the campaigns against drink driving and for belting up. His problem was that, no matter how graphic and compelling the advertising of the dreadful statistics were, this could not make up for the lack of a visible police presence.

The RUC traffic branch have to use unmarked vehicles in many areas and the highly visible police motorbike has been an endangered species for many years. Police officers are 'legitimate' targets to the IRA and therefore are denied the chance to police the province's roads. Their priorities have understandably been concentrated elsewhere. One of the horrible by-products of terrorism is the number killed and maimed on the roads. If the motorist is unlikely to be caught for breaking the law, he pays for this dubious privilege as Ulster's insurance rates are the highest in the UK. Despite all Ronnie and his team's efforts those killed in motor accidents remained stubbornly high: 177 in 1985, 214 in 1987, 181 in 1989, 185 in 1990. This was double the number murdered by terrorists, a fact that was rather morbidly used by the advertising agents for the Industrial Development Board as showing how 'safe' Northern Ireland really is from terrorist violence.

18

WATER, WATER, EVERYWHERE

ANY ULSTER MIGRANTS TO AUSTRALIA and the United States wrote home to their families expressing their unhappiness at being cut off from their dear ones, but the thought of Northern Ireland's weather deterred most of them from taking the next boat home. In the Silent Valley in County Down, it rains more in August than in February or March and it rains more in February and March than it does in most other places.

My first ministerial confrontation with rain and tempest came in November 1987, when days of torrential downpour led to calamitous flooding in Omagh and Strabane. Tom King made me co-ordinating minister between the different departments to clear up the deluge. I decided to adopt the management approach that I had learnt earlier that year from Yukio Satoh, the chief of police in Myazaki, Japan. Yukio, now Japanese ambassador at the United Nations, is a senior diplomat who had been seconded to the police to broaden his experience. Satoh realised he was an unwanted outsider who would find it hard to gain the confidence of his men. So he summoned them all together and explained that, while he knew nothing of policing, he knew a great deal about diplomacy. He therefore would represent his men to the general public, explain their actions, support them in every way and refrain from interfering with their professional duties. His strategy appeared to work and he became popular with both his men and the local people. There have been a few RUC senior officers over the years who might have benefited from a short overseas posting to Japan.

I decided to follow the same path in dealing with the flooding. I did not want to interfere with local efforts by 'parachuting' in and using up the time of hard-pressed managers reporting to me on what was happening and distracting them from their real work. I ensured that there was a co-ordinating committee of local officials drawn from various departments and agencies under a senior DOE official whom I rang regularly to check on progress. Everything appeared to be going swimmingly, despite some alarmist reports in the press, until the Secretary of State paid a personal visit and reported back that chaos still reigned. A week later my colleague at the Department of Agriculture, Charlie Lyell, who had been visiting flooded farms, was more graphic in his descriptions.

I decided to put Japanese management methods to one side and see for myself. Tom and Charlie were right. They were all doing their best, but because officials had to report back within their departments and had few if any delegated powers, there was little a local co-ordinator could achieve. Local councillors were not satisfied with local brush-offs. They wanted action and money for their constituents. Many of those hardest hit had no insurance, yet it would have been unfair to give hand-outs to the two-thirds in Strabane and the one-third in Omagh without cover while giving nothing to those who had taken sensible precautions.

We managed to find an EEC pot which paid £126 to each flooded household and we paid out £210,000 under the social security system for distributing free coal and funding temporary homes provided by the voluntary and statutory organisations. I disagree with the proponents of minimum state intervention in instances of individual loss. Of course, insurance is an option for those who can afford it. But the flood at Strabane and Omagh was as much a result of departmental failure to provide adequate protection as it was an act of divine outrage. In such circumstances it is a cop-out for government to deny responsibility and it is open to taxpayers to take their revenge through the ballot box if their politicians are proved incompetent – admittedly an easier remedy for those in Britain than those in Northern Ireland.

Once a ministerial directive had established that the local councils, the DHSS, the DOE and the voluntary organisations could report back directly to me on any further administrative or financial hurdles, the difficulties started to ebb away. The network of voluntary bodies reacted fastest and most sensitively in bringing individual relief and highlighting individual hardship. Because they can call on large numbers of unpaid helpers to turn out without a rule-book and an overtime embargo to hinder them, voluntary organisations can get to the coalface much faster than those employed to interpret the rules and wait for the complaints from behind their desks. A full survey assessing the level of commercial and domestic damage bought us time, and time as usual bought us solutions. By the end of 1987 we had established very effective teamwork in the west of the province.

Disaster planning has always been a civil service prerogative. Many was the time, I was told, that Stormont House was sealed off because the NIO was playing doomsday scenarios on how to react to nuclear war or a possible chemical attack. It appeared that if the going really became tough, ministers really became irrelevant. They could not be trusted with organising or influencing the response. There was to be no room in the bunker for us. The lessons from Strabane showed the nonsense of such a tactic, provided, of course, ministers were prepared to ignore Japanese work practices.

THE WATER WORKERS

One of the quaint and nonsensical subsidies afforded to Northern Ireland industry but not Northern Ireland commerce was that the latter paid business rates and the former did not. The DOE's income from water was based on two sources, metering and a percentage of the rates. Commerce therefore paid twice, being metered and rate-assessed, while industry was only metered. The civil service, particularly the Department of Economic Development egged on by the Industrial Development Board, were determined to prevent this double whammy on the service sector being openly debated. Indigenous industry had to be protected; the linen industry and the food-processing industry would be bankrupt if they had to pay a proper price for their water, we were told.

The side-effect of this ridiculous distortion was that the DOE's water service was immune from privatisation, from pressures to reduce its costs and prune its workforce or from pressure from its customers to improve the quality of its service. The water service was unable to borrow capital except from an ever more reluctant Treasury. Although water consumption had dipped after the closure of the chemical plants in the sixties and seventies, by the eighties it was on the increase. Sooner or later, extra investment would have to be found. Fixing cracks in the province's 12,500 miles of pipes and mains would not suffice.

Two great round-table conferences were called in the Cabinet Room at Stormont as London pressed for a sell-off. But Tom King, Peter Brooke, Peter Viggers and I were not sure enough of the consequences of reducing Marks & Spencer's water rates while increasing Harland and Wolff's metering charges. We decided on one chew at a time. So Shorts, Harland and Wolff and Northern Ireland Electricity appeared easier and more profitable privatisation targets. In retrospect we were wrong, for although water was an important element in some companies' costs, it was as nothing compared with the improvements that were achievable through more productive use of investment, better management practices, better design, better marketing and a better trained and motivated workforce.

Northern Ireland's water service was not badly run, but it was not that well run either. One of the dispiriting aspects of engineer-dominated scientific management teams is that they hate being wrong. In order to avoid being accused of being wrong, they never take a risk. So it was with the Silent Valley.

The Silent Valley had belonged to my great-grandfather and is one of the national treasures of Ireland. The Belfast Water Commissioners purchased it in 1893 from my great-grandfather and then spent forty years turning it into the North of Ireland's largest reservoir. It was in reality two reservoirs, one lake feeding down an imposing concrete face, via a waterfall that resembles shimmering lace, into a second lake in the valley itself. The water then passes down through the dam into a series of filtration and cleaning chambers until it disappears into pipes and wends on its way to Belfast. The main dam took ten years to build, and so for a decade a standard-size railway ran from the site to Annalong, bringing men and materials. The piles had to go to a depth of 170 feet, which bankrupted the first contractor. It was Northern Ireland's largest ever infrastructural development and it is very beautiful.

Before the construction, the place was known as Happy Valley. Now above the dam the silence is deafening; not even trout seem to live in its black, peaty depths. On the hilly banks there is nothing but rock, heather and the occasional whin. But from the top of the dam looking south there is a green Garden of Eden with lush grass, rhododendrons, escallonias, Scots and Japanese pine, birch, larch and laurel. The dam wall stands between two climates, both spectacular. The public could enjoy one but not the other, because they were denied access above the dam. For twenty years, no one other than water workers had been able to witness the most spectacular wilderness in Ulster. It was closed off, I was told, on security grounds. Apparently the IRA in the late sixties had placed a bomb in the two-and-a-half-mile tunnel connecting Slieve Binnian with the Silent Valley. After this incident the DOE had felt it was too risky to allow continued public access which might put Belfast's water supply at stake.

There was only one fault with this arrangement. I discovered it was not the IRA who had placed the bomb, but a Protestant terror gang supposedly from Kilkeel (perhaps the ones that around the same time had tied up my great-aunt and made off with all the Needham silver from Mourne Park next door), pretending to be the IRA. The belt-and-braces boys of the DOE water service had never enquired sufficiently of the truth, and as a result, for a generation the public had been forbidden to visit a most entrancing piece of their heritage.

Furthermore the drive up to the base of the dam had been laid out like a second-rate municipal garden. There were no proper facilities for tourists, only a sullen security guard at the gate who gave the impression that anyone entering was doing so at not inconsiderable personal risk.

I was determined to change the rules or demand the return of my family's valley. Luckily I was supported by Maureen Grant, the tourist officer of Newry and Mourne District Council, and by the Nicholson family who ran the estate and were formidable gardeners as well as highly trained water workers. I invited over Arabella Lennox-Boyd, Europe's greatest landscape gardener. She said, leave it to Mr Nicholson and nature, and all will be well. We took her advice, and we also left it to Mrs Nicholson to manage a visitor centre and a tea-room. Access to the entire valley was restored to the people of Northern Ireland, and the number of visitors to the Silent Valley Mountain Park rose from 60,000 to 122,000 between 1985 and 1990. To the horror of the officials, my cousin, Julie Ann Anley, persuaded me to allow dogs on leads in the valley, but to my knowledge no one has abused the privilege that belongs to all who visit there.

If the Silent Valley showed the water service at its least adventurous, the sewage works at Newcastle demonstrated its capacity for imaginative solutions. There is not much room around Newcastle for a sewage works and Northern Ireland's record for clean, European-standard beaches went relatively unchallenged because few braved the cold let alone the dirt of the Irish Sea. It was decided to build a new works by the shore on rocks between the road and the high-water mark. It was brilliantly executed, fits cleverly into the background, is entirely undercover and never smells. Deservedly, it won Europe's most prestigious annual environmental award.

If only we ministers could have overcome the natural fears of our advisers to continue supporting the economically insupportable and pushed ahead with privatisation, I am sure Northern Ireland's water engineers would by now be roaming the world after business, as do Northern Ireland's doctors and nurses.

19

REBUILDING BELFAST

And have not here our souls with Freedom glow'd,
Has she not here long fix'd her lov'd abode?
Yes – and old time shall yet, with glad surprize,
View in Belfast a second Athens rise.

Hugh George Macklin, 1793

BELFAST IS A TOUGH, RAW, WORKING–CLASS CITY built on the success of the industrial revolution. Not much grass, but terrace after terrace, row after row, estate after estate cascading out from the city centre towards the heights in the west, across the Lagan to the east and towards the leafier suburbs to the north and south. It is surrounded by hills, so everyone has a view.

Its industry, its port, its universities, its commercial and shopping centres, and most of its 500,000 people are crammed within a mile of the City Hall. When the heart of Belfast was reconstructed in the late nineteenth century, it was filled with fine, confident and powerful empire-style buildings. All the main roads in Ulster from north, south, east and west lead to Belfast. In its heyday the city was the world's 'Linenopolis' and it boasted the world's largest rope-works. It was home town to Gallahers and to Harland and Wolff. During the early years of this century, the shipyards headed the world league for tonnage built. They constructed liners that cruised and cruisers that fought. Hamburg, Brest, Baltimore and Yokohama followed the designs and learnt the skills of Belfast's engineers and shipwrights.

Belfast was one of the five mighty hubs on which the British empire's trade and power depended. At its peak, it was without equal. Its merchants roamed the world, their products unmatched by those of their competitors. John Boyd Dunlop set up in Belfast, as did Harry Ferguson, partner of Massey. Queen's University produced the best-qualified doctors and the most competent and incorruptible of administrators for service in every country in every continent. It was and remains a very tough city whose folk like their drink and do not duck a fight. It still produces the hardest boxers in Europe. Its citizens are funny, brave and loyal, often blindly so, to their traditions. Neither side will ever defeat the other in Belfast. They are so similar in outlook, humour, language, attitude and sometimes name, that for an outsider to understand their ancient, bitter differences is well-nigh impossible.

It is a radical, sometimes revolutionary city. Founded by the Anglo-Irish ascendancy and owned by the marquis of Donegall, the modern city of Belfast, despite its Gaelic name, was at first an Anglican settlement that soon relied on the incoming Presbyterian Scottish planters for its commercialism and its drive. Its young men went to Glasgow and Edinburgh to study medicine and religion, and it was the politics and philosophy of Scotland that dominated the city's liberal outlook. At the end of the eighteenth century, Belfast supported the American colonists; many of those who had fled to Virginia left their parents, brothers and sisters in Ulster. The leaders of Belfast enthusiastically hailed the fall of the French monarchy. The first meeting of the revolutionary Society of United Irishmen was held in Belfast in 1791. The Belfast radicals wanted to run their own affairs and be responsible for their own taxes. They were overwhelmingly Protestant, for Belfast was not a Catholic city. The first Roman Catholic church, St Mary's in Chapel Lane, was not built until 1784. Belfast has always had much more in common with Glasgow than it has ever had with Dublin. But in the first one hundred years since the city's incorporation in 1613, the city's fathers showed greater tolerance of Catholicism than did any other place in Ireland.

If the intellectual drive of the city focused on industry, medicine and commerce, it did not exclude art or literature. For a town of 45,000 in 1835 that had become a city of 350,000 by 1900, it was astonishingly sophisticated. The poets, artists, actors and sculptors may not have become world names, but they were numerous, eclectic and successful. Compared with the output of the modern 'new towns', Belfast's settlers in an age before technology and television were astonishingly creative and often very poor:

> See Belfast, devout and profane and hard,
> Built on reclaimed mud, hammers playing in the shipyard,
> Time punched with holes like a steel sheet, time
> Hardening the faces, veneering with a grey and speckled rime
> The faces under the shawls and caps . . .
>   *from* 'Valediction' by Louis MacNeice

I love Belfast.

REPAIRING THE HEART

By the early 1980s the city was in trauma. Although much of the housing had been splendidly replaced, the roads were adequate, the water was clean and the lights worked, nearly every other aspect of inner-city life fell way below the standards of its peers. The centre had been bombed relentlessly for ten years. Most new buildings were tasteless, cheap, concrete and characterless; they reflected the mood of the people. The Lagan was dirty. There was no private housing in the city core. The hotels were few, their accommodation barely above adequate, their service indifferent, and their food often stodgy and overcooked. Restaurants, with pitifully few exceptions, came and went. Those with money ate outside the city and shopped in England. Confidence had been drained away as barbed wire spread like ivy. Security checks delayed shoppers, while armoured cars rumbled through the streets, the soldiers with blackened, unsmiling faces. The City Hall and the city fathers had had their powers castrated by the British government. They spent most of their time denouncing each other with sectarian abuse. Self-reliance remained, self-confidence had vanished. Yet these were the grandchildren and great-grand children of the builders of an empire on which the sun never set. Surely they were no different from their predecessors?

The law demanded the publishing of a new City Plan and we decided to use it as our strategy for conservation, redevelopment and renewal. In early 1987 we commissioned separate studies into retailing, the Lagan, conservation, office accommodation, transportation, population projection (the population had been declining due to the

Troubles) and tourism. The drafting of the plan allowed us a chance to fit all the jigsaw pieces together to give us a whole, which we would then rigorously promote as the biggest series of opportunities for over a century. We were determined to make the plan the vehicle on which would ride the hopes and dreams of the citizens. Although statute confined us to describing strategic land use, we had to find ways of capturing the public's imagination.

The area covered was the whole of Greater Belfast and we publicised the proposals and mounted displays at every opportunity. Of course, I wanted as much public participation as possible, but I had three other motives. First I intended to flush out opposition at an early stage, lance any boils, isolate objectors and gain widespread public backing. Uniquely, I believe, we provided £50,000 to the voluntary organisation Community Technical Aid so that local pressure groups opposed to the plan could have their criticisms properly co-ordinated and debated before the Planning Appeals Commission. My second objective was to isolate and bring pressure on unionist councillors to end their boycott of government ministers and re-enter political dialogue. If they excluded themselves from shaping the future of their city, there was little point in them remaining councillors. They were told that, although final decisions would be mine, they were free to discuss the issues with my officials and I was always available. As the months rolled by and more and more exciting programmes were announced, a mixture of curiosity and a genuine wish to become participants led to an ever-increasing number of taps on my door. My third objective was to isolate the terrorists by proving that it was they in both east and west Belfast who were the villains, delaying progress and strangling investment.

Most of the objectors and objections dealt with the particular hobbyhorses and prejudices of single-issue pressure groups. They were nonetheless real for that. There was concern over breaching the stop line and allowing an ever-larger number of mock-Tudor residences to invade the green belt. We pointed out that only six thousand of the twenty-five thousand increase in housing provision would be outside the line and we wanted private flats, of which there were very few, to be built in the city centre. Was this a plan to bring in yuppies? the Workers' Party demanded to know. The answer was, yes, this was definitely part of the plan.

If there was much middle-class discussion about the stop lines, there was little or no public debate about the dividing lines that criss-crossed the city. The Catholic population was growing and the Protestants, in the districts most isolated, most deprived and most terrorised such as the Upper Shankill and Tiger Bay, were leaving. The flashpoints of violence that so often made the headlines were due to a battle to capture or defend territory. The Catholics needed space and the Protestants would not give an inch, even though in many areas houses were deserted and boarded up, school rolls were declining and some churches were empty. Berlin walls were the most depressing and eloquent monuments to two decades of failure by British and Irish governments to bring peace to those entitled to be citizens of both states. We did not advertise it but wherever we could we tried to find neutral uses for the no-go land. Factories, offices, warehouses, old people's bungalows, schools, leisure centres – all were used to make the divisions less obvious and provide possible links for any future reconciliation.

A much more contentious criticism came from the bishop of Down and Connor, Cahal Daly. Research had shown that, small as Belfast is, very few of those living in west Belfast ever went near the city centre unless they worked there. Both the SDLP and the Catholic clergy argued that to stop parts of the city becoming no-go ghettos as far as employment and investment were concerned, we should concentrate on a programme which would provide local jobs for local people.

I believed that such a plan could lead to disaster. Not only did the levels of lawlessness make success highly unlikely, but failure would reinforce isolation in what were already slums. We had to find alternatives that would create 'safe' areas where both communities could mix and match. The tribes already lived apart and I could think of no way to attract private capital into districts that were skill-less as well as lawless. The political pressure on the Church partly came from Gerry Adams's constant reiteration of the need for two thousand industrial jobs in his constituency, a bleat that he knew to be fatuous. What we could prove was that 50 per cent of those in west Belfast who did have jobs worked in the city centre and what we had to do was provide thousands more jobs which would attract the alienated young and provide work that they could do and be properly paid for. We also knew that the IRA would use their newly acquired hoard of Libyan Semtex to stop us. Laganside, Royal Avenue and Great Victoria Street would be the hub of our effort to provide offices, shops, cinemas, opera, concerts and food.

We had to create a quality of life that everyone from everywhere would enjoy and remember.

By the end of the 1970s shopping in central Belfast was a mess. With a few notable exceptions, the great retailers from across the water had boycotted Belfast out of fear of the bomb and ignorance of the opportunities. Marks & Spencer and Boots had kept faith and had prospered, but many of the old established retailers and department stores had closed. Their frontages were boarded up, the offices above deserted, the ledges home only to hardy pigeons and hardier weeds. Anderson & McAuley tried to keep up appearances but what money they had they put into their out-of-town supermarket at Supermac. North of Donegall Place, scruffy shops with scruffy contents were hardly worth the inconvenience of enduring the security checks that ringed the core. But there was a golden opportunity and it came to be known as Castle Court.

On the west side of Royal Avenue was a massive area dominated by the army-occupied, barricaded Grand Central Hotel, while beside it was the vacated head post office site. Behind them both was the burnt-out Smithfield market, filled occasionally with temporary stalls. Between Smithfield and Millfield there was empty space. After six o'clock, despite the efforts of the traders to inspire late-night city centre shopping, there was nothing to do, nothing to eat and nothing to drink, although a few resident alcoholics must have found somewhere to provide them with sustenance. In 1978 the DOE had realised that there was enough spare cash in Northern Ireland to fill the 'big hole' alongside Royal Avenue, but confidence was low and investors nervous.

By the time I arrived in 1985 there was something in the air. There were two very grand committees that met regularly under the minister's chairmanship to review all major aspects of Belfast life. They were too diffuse in membership and too parochial in interest to be more than talking shops. We wound them up. The real dynamo that drove the dream forward was the DOE's Belfast Development Office, which worked with the Belfast Chamber of Commerce and the large traders. The boss of the Belfast Development Office was Eddie Simpson. Five minutes with him and any investor was convinced that he was being offered prime space just as lucrative as Knightsbridge and at a fraction of the cost. Unfortunately, soon after I became involved Eddie was appointed clerk of the court service – a career progression that did much for his golf handicap but nothing for Belfast. Luckily for me, his successor was Gerry Loughran who became the under-secretary in charge of urban regeneration at the DOE. He was one of the few Catholics at or near the top of the Northern Ireland civil service. He is exceptionally able and can be exceptionally provocative. He and I started off with a ferocious row when I altered the final paragraph of one of his draft press releases and he altered it back again and issued it. Peace was brokered, and for the next seven years Gerry was to be my right-hand man in almost every initiative that we promoted in Belfast. Moreover, those Gerry had around him had humour, optimism and guile against which no obstacle stood a chance.

Many of the bombed sites had been turned into profitable car parks by the IRA or UVF. We could not persuade NCP to invest in new multi-storey parking, but the transport holding company came to the rescue and together with a local developer and former hairdresser, John McIlroy of Ewarts, they put up the money for the first combined shopping and multi-storey car park complex in Victoria Street. Crazy Prices was the anchor tenant. It was hardly Fortnum & Mason but it was a start. It was also brave. As the *Belfast Telegraph* reported, 'the opening comes just two months after the last major IRA city centre car bomb. Just three weeks earlier another car bomb caused an estimated £3 million worth of destruction in James Street South.' Not many months would pass before the IRA turned their attention to the Victoria Centre, which by then had been sold on.

Meanwhile developers Sheraton Caltrust applied to demolish the old Robbs building in Castle Place and spend £10 million on a new shopping mall. In October 1988 the company's managing director, Gordon Thoms, remarked: 'We would not be building this unless Castle Court was going up.'

But could we get Castle Court up? It was an enormous project: 350,000 sq. ft of shops, 180,000 sq. ft of offices, parking for 1,600 cars. It would cost around £65 million to build and a further £20 million to fit out. But without an anchor tenant and without a government grant, the project was doomed. There were other questions. Who would become the long-term investors once it was complete? Could Castle Court compete with new edge-of-town developments? Could we entice the people of Belfast back to their city centre? Most fearsome of all, what would the IRA do to Castle Court?

Architect and planner Alwyn Riddell had started the ball rolling. He had been asked originally by the Smithfield traders to help redesign and rebuild their market. He brought together two other developers and together they persuaded Laing's to put up the money to build on the entire site. Laing's has a long and powerful presence in Northern Ireland. In Ronnie Dunn, their local manager, the company found – despite his cheery chappie English accent – a no-holds-barred, determined operator who did what was required to fund and finish the business. Martin Laing and his company never flinched in their support for Castle Court. In the end they made money and they deserved to.

Selfridge's was arm-twisted into becoming the anchor, and in early 1986 I was invited to inspect the plans agreed between the department and the developers. It turned into a long meeting. Selfridge's pushed hard during negotiations. They had demanded a ninety-nine-year, rent-free lease plus a premium of £1 million. The effect of this would have been to funnel government support into the pockets of Selfridge's and not into improving the quality of the architecture or the surrounding environment. I knew that I would be open to immediate and unanswerable criticism from my ministerial colleagues. If Belfast's shopping was underprovided, why should we be subsidising the likes of Selfridge's? My colleagues could demand the money for their budgets, and I as Minister of Health would have an unenviable conflict of interests. I would not be able to persuade the Department of Finance or the Secretary of State to underwrite the grant.

Furthermore the demands of Selfridge's and the costs of providing proper store security had so squeezed the budget that the first designs more closely resembled Crumlin Road Jail than the '*beaux-arts* Grand Canyon' of graceful Victorian buildings that were also awaiting restoration along Royal Avenue. I was alarmed at the prospect of a 300-metre unadorned brick frontage. I was determined only to agree to a building of international significance backed by the finest street furniture and street lighting. Ministers have little enough chance to be remembered by history for what they do or do not do, and I was not keen to be remembered for wrecking an immense opportunity for Belfast. The development team would have to go back to the drawing-board and I pledged to find another anchor tenant. I also demanded the building should be faced in glass: Castle Court was to be the defining landmark of the city's new confidence.

171

At the end of the discussion there was silence, followed by disbelief. 'Our surveyors have told us, Minister, that the demands of Selfridge's are entirely reasonable,' chimed in one voice. 'We will never find another anchor tenant, we have already been round every house a dozen times,' claimed another. 'Glass, Minister, you must be mad. What will happen to all the shoppers when the IRA blow it up?' interjected a third.

'Should we build it out of concrete blocks?' I responded. 'The shoppers will not differentiate much between being decapitated by flying glass or crushed to death by falling masonry. Why should small tenants have to pay £165 rent per sq. ft annually while Selfridge's so condescendingly pay nothing?' I was not to be budged. Roy Adams, now managing director of BDP, one of the UK's most original architectural practices and then chief of its Belfast office, supported me. Within a few weeks he had come up with a spectacular design and we had come up with another anchor, Debenhams. The developers agreed to pay Debenhams a contribution towards their fitting-out costs and Debenhams agreed to pay a reasonable rent. In return I accepted that the DOE should find £10 million of Urban Development Grant and a further £5 million to improve all the areas surrounding the site. The DHSS agreed to take the office space and move nine hundred staff who had emigrated to the Stormont Estate many years earlier back into the heart of the city. The total development covered a massive eight and a half acres and when completed would create two thousand new jobs. I was also determined, while the city centre's glory was being restored, to steer the planning guidelines away from massive out-of-town supermarkets.

Castle Court took over three years to build. One of the first ceremonies in January 1988 was to witness the removal of the nineteenth-century piles, seven hundred 45-foot-long pine trees which were drawn out of the ground like reluctant teeth and which had been perfectly preserved by Belfast's mud. Dixie Gilmore, the lord mayor, came along with me and was roundly abused by the city's DUP councillors for breaking their boycott. I was grateful to him, for I could escape from his colleagues while he could not.

Our secret fear was that the IRA would not let us complete the building without destroying the confidence of future tenants. During the three construction years we held our breath. Despite the best endeavours of the RUC and the builders, the IRA did what they could to destroy our dream. In all there were four bomb attacks and endless numbers of hoaxes, the last one a week before we were due to open. The department had insisted on the most rigorous security monitoring and the car park was built like a fortress, but the fear of an uncontrolled fire before all the systems were in place was a constant worry. We had, however, devised another strategy to try to neutralise the terrorist menace.

Adams and his followers had criticised the project for underwriting low-paid service jobs while the profits found their way into the tight fists of greedy English shop owners. We persuaded Debenhams to take on one hundred and fifty young trainee shop assistants from west Belfast, many of whom came from families with republican connections, and send them over for training in their Liverpool store. When they started work, the attitude in west Belfast changed. On the opening day in 1990, the winner of a free hamper as the first shopper through the door happened to be the mother of a Maze inmate. The only downside to the success of this neutralising plan was that every time I was seen in Debenhams there would, within ten minutes, be a coded bomb threat from the IRA. But we had Castle Court up and running. We had at last the foundation stone on which to expand the city, east, west, north and south.

Urban Development Grant was an incentive that worked wonders. We divided the city centre into zones and then we invited companies or individuals to come up with proposals to turn buildings they owned or were bidding for into profitable commercial businesses. They had to present the department with a realistic business plan detailing what needed to be spent and what income they could expect once the refurbishment was completed. The government would then contribute a certain amount of capital to allow the applicant an economic rate of return.

When the grant was first introduced there was a maximum limit of 50 per cent of the total cost of the project and it was paid out over a wide area of the inner city. We decided to increase the maximum pay-out to 75 per cent and narrow it to particular streets over a short time-period. With Castle Court out of the way, we focused on the dilapidated jumble of cobbles and buildings around St Anne's Cathedral to the east and Upper Library Street to the north. The property men came like ducks to winter barley. An imaginative and creative owner on a site and in business immediately attracted others next to him. As property prices soared, we cut off the grants. Barrie Todd, an architect, and Nick Price, a restaurateur, re-created the nineteenth-century, Victorian atmosphere of Hill Street. We stopped John Whitlaw's road men ripping up the cobblestones and two of Northern Ireland's most successful and interesting businessmen turned two rotting warehouses into cleverly designed, thriving successes which brought in custom and customers from all over the island. I told everyone that the red brick, cobbles and narrow alleyways overshadowed by the mighty St Anne's Cathedral reminded me of Siena – though not many agreed. Bewley's, the Dublin coffee house, moved into Donegall Arcade, as did ice-cream parlours, chocolate shops, ladies' boutiques and Dixon's electrical store. By 1990 we had all the major UK multiples except Sainsbury's and Tesco, and I was not too keen to have them undermining the new city centre with peripheral megastores.

Not every shop or every new centre was a success. The conversion by the Presbyterian church of their old Assembly Buildings into the delightful new Spires Centre at the corner of Fisherwick Place and Howard Street might have become more profitable for all concerned if they had allowed the restaurant a licence. Ross's Court, a wonderful new three-storey retail precinct off Victoria Square which would have made an ideal craft centre, has still not succeeded in attracting the right kind of tenant. Craft Works, which displayed the designs of Ulster's most talented craftsmen and women, had neither the imagination nor – they claimed – the funds to move from a remote cubby-hole in Linenhall Street to custom-made Ros's Court, where they would have attracted a wide clientele which in turn would have allowed the most successful designers to move into their own outlets alongside their original parent.

As well as the Urban Development Grant, the Belfast Development Office had a significant budget for environmental improvements. We had to work with Belfast City Council, who were responsible for building and maintaining wooden planters which were dreadful, plants which they grew with style and litter which they often left uncollected. I tried to encourage modern sculpture, but after the city fathers had acrimoniously rejected one young artist's plans for a life-size model of a lady of the night who had once plied her trade in Amelia Street, I decided to return to convention.

There were three remaining sores at the entrance to the city from the north. First there was the splendid old Gallaher tobacco factory, an enormous heap which, although it had a protection order attached to it, I thought could only be fixed by demolition. Second there was the Coop store in York Street which was both remote and covered in an extraordinarily ugly white cladding. Thirdly there was a horrid 1960s box which housed the Ulster University's art department; I hoped that the design of the building outside did not rub off on those designing inside. John McIlroy came to the rescue again with a proposal to redevelop the whole of Gallahers into the 'Yorkgate' centre which would have the relocated Co-op as the main store, together with a twenty-four-lane tenpin bowling alley, an eight-screen multiplex cinema, a leisure pool and 1,400 free car parking spaces. It would, he claimed, provide 1,500 jobs when finished and 300 during the construction phase. He asked me to produce £1 million towards infrastructure against his total investment of £30 million. There was a long argument about whether this new district centre would harm Castle Court, but we were keen not to lose the Co-op and it was an ideal site for an edge-of-city, mainly food store, development. In went the £1 million and up it went. It was a brave investment and I suspect the investors have yet to see much of a return on their money. Moreover we did not have to demolish the fine old factory building.

We were then left with the white whale of the old Co-op building in York Street. Shorts found a solution. The company had long been concerned about the difficulty of finding young Catholics to be apprenticed in east Belfast. Their human resources director, Brian Carlin, himself a Catholic and a man of real guts and foresight, hit on the idea of turning 'the whale' into an apprentice school which, because it was on neutral territory, would hold no fears for either community. Father Myles Kavanagh said he could make use of most of the rest for 'incubators', which were low cost starter units for small businesses providing common support services. The 'peace process' led to the conversion of the remainder into the venue for the seemingly never-ending talks. That then left the horrible art school, surrounded by a maze of scrubby shrubbery which housed all sorts of rubbish as well as a few unlovely buoys whose life in the lough had ended. Some city planners had thought they might look decorative on dry land. They do not. But both they and the art school defeated my best endeavours at removal and rehabilitation.

There were two other ideas that we hit upon to make the city centre more enticing. We decided to floodlight as many buildings – old and new – as we could. Floodlighting can hide a lot of wrinkles and can pick out architectural masterpieces that the busy pedestrian would never notice at street level. My Neapolitan sister-in-law Marina had told me that Naples was a city of few diamonds in a muddy pool. I wanted to make the Belfast diamonds take over the pool, and floodlighting, together with cleaning and restoration, has made a spectacular difference. (Several years later I used the Belfast experience to persuade the Indian government to adopt a similar plan for lighting up the great Victorian buildings in Bombay, Delhi and Calcutta – the empire strikes back.)

The second idea concerned tasteless, colour-clashing shop fronts which were common in the city centre. Whoever designed these gaudy eyesores had no feeling for matching the fascias with those of their neighbours or the buildings into which they were studded. I wanted to return to traditional sign-writing, with gold leafing on hardwood panels. Gerry Loughran agreed to us issuing a code of good practice and allowed me to promote a competition where members of the public who chose the best designs would be awarded £500 prizes. I also wanted a competition where I would give a prize to those who pointed out the worst and shame their owners into action. We compromised. We provided alternative designs for the most offensive shop fronts. I am afraid that we did not always succeed in getting rid of these eyesores, even though we offered the owners a 100 per cent grant to implement the ideas of professional designers. As always the Belfast Civic Trust supported me in every way possible, but ultimately the only solution was to change the planning laws and, as usual, a parliamentary slot was not available.

If there was a dearth of anything in Belfast by the end of the eighties, it was good hotels. This was despite the efforts of Diljit Rana to develop smart new hotels and the understandable opposition of Billy Hastings. Diljit and his wife Uma came to Belfast in the early fifties and from very humble beginnings worked their way up the property and retail ladder. The Ashoka restaurant is a very good Indian restaurant by any standards and when mink and leather were in fashion Mrs Rana's boutique matched anything in Bond Street. They never ever gave up despite a terrible personal tragedy and the ups and downs of trying to do business in Belfast. They were bombed out, burnt out and intimidated out, but they always came back for more. There was always some new idea, some new unthought-of (and sometimes unthought-out) plan to do something different in Belfast. What money Diljit and his family had was where his mouth was, although some creditors might have complained that it was occasionally trapped at the back of his throat. He once came to see me with some new idea which would require dollops of government funding and I was determined to be tough with him. He came through the door with his usual captivating smile and presented me with a series of attractively designed, numbered, colour prints of Northern Ireland. I melted, and so did my resolve. Belfast needs many more Diljit Ranas. He never lost faith in his new home or in his iron determination to make a success of his business and the city he adopted and which now has adopted him. He has now enticed Sir Brian Mawhinney to become chairman of his expanding hotel group.

There were other remarkable characters who made up the city's Chamber of Commerce. Sandy Brown was a gentle, large, amusing and very clever Scot who had masterminded Marks & Spencer's Belfast survival and expansion so that by the end of his time his store was one of the largest and most profitable in the whole M & S group. He believed his customers to be always right and his customers were the people of Belfast. If there was a panic Sandy calmed it down, if there was a rumour he quashed it, if there was a row he sorted it. Sandy was also a philanthropist; nothing was too much trouble and every worthy cause would have Sandy as a champion. He retired in Belfast in 1990 but tragically died in early 1993 before he could enjoy, influence and improve the voluntary and business groups which had captured his heart and his imagination.

Once the city had started to put its new clothes on, I was determined to show it off. Every visiting dignitary, every group of businessmen or politicians – I walked them all round the city centre, often puffing a large Havana cigar to show how prosperous we all were. Many of them gave the impression that they were visiting Beirut and suggested Saracens and flak jackets. Southern Irish ministers and British MPs were particularly apprehensive. I explained that 99 per cent of Ulster folk would not have a clue who they were, and even if they did they would be greeted with warmth and enthusiasm. I always tried to ensure a minimum police and army presence, although as the delights of Belfast grew so, it seemed to me, did the number of army patrols wanting to visit it. After a walk round Castle Court and a cup of coffee in Bewley's, Seamus Brennan, a Southern minister, explained to us that most Dublin ministers knew more about Brussels and Paris than they did about Belfast – a city they viewed with fascination and fear.

DOWN BY THE RIVERSIDE

Castle Court was big but it was not 'the big one'; that was Laganside. Bob Crane, who was managing director of the *Belfast Telegraph*, asked me in my first fortnight in Northern Ireland to meet and have dinner with a few of his senior managers and reporters. His boardroom wall was covered with a massive painting of the city which so fascinated me that I failed to take in the erudite and subtly phrased briefing they were keen to register with their new apprentice minister. Through the centre of the tapestry ran a great silver sword – the Lagan – and yet on each bank there was, in reality, nothing but dereliction, scrapyards and coal tips. The city had turned its back on a treasure and allowed it to become dark, dirty and smelly. Here was a chance to do something.

I was not, of course, the first to have thought of it. Chris Patten's hasty *au revoir* had included a mumble about the Lagan. What had been happening in London's Docklands and Boston's waterfront had already been advertised by Eddie Simpson and his team at the Belfast Development Office as a benchmark for Belfast – for Belfast!

'Why not?' said Eddie's successor, Gerry Loughran, in a matter-of-fact, mid-Ulster snap, and off he went to organise how we could attract hundreds of millions of pounds of private investors' funds to make a vision come true. Up to the mid-eighties, capital investment in the city had been paid almost entirely from the British exchequer. Now we had to market ourselves in competition with a hundred other cities (including Dublin and Glasgow) to persuade investors to pour their money into Belfast. We had schemes such as Urban Development Grant and we had funds for clearing sites and putting in basic services, but if Laganside was to succeed the ratio would have to be at least £5 of investors' cash to £1 of the government's.

My first lead was to save an old flour mill which was likely to be part of the earliest Laganside redevelopment site. McCausland's building in Victoria Street was one of the last examples of buildings that breathed the belief and self-confidence that the Ulster-Scots had in themselves and their businesses. It was beautifully proportioned and crafted with ornaments and intricacy. The DOE proposed knocking it down. I refused. I may, as Charles Brett used to chide me, be guilty of 'façadism', but if it is legitimate to alter the inside of a building to suit modern commercial practice, it is inexcusable to destroy a beautiful link with the past. I believe that my stand on McCausland, supported by Belfast's articulate conservationists, helped strengthen an already growing mood within the department that even if conservation did not mean preservation it certainly did not warrant destruction.

The next task was to see what others had been up to. I spent some time with Sir Nigel Broakes, chairman of Trafalgar House and also chairman of the London Docklands Corporation, and his imaginative chief executive, Reg Ward (whom Nigel once described as having both feet planted firmly in the air!). What they were doing made Laganside look like a village, and yet, impressed as I was, I felt that the Thatcherite restrictions of only using private funds largely excluded the views of local councillors and the local people. That would not work in Belfast. Ours had to be a community effort. What we were attempting had to be part of a healing process and we had to provide a safe haven for all Belfast's people, haves and have-nots.

Gerry Loughran and his team started on a search for consultants to help us design and promote our plan. A group of us went to Baltimore and Boston to see how Jim Rowse and Steve Coyle had reworked their waterfronts. The Americans are so brash, so certain of success, that nothing appears inconceivable to them – and as a result often nothing is. As many of those involved in Boston were of Irish extraction, our boys were determined that anything they could do, we could improve on. Gordon Irwin of Belfast port, who hates 'abroad', said he had seen nothing that had surprised him. Cecil Ward, the incorrigible Belfast city clerk who had done more to keep the city council from degenerating into open sectarian warfare than anyone else by keeping open the channels of communication between the council and ourselves after the signing of the Anglo-Irish Agreement, went home determined to educate his flock on what could be done, if only they could be persuaded to look beyond their navels. We all realised that we would have to build one step at a time, and that the key would be how we organised ourselves, how we advertised ourselves and how we could make a success of the first site. If that went well the rest, we believed, would follow.

After his involvement and success with Castle Court, Roy Adams was an obvious choice as architect, but we needed a Belfast equivalent to Boston's energetic Steve Coyle. Gerry came up with Peter Hunter. I could not really believe that Gerry was serious when he introduced me to a bespectacled, shy, slightly dishevelled, unassuming, uncertain, uncharismatic man. Then Peter started to tell me what he proposed to do.

Step by step he took me along the Lagan. There would be a weir here, a private housing estate alongside a river walk there, a massive new theatre complex, an international hotel, a leisure island, a marina for seagoing boats, a working maritime museum, 200,000 sq. ft of office space, 100,000 sq. ft of speciality shopping, a riverside garden, a closed channel for canoeing, a Gateway centre for schools and tourists, cinemas, bars, discos, restaurants, health clubs. The traffic would be redirected, and new rail and road bridges would be built. 'This, Minister,' he concluded, 'will make the Lagan one of the most attractive rivers in Europe, and I am sure, Minister, together we can sell it both to investors and to the dear people of Belfast.' The man was a genius.

To turn Peter Hunter and Roy Adams's architectural inspirations into life we founded the Laganside Company. For the chairman we picked James, duke of Abercorn. Jimmy the Duke, as he is occasionally irreverently referred to by his escorts, is no patronising, patrician figurehead. He is a super salesman. A 6 foot 2 inch Grenadier, for much of the sixties MP for Fermanagh–South Tyrone, entrepreneur and landlord, he exudes enthusiasm, optimism and energy. He also knows a lot of people around the place. Once he had taken up the challenge, there was no suitable city not visited, no property developer left unassailed, no conference opportunity ducked: wherever and whenever there was the sniff of something that could help our cause, James would be after it. He needed to be kept to the scent, as occasionally his eagerness would lead him down false trails. His chief executive was the opposite – a solid, reliable, careful former head of the North's Local Enterprise Development Unit (LEDU). George Mackey and the Duke were an irresistible double act.

We launched Laganside officially on 10 March 1987. We claimed the plan would bring £280 million of investment into a one-and-a-half-mile stretch of river. Sammy Wilson, the DUP lord mayor, boycotted the launch but the incoming mayor, Dixie Gilmore – whom I had made a director of the new company – came, together with various landowners, estate agents, banks, builders, lawyers and accountants who could see the potential pickings.

Two months later we gave permission for a £60-million cross-harbour road and rail link, and in December 1987 we disclosed the details of the new £7-million weir which would control the tide and hide the smelly mudflats. The weir and bridges were the catalysts for redevelopment, and as the work started, even the coal and scrap men around the Abercorn basin began to accept we were in earnest. They were the most difficult to persuade. Some of them perversely believed that a scrap-iron wharf was a visitor's attraction. 'Have you not noticed people lining the Queen Elizabeth Bridge watching the coal being unloaded?' I was asked by one slightly tipsy interested party at some official function. 'If that's the only entertainment they can get from their river, it's high time we moved you out,' was my answer.

In February 1989 we revealed that Farrans were the successful bidders for the McCausland site. The main feature of the development brief had been the retention of the McCausland building and the scheme comprised 120,000 sq. ft of office space and 24,000 sq. ft for private flats, the first in Belfast for a century. Also that month I introduced an order establishing the new Laganside Corporation. The Labour Party, as usual, damned me with qualified praise. Jim Marshall, their front-bench spokesman, said the money for Laganside could perhaps be better spent elsewhere; it would, he claimed, provide a new ghetto for well-off yuppies (whatever that might mean) and be a property bonanza. He complained that local people were not being sufficiently consulted. Fortunately Cecil Walker, North Belfast's MP, came to the rescue: 'There is no such thing as a "yuppie" in my opinion in Northern Ireland. We may witness this development bringing some yuppies. If they come into this area and they bring yuppie money I will not be unduly worried.' I suspect that even now under the skin of New Labour the envy of Old Labour lies not too deeply hidden.

From 1989 onwards, when I became Minister of Economic Development as well as of the Environment, it became very much easier to co-ordinate the activities of the Belfast Development Office and the Industrial Development Board in focusing on and inviting in potential investors. The Laganside Corporation could identify the needs or the potential sources of capital, but it was the IDB who could seduce the potential back-office tenants through grants and interest-free loans. We had a seamless marketing strategy by the early nineties, which could have been undermined if my ministerial responsibilities had been altered.

The combined efforts that we made to bring the largest area of Laganside – Laganbank – to completion were as good an example of interdepartmental and interagency co-operation as I witnessed during my years as a Northern Ireland minister. To find an international hotel we needed the contacts and the knowledge of the Tourist Board, whose sponsoring department was the Department of Economic Development. To be successful in bringing back-office jobs from British Airways and British Telecom we relied on the IDB. We had to move the Oxford Street bus station, who were none too keen to be shifted; for that, the transport division of the DOE was involved. The High Court and judges' chambers were immediately opposite the Laganbank site and they were constantly being mortar-attacked, bombed or rocketed. We had to persuade the judges not to demand sangars, barbed wire and pillboxes around the courts and not to change the line of the existing road to take it further away from the court house and on to the Laganbank development. This could only be done through the NIO talking to the judges, who had a much higher view of their own importance and safety in the scheme of things than they had of our desires to build a hotel and a concert hall.

Belfast needed a modern concert hall; the Ulster Hall was adequate in its day for Craig and Carson but not for the Berlin Philharmonic. The total cost for a new hall was £27 million, and even with European money the charge to the ratepayer amounted to £13 million. There were those in the DUP who distrusted the government's motives in promoting Belfast and would have welcomed a scorched-earth policy rather than co-operation with the NIO. There were also radical socialists who distrusted entertainment for the well-to-do even though the Waterfront concert hall was specifically designed to attract all Belfast's people, young, old, poor or rich. They were unmoved that the money had been set aside by the crafty Cecil Ward and his allies over the years. The DOE was the liaison agency with Belfast City Council, and the Belfast Development Office seduced the majority of the council on to our side against a strange DUP/Sinn Féin alliance.

None of us was prepared to see Laganbank fail. We all became networkers, allocating specific roles to key people in each department to deal with each specific hurdle that confronted us. I argued with the lord chief justice. I went to see the chairman of British Telecom and British Airways. As far as the hotel was concerned, I called on the Anglo-Irish ascendancy to see us through.

It so happened that Lindy Dufferin (the marchioness of Dufferin and Ava) had a very close friend who was the art adviser to the Pritzkers who own the Hyatt Hotel Group. So Lindy had Tom Pritzker and his wife to stay at her memorable home, Clandeboye. The duke of Abercorn was summoned from Baronscourt in County Tyrone and Hugh O'Neill from Cleggan. We had an idyllic Saturday in wonderful July weather: tennis, followed by tea and cake, then dinner, then port and then the hard sell. The following day I thought Belfast would have a Hyatt. We took a picnic to Strangford Lough. Tom Pritzker's wife looked nervous and said she did not like boats, particularly speedboats. I did not hear this, took command, increased the power, put the wheel hard over and in ten seconds nearly wrecked everything. The Duke shoved me into the bilges and goodwill was restored. We never did get a Hyatt, but the Duke and Hugh had been working separately for years on a Hilton. And now it's there, next to the Waterfront and British Telecom's new offices.

The success of Laganside did not happen by accident. It was due to a group of people, some unremunerated, some poorly remunerated, all of them certain that what they were doing was creating a once-in-a-life-time opportunity for a city they cared for. Their names should be placed on a roll of honour in the City Hall as an example to the future.

But the new Belfast had to be used in a way that would improve the lot of all. Parts of the city remained in deep shock, depressed, under-mined by violence, with rates of sickness and unemployment that were unacceptable in a civilised country. What were we to do to try to bring economic and social freedoms to a people under the rack of terrorist tyranny?

20

THE ACTION TEAMS

B Y THE END OF THE EIGHTIES the centre of Belfast may have been buzzing but many of the suburbs were destitute and depressed. Sir Kenneth Bloomfield had commissioned a study on the extent of inner-city poverty and the results were dreadful. There were massive levels of male unemployment and desperate levels of educational attainment (in the Shankill only nine pupils a year passed their eleven-plus). Large families, poor diets and marriage break-ups were as much the norm as the exception. Most of those with talent left. It mattered not whether you were a Protestant or a Catholic. Tiger Bay was no better than the New Lodge, Rathcoole every bit as awful as the Ardoyne. Although state housing conditions had improved, the quality of life of the tenants was as drab and as hopeless as ever. Some 15 per cent left school with no qualifications; 15 per cent suffered from a long-term illness; 64 per cent of those unemployed had been out of work for a year or more, and of those, 49 per cent were known to be Catholics and 37 per cent Protestants. Those in work were often poorly paid and insecure. Crime rates in the city were 20–50 per cent higher than elsewhere in Northern Ireland. The man responsible for the Bloomfield findings was Douglas McIldoon, head of regeneration initiatives in the DOE.

In 1986 I had decided to find ways around the Chancellor of the Exchequer's rules on additionality; this was the doctrine whereby any money from Brussels that was considered part of the government's main line expenditure programmes led to offsetting reductions in the corresponding national budgets. As we were net contributors to the European Community's coffers, the Treasury argued that the Commission was only returning money that was rightfully ours. As net beneficiaries, Ireland and Italy could, of course, spend as much as they could grab – and very good at grabbing they had become. In the DOE we had managed to find a few loopholes to this dubious principle. (It was dubious because the Brussels accounting officers knew what London was up to and merely reallocated even more money to other countries' programmes.) The ports, the airports, the railways and the buses were not covered by the rules because although they were publicly owned companies, they were not directly managed by the state.

I longed to see how the Italians of the Mezzogiorno organised their budgets and so I suggested we visit Naples in February to discuss a possible twinning of our two great cities. Douglas came along as the DOE's brightest, most free-ranging intellect. At first I thought he was a gangly, rather vague left-over from the socialist seventies who had only got round to having his hair cut because civil service rules demanded it. I was mistaken. He had fire, resolve and a readiness to learn anything from anywhere which he could adapt to Northern Ireland conditions.

We had an interesting time in Naples. We were apparently the first delegation led by a British minister ever to ask the city leaders how they ran their city. As soon as we arrived we were rushed off to a harbour restaurant, where for three hours our Italian hosts shouted at each other. Then quite suddenly, over coffee, their leader embraced me. He explained that there are different tiers of public governance in Naples: La Regione, La Commune and La Città. Before our visit the representatives of all three had been fighting for years like cats and dogs over both who should control the money from Rome and Brussels and who should be responsible for doling it out. Our arrival had forced them to work out an agreed position prior to their post-lunch presentation. This 'historic' accord had been finally agreed over the grappa. I had become an instant hero.

The presentation showed that the problems of Naples were more intractable even than Belfast's. At least the IRA or the UVF had not infiltrated every level of the police, the civil service and the political establishment. The Cammoristi, the Neapolitan Mafia, had influence if not control over most aspects of normal life in the city and its suburbs. There was always a financial crisis – while we were there, the police wore jeans because there was no money to dry-clean their uniforms. No one knew who was straight or who was twisted. They showed us grandiose and exciting plans to clean up their city, sort out the traffic chaos, build a proper underground public transport system and develop new community centres of housing, offices and supermarkets. But the administrative and political structures were chaotic and if the Cammoristi did not receive their cheques in the post, the letter-bombs came by return. However, the city knew how to board the Brussels gravy train. They had cleverly placed key officials in many of the cabinets of the highest-spending EC commissioners and they had a shrewd awareness of how to tap into and extract Community funding which was much more sophisticated than ours. We determined that on our return home we would bolster our presence in Brussels, which we could only do by setting up a Northern Ireland Chamber of Commerce office there. We could not compete with the Republic, and London would only allow us a quota which would not antagonise the Scots or the Welsh; so we would have to try to represent ourselves, which we duly did.

My Neapolitan excursion to seek alternative ways of securing funds was met with a terse interjection from an angular lady sent by our embassy in Rome to watch over me. 'This is the first time I have ever met an English Minister trying to find ways of circumventing his own government's policies,' she rasped. 'I am not English, I am Irish,' I responded.

We stayed with the British consul general, who was as perplexed by our arrival as the Italians or the lady from the embassy in Rome. His responsibility was primarily concerned with liaising with his NATO colleagues and keeping visiting British sailors on Mediterranean exercises out of Naples's brothels. His office had a magnificent set of naval ships' name plaques. Among them I spied the crest of the HMS *Kilmorey*, Belfast's former minesweeper. Very generously he allowed me to take it home, where it hangs in its rightful place next to a photograph of Northern Ireland's contribution to the Royal Navy leaving Portsmouth. A few weeks later I enquired from the naval records office in Belfast when HMS *Kilmorey* had called in Naples. There was no record, although it appeared that she had disappeared for a few days after a minesweeping exercise around Malta. My great-uncle, Rear Admiral the Earl of Kilmorey RNR, had, it seemed, used her for a short period as his private yacht. Many were the elderly, matronly and retired Wrens who with a twinkle in their eyes told me how much they had enjoyed sailing on the *Kilmorey* under the command of the captain who bore her name.

The Minister for the Mezzogiorno, Remo Gasperi, had come to hear about our expedition and requested a return visit for him and his officials so that they might discover what they could garner from Belfast. Remo Gasperi was a tough former Christian Democrat mayor of Bari who had made his way up the political ladder by locking up all his Communist opponents. He was later found to have siphoned off a large sum of money which had been set aside for earthquake victims in Calabria. It had turned up in Padova, where he hoped to further his North Italian political connections. He then suffered the same misfortune as his erstwhile opponents.

He arrived in Belfast in an Italian airforce jet with a formidable delegation and an interpreter who soon decided that her opinions were of greater importance than his, and proceeded to give her own responses to questions rather than translating her minister's. Gasperi spent a considerable part of his time with the Catholic clergy of Belfast, and I am sure they benefited from his colourful tales of life in the south of Italy which they could follow without help from the interpreter. To our astonishment we discovered there were around one thousand Italians living in Northern Ireland. Many were wives or husbands of Ulster soldiers or sailors and most came to take wine with their minister when we invited them to Stormont Castle. After he returned home the accompanying journalists from one local paper gave him a fulsome two-page spread on his visit to Northern Ireland, praising his bravery for undertaking a hazardous journey, although to him it must have appeared at times a rainier version of home from home. Unfortunately a typo appeared throughout the piece telling the people of Naples that Signor Gasperi had enjoyed three days in Islanda del Nord rather than Irlanda del Nord.

Douglas McIldoon then spent the following year researching what redevelopment work was being done in English and Scottish cities. When he had completed his work in July 1988 we launched the Making Belfast Work programme. The aim was to increase job opportunities for the unemployed and improve their quality of life in unconventional ways. Our aim was to give local people greater direct influence in the provision of those public services that dominated their daily existence. We divided Belfast into blocks covering several thousand electors. In each we introduced an 'action team'. These comprised a leader and three or four young civil servants who were supposed to be the best and brightest in their departments. They would, we believed, gain real experience in the harshest of environments before returning to their mainstream careers.

As each team was drawn from different departments, we knew that between them the members of a team would have sufficient knowledge to hunt out the relevant section in each government office when they came across a service failure or a bureaucratic muddle. They were to be gamekeepers turned poachers on behalf of their new community clients. Even those from the Department of Agriculture, who might have been expected to struggle a bit in an urban environment, found that their knowledge of the system saw them through.

Because the city's politicians had had their responsibilities siphoned away by direct rule, councillors and MPs could do little to influence decisions on the allocation of housing, the provision of local health centres, the level of social services, the quality of education or the state of the pavements. They were impotent. Our intention was to use the action teams as a focus that the deprived and the alienated would call upon to sort out the problems that beset them. The teams were to promote community groups and work with the local councillors and MPs to bypass the red-tapery that inevitably exists in monoliths, such as the Housing Executive, the Eastern Health Board or the Belfast Education and Library Board. We gave the teams a considerable additional budget of some £20 million a year beyond and above the public funds already committed in the main line spending programmes.

The action teams were to concentrate their work on the voluntary organisations. Every effort was designed to bear down on the most intractable of problems. Some of the initiatives provided services that would have been unnecessary in normal communities: providing homework centres for children who could not study after school; introducing boys and girls to information technology; involving youngsters in after-school sports of a different kind to those they had become accustomed to on the streets after dark; giving adolescents education on safe sex; providing women's groups with premises and administrative support. The action teams had to steer clear of politics and security and they had to ensure that money did not end up in the pockets of terrorist-infiltrated organisations that had sprung up to suck off funds wherever they could. The programme was managed and led by the Belfast Special Action Group which comprised some of the most powerful civil servants in the province and was chaired by the head of the Northern Ireland civil service.

Did the initiative work? In the main, yes. Some young civil servants thrived on it. Ritchie Warburton, for instance, gave up his suit and his conventional career, put on his jeans and his trainers and soon had the New Lodge, Duncairn and Skegoniel heaping him with praise. He suggested a community festival with seed-corn funding. He sponsored an unemployed student to put together a photographic exhibition of the area. He helped run and finance the Unity Flats community newspaper. He advocated local policing and helped to set up groups for pensioners, the young, mothers and toddlers. He enlisted everyone in promoting their community in order to attract new private investment, new shops and extra services. He now runs the Belfast Development Office.

Another extraordinary team leader was Kate Kelly. Her father was a prosperous Catholic businessman who had been burnt out of east Belfast. Kate had learnt her community work in Watts County in Los Angeles. The Springfield Road therefore held no fears for her. Her mission was to work with the women of Belfast. She saw in them the most rational and most determined groups that could articulate effectively to their menfolk, to the army, to the police, to officialdom and, not least, to the Church what needed to be done. She trod on many toes but I was determined to support her in all she proposed. She truly worked wonders for the women's groups across all Belfast. Her courage in standing up to those in authority, be they in the Church, the security forces, the NIO or the IRA, gave her women the courage to do likewise. She showed how an action team should be run, though unfortunately in the end her efforts cost her her health.

There were a few others like them, but unfortunately not all were. Some never let go of the umbilical cord that tied them to their departments and were scared to take a risk that might lead to a failed project and a career black mark. Some others did not always account for their expenses as rigorously as they should. Yet the vast majority were brave and dedicated young men and women.

For my part I found the action teams an invaluable asset in discovering what was really happening and in forging partnerships with local community leaders which improved the government's reputation for action, caring and commitment. The Making Belfast Work initiative was a vital part of our strategy to talk to and underpin those who lived in terrorist-dominated areas: it gave us access to them and opportunities to wean them away from violence. In unionist territory our programmes helped undermine opposition to the Anglo-Irish Agreement. In nationalist wards we were able to support discreetly those antagonistic to republicanism. The projects gave us a direct entry into every area of city life.

Our objective was to encourage the good and to vilify the evil. Dr Joe Hendron was one of the former. He is one of the most decent and courageous of Irishmen, and he has never given up on west Belfast. Though often verbally and sometimes physically abused by Sinn Féin supporters, he always maintained a balance in his views. He measured his words, he always smiled, he listened, he charmed. I never saw him lose his temper. He beat Gerry Adams in West Belfast in the 1992 election despite the voting impersonations, the threats and the bullying. Had he not been so dreadfully let down by the government's failure at Drumcree in 1996 and undermined by the American funds that Sinn Féin relied on after the ceasefire, I suspect he would have kept Gerry Adams out. I used every means to support Joe and his supporters in their commitment to bring normality and decency back to west Belfast life.

Another exceptional man I was equally determined to bolster was Father Myles Kavanagh, together with his 'managing director' at the Flax Trust, the charismatic Sister Mary Turley. Myles would have as many new ideas as there are minutes in an hour. Sister Mary would weed most of them out, the NIO's obstructionism, as he saw it, would kill a few more, and then he would be in to see me, using a mixture of humour, threats, cajolery, beggary and flattery. Whatever remained were gems. Myles used the best of ideas from America to start business incubation units and to encourage business start-ups in west Belfast. He befriended some of the most powerful men in Washington, Boston and New York and brought them regularly to Belfast to see for themselves what he was doing. He played a major role in supporting my attempts to tease out new ideas and take on new ventures. When he goes to heaven there will be a strong lobby that he be given a halo – and there will still be some in the NIO who would have preferred to see him go the other way.

On many occasions the team leaders found that the orders given to the security forces on the ground made matters more difficult. Although the co-operation between the action teams and the RUC on the street was hardly ever a problem, the lack of co-ordinating machinery further up helped not at all. Furthermore there is a limit to what can be done for people living in multiple deprivation. A survey in 1991 showed that those disadvantaged in 1981 remained in much the same state a decade later, and that if anything the gap between the richer and the poorer wards was getting wider. The theoretical trickle down from rich city centre to impoverished near neighbourhood was not in evidence. A recent review has suggested that the Making Belfast Work initiative should be continued and that although the programme is expensive, on balance it has worked in improving the lot of those it has targeted. What the review did not analyse was the amount of political leadership, or lack of it, given to the programme over its entire lifespan. Had we been without the action teams, the state of the poorest would, I believe, have been much direr. Unfortunately, surveys do not deal with hypotheticals.

21
DERRY / LONDONDERRY

THE FIRST GLIMPSE OF LONDONDERRY from the east bank of the Foyle is unforgettable: a walled city with a magnificent cathedral surrounded by Georgian terraced houses. If it were not for the barbed wire and the army pillboxes, it could compare with Windsor. In recent years the city has become deeply divided. The west bank is now over 90 per cent Catholic and only a small and poor Protestant community still hangs on in the Fountain Estate. The Shantallow and Creggan estates, neat and modern, belie a male unemployment rate of 60–70 per cent. The SDLP have a hard grip over the middle class, the middle-aged and the elderly. Sinn Féin have a worryingly high level of support among the young.

Derry's history is a roller-coaster of success and hope followed by failure and despair. Geographically a backwater, the city was strategically at the hinge of the centuries-old battle between British domination and Irish resistance. Every paving-stone has a story and the suffering of both sides requires no embellishment to convey its awful authenticity.

When St Columba founded Derry in the sixth century, he scribbled a verse:

> This is my reason for loving Derry. It is in all its width and length
> Filled with shining peace for it is peopled by God's angels only.

In July 1689, deep into the city's third siege, the defending commander,

General Walker, recounted a grisly shopping list in his diary:

A quarter of a dog fattened by eating the bodies of the slain Irish	5s 6d
A dog's head	2s 6d
A cat	4s 6d
A rat	1s 0d
A mouse	0s 6d

The history of the city and its place in the pantheon of both communities are imbibed from birth. In the nineteenth century it was the port through which many of the starving passed on their way to America. Later, it became a world centre for shirt making (and still is).

Much of the latest Troubles have centred on Londonderry and by the end of the seventies the *Guardian*, in a major centrepiece article, was describing the city centre as 'Tumbledown Derry'. A BBC news correspondent described sitting in his studio waiting to do a piece on the one o'clock bulletin when a building next door collapsed with a loud thump. Determined to get a vox pop reaction to the blast, he went out and stuck his microphone into the face of a bemused onlooker who told him: 'That there was my shop. Some boy come in with a television set and dropped it on the counter. "How long does it take to mend?" he says. "About a week," I said. "Well you've got two minutes," he says, with me running out behind him.'

Yet for all those promoting the division there had always been a corresponding group of powerful and determined characters who never gave up on reconstruction and reconciliation. It was the city's good fortune that in the mid-eighties such a body was just waiting for a signal.

There was Paddy Doherty and there was Glenn Barr, a Protestant version of Paddy. He had been one of the leaders of the Ulster Workers' Council strike in 1974 and had later turned his blue-eyed, boyish charm, together with his formidable organisational talents, to helping the young unemployed on the east bank of the Foyle. He bubbled with enthusiasm and his imagination led him to ideas, some of which were fanciful but most of which were practical. Though red tape and bureaucracy constantly confounded him, there are many young Protestant men and women in well-paid work today who would not be there but for Glenn Barr's purpose and leadership.

Bishop James Mehaffey of Derry and Raphoe had been vicar of

Kilkeel for several years and therefore knew all there was to know about the Needhams. Dark and slight with a captivating smile though sometimes very sad, he was a powerful example to his fellow Anglican clergy. I never heard him raise his voice, I never saw him angry, I never met anyone who had anything other than good to say of his judgement, his intellect or his character. He should be a paradigm to those who bellow instructions from the pulpit.

There was another remarkable bishop in Derry, in some ways more so, for Bishop Edward Daly stood for the majority nationalist community as God's representative against atheistic terror. It was he who had to console those who had been beaten and threatened; it was he who had to counsel the families of the young men sent to the Maze, many of whose parents would never have dreamed that their children had been seduced into terrorism. He will forever be remembered as the priest pictured waving the white but bloodstained handkerchief while leading a group carrying a dying man towards an ambulance following the infamous and, in my opinion, despicable behaviour of some members of the Parachute Regiment on Bloody Sunday.

There are some reasons for being critical of how the Catholic Church has handled the divisions in Ulster, but Bishop Daly was an inspiration. He saw all sides, he listened, and he interjected always with the greatest politeness. He saw good wherever he could, and he never failed to be where there was trouble or grief or anger. Over many years he was a granite rock which saw the city through. He once told me how, dressed in a sweater and slacks, he had gone down to the Strand Road police station to chat to the new RUC commander over an informal lunch only to be met by the chief superintendent in full dress uniform bedecked with braid, wearing gloves and clutching a cane, who greeted him with a formal salute and an icy glare. Bishop Daly had a very long war and in the end, with his health broken, he was forced into early retirement. I only wish he had been allowed more happiness and more joy.

Alongside these remarkable men were many others from the city council (the first to share power), commerce, industry and voluntary groups, and above them all towered Northern Ireland's only internationally recognised statesman, John Hume. He is a man of prodigious physical and intellectual capability. He smokes too much, he eats too much, sometimes he may drink too much. He does not sleep enough and he does not exercise enough, but he works like a man possessed.

He drives tens of thousands of miles from Aldergrove to Derry to Dublin to Donegal. How he has ended up in the ditch only once is a miracle. He has no protection because he does not want it and because any young RUC officer would, in John's judgement, be more at risk than he. He and his family therefore are enormously courageous in the face of loyalist threats and Sinn Féin blackmail. Like all great men, behind him stands a great woman; his wife Pat has looked after him and his constituency and maintained his morale when the black dog of depression has threatened to overwhelm him.

He has a vision of bringing the two cultures together through respect and understanding, and he has promoted that vision in Northern Ireland, London, Dublin and Washington with consistency, conviction and flair. Like every really good schoolteacher, he can explain and illustrate in ways that even the most hardened sceptic can find difficult to resist. By his reason and his force of personality he has dominated and dictated both the Washington and the Dublin approach to the problems of the North. Single-handedly he has wrested the initiative towards his corner and kept the arguments to his agenda, despite the relentless opposition of the unionists, the distrust of the Northern Ireland Office and the ambivalence of the Foreign Office.

He can infuriate the British by his refusal to be specific, by his use of generalities, by his change of tactics, venues or times, by what they perceive as his inconsistencies. But John knows what he wants. It is power-sharing in Northern Ireland acceptable to both sides, underwritten by both governments, with as many cross-border institutions as possible, which one day, with the support of unionists, could lead to a political system covering the island of Ireland. He has all the attributes to succeed. He is the one political leader in Northern Ireland capable of forging an acceptable way through for both communities. But sometimes, at the crucial moment, he fails to go that extra inch with the unionists. Somewhere in the recesses of his psyche there is a nationalist Derry reflex that gets the better of him, and sometimes he appears ready to risk offending his colleagues and losing his supporters by courting Sinn Féin while he temporises on attracting even moderate unionists to his view.

For years he had been demanding a bigger input into attracting investment to Derry and harnessing his contacts in America to that cause. No one had better qualifications, yet he was left by the Industrial Development Board to struggle on his own. But as always with John, the struggle intensified the effort. The beginnings of the regeneration had begun in the early eighties with the building of the Richmond shopping centre (to a design which did little to flatter the city's remaining historic architecture) and the opening of the Foyle Bridge. But whenever I went to Londonderry or deputations came to see me, I was always reminded of what was happening in Belfast and how little Derry received in comparison.

I knew that regeneration in the north-west of the province would provide the SDLP and their leader with the proof they required to show their people that co-operation with the British government could bring results and that economic and social improvement could bring opportunities denied them by violence and deprivation. We also observed that the IRA were finding that a bomb in Derry brought a very much stronger reaction from their own community than one in Belfast city centre, and if we could halt the bombs in the north-west it would become more difficult to justify destroying 'economic' targets elsewhere.

In April 1986 David White, the Department of the Environment development officer, retired and I insisted that we replace him with the very best, the very brightest high-flier we had. Joe Cowan turned out to be better than I dared dream. He loves the north-west, he has all the guile required to work the system, he speaks well, he is a conciliator and he was determined to do for Londonderry what the Belfast Development Office was doing for Belfast.

From 1985 to 1987 I was scratching about to find schemes for Derry that compared with the monthly announcements that I was making about Belfast. Industry had suffered grievously with the closure of the enormous Courtauld's Maydown plant. One million sq. ft stood empty. Michael Black, a local businessman who had bought the site, was doing all he could to attract new small industrial entrepreneurs but an empty space of that size can soon become a gigantic, decaying monument to industrial failure. The shirt makers were struggling against Asian competition. Dupont was a big, bright hope but chemical plants are not massive employers. United Technologies, making electrical harnesses for Fords, were the largest employer of Catholics on the west bank, but their declining fortunes coincided with those of their industry. Most industry remained around the Maydown industrial estate to the east of the city.

We needed a strategy that we could sell to the people and we needed an organisational framework where we could bring the city leaders together as a team to drive the plan forward. The establishment of Derry Boston Ventures Ltd in 1987 proved to be the catalyst. The venture came out of an initiative John Hume had arranged with Boston's mayor, Raymond Flynn, to forge business links between the northwest and east coast America. It was originally funded by the DOE and then supported by the IDB. The New World was brought in to heal the divisions of the Old.

I had met the O'Connell brothers, two of Boston's most prolific and successful developers, for the first time when I had been to the city looking at waterfront projects for Belfast in 1986. They had shown me what the future might look like along the Lagan but I had not thought of them being the key to unlock the potential to redevelop Derry. Quite separately John Hume had befriended the O'Connells and his son Aidan had been offered a job with them. The Boston Irish were stern critics of the British government. Their actual understanding of a European conflict was limited by their understandable, intertribal historical prejudices and an American predilection to see everything in terms of 'good' guys and 'bad' guys. If we could persuade them to invest with us rather than lecture us, we could turn a previously conflicting triangle of British, Irish and American interests into one of successful partnership and cooperation. The O'Connells' name was the vital American ingredient, even if, as the recession bit at the end of the eighties, O'Connell dollars were in increasingly short supply. It had been struggle enough to persuade mainland and Irish investors (North or South) to put their money into Belfast. Derry was another proposition altogether. Its remoteness, reputation, size and lack of economic buoyancy made it almost unsaleable as a retail investment proposition. None of this seemed to bother the O'Connells, and with their typical American ebullience and efficiency they were the catalyst we were looking for.

Economic and social commentators were quick to claim that our plans for both Belfast and Londonderry were attractive for the better-off but offered little prospect of stable, well-paid work to the very large numbers of long-term unemployed. I never agreed. If we were to interest outside investors and retain our best and brightest, we had to offer facilities that in every respect – from education to entertainment – would provide a quality of life that matched those of our competitors elsewhere in the poorer parts of Europe, for they were fighting similar sorts of regeneration battles. Our great advantages were the English language and the Irish-American connection.

Arthur Casey, the small, tough, tightlipped, tenacious, scuba-diving development director of O'Connell's told me that Marks & Spencer had to be the anchor tenant. There was no one else with the prestige and the pulling power to compare with them. If they would set up in Londonderry, the city would take off. But it would not be simple. M & S had stood by Northern Ireland when all other English multiples except Boots had fled or were too frightened to come. They had a plan for expansion which involved a number of stores spreading out from Belfast over several years. Derry was not on their immediate hit list; neither was the nearby Coleraine, but it came before Derry.

I was lucky and I played on my luck. I knew M & S well from the days I had worked with them as a parliamentary secondee sponsored by the Industry Parliament Trust; moreover, by placing Roger Aldridge, their new store development director, on the board of the IDB, I had a friend at court. But the key was the chairman, Sir Richard Greenbury, the shrewdest retailer in Europe. He was torn commercially between conflicting investment opportunities. On the one hand, the South had not been a happy hunting-ground for M & S, mainly because they overpriced themselves there; furthermore Dunnes Stores was a down-market but well-organised copy of Marks. On the other hand, there was no competition in the North from other mainland department or food stores. M & S-type outlets for the better-off Northern Ireland consumers did not exist outside of Belfast. If the island of Ireland could be made into a billion pound market with a single distribution network, it could rival Wales or Scotland. But as always there were the local critics. They suggested that bringing in Marks amounted to bringing in imports and closing down the local retailer with his locally produced merchandise. I reckoned the opposite to be true. Even in the early 1980s Marks were buying as much in Northern Ireland as they were selling. If M & S could retail half a billion pounds worth of goods in the North they could force their British suppliers to set up in the province and could also encourage Ulster companies to raise their quality to meet M & S requirements. Food and clothing were what M & S sold, and food and clothing were the basics of Northern Ireland's industry. It just had to be done.

Fortune smiled on us, for Rick Greenbury had a daughter who had married a Derry man and who ran a riding school outside Dungiven. Underneath Sir Richard's fearsome gaze and his lashing tongue is a decent man who will sometimes take a risk as much out of emotion as logic. He backed Roger and I over Londonderry, and I will always treasure the faith he put in us, for the arguments were nowhere near as strong as I had made them out to him – though I refrained from taking the advice of one local wag who told me to tell Greenbury he would have M & S blown up if they refused to come.

Marks & Spencer are now the biggest single purchaser of produce in Northern Ireland and buy twice as much as they sell there. Changes in technology mean that as a dressing-gown is bought in a Swindon store its replacement is already rattling down a line in Desmond's factory outside Londonderry towards a container that will deliver it to Swindon the next morning. Furthermore Rick brought over mainland suppliers such as Northern Foods, run by Irishman Chris Haskins (now Lord Haskins). He backed us in trying to persuade them to set up manufacturing subsidiaries, and although we did not persuade all of them, the spin-offs for those that did invest in supplying M & S from Northern Ireland were princely.

During the first half of 1988 'Uncle Joe' Cowan, as we nicknamed him, drew up his plans. In August I let drop a hint that it would not be long before Derry would have its own Laganside. In September the O'Connells came over with Arthur Casey. By December we were ready to go. John Hume quite rightly jumped the gun and announced that in a couple of weeks we would introduce a 'Making Derry Work' initiative on similar lines to Belfast. On 14 December I called the city leaders together for a day-long conference entitled 'Your City, Your Future 1992'. Joe outlined the structure. We would increase the budget of the Londonderry Development Office by £1 million a year. We would put together new co-ordinating machinery on how we could help the needy and the deprived. We would arrange new ways for consulting and involving the business and elected representatives in the regeneration proposals. I told them that they were amongst the cleverest, funniest and most interesting group I had ever met but I was fed up with their constant complaints about lack of government help for this, that and the other. It was always our fault not theirs. Everything depended on state funds and departmental resources. I told them to stop squawking and develop for themselves a new image, a new creativity, a new strategy for increasing prosperity and celebrating their cultural diversity. I told them that 1992 was to be a year of celebration and they were to run it. After a moment's silence they were away and there was to be no stopping them. They were determined to outdo Belfast.

Tom King supported the transfer of three hundred civil service jobs into a new office block alongside the old railway station on the east bank. There was a strong reaction. It was difficult to persuade civil servants to move ninety miles to the north-west. Londonderry had a reputation as a closed, Catholic-dominated town. Protestants were worried about reverse discrimination, about losing out on promotion opportunities, about a perceived shortage of good Protestant grammar schools and about forsaking their friends and social position. All these arguments cumulatively made the decision more awkward in value-for-money terms. And since value for money preoccupies the Comptroller and Auditor General and the Public Accounts Committee to the virtual exclusion of all other considerations, the Secretary of State was called upon to give an instruction to relocate in order to protect the departmental permanent secretary against possible criticism from these august bodies, which he duly did.

I had once been a member of the House of Commons' Senior Select Committee and was one of the few to study the mountains of paper assiduously before every meeting. I had come to the conclusion at that time that most of Northern Ireland's spending was dubiously controlled, but what more could one expect of the Irish! Only after I became a minister did I realise what a baleful influence the Public Accounts Committee has on innovation and risk taking. Public servants hate the limelight and hate criticism. They will nearly always do nothing rather than court either. The Public Accounts Committee takes a perverse delight in making judgements far divorced in both time and reality from the events it investigates. If it wishes to continue to issue reports so damning on pure 'public expenditure' grounds and so partial and ill-informed on the political and social background, it should stop the one-sided practice of grilling civil servants without calling the responsible ministers before it to face the music. It is ministers who are responsible, not their civil servants. If the Public Accounts Committee continues as it is, it will act as a damaging brake on good and imaginative government, and parliament will be to blame as much as ineffective ministers and overcautious permanent secretaries.

In May 1989 another team went to Boston. These visits became a 'wok' of sizzling ideas, widening the perspectives of the Derrymen and women, inculcating a new sense of self-help, self-esteem and selfless teamwork. The good news reached the front page of the *Boston Globe*, and from there to the front page of the *New York Times*. Everyone wanted to be associated with the success of the O'Connell Foyleside development. The problem was the O'Connells had run out of funds. Even though we increased the government contribution, their demands on us for subsidy became too much. I suspect Boston bankers viewed an investment in Londonderry with the same degree of frightened reticence as did bankers in London.

We had to keep the O'Connell front, but now that Marks & Spencer had signed up we were able to put together a group of Northern Irish investors to come up with the money. As the amount of government support increased, so did the controls and so did the amount of cheeseparing on the design and the materials to be used in the £65-million Foyleside development. D.Y. Davies, the first architectural practice in the UK to go public, had been chosen as the architects. They may have been quality financiers but to my mind they were far from being quality architects. Their design had little empathy with the walls, the city or the hill around which it was to be built. It had too much brick, too little imagination and did not fit with its surroundings. It might just have passed muster in Harlow but not Derry. Gerry Loughran said nothing could be done; there was no more money and no more time, as a planning appeal was due to begin and we needed to strike while the mood of excitement was keeping all the players together as a team. Luckily I found one of London's pre-eminent architects, Jeremy Mackay-Lewis, who weekends in Northern Ireland, and I asked him to try to make something remarkable out of a sow's ear. He came up with a wonderful new creation, embedding the enormous development into the side of the hill and blending it in with the walls rather than dominating them. Unfortunately it was too late to start from scratch again, and so Jeremy came up with a second proposal which, by clever use of materials and sight-lines, mitigated the worst of D.Y. Davies's mediocrity. Today Derry is rightly proud of its new Foyleside, which far exceeds anything similar in a city of comparable size on the UK mainland. After I had ceased to be minister, the developers reduced the amount of stone and increased the number of bricks on grounds of cost. I would not have allowed it.

Meanwhile the 'community' dimension had taken off. Paddy Doherty and his Inner City Trust had refurbished the old Foyle College together with many of the derelict buildings in the city core. He opened a craft village and helped construct the Tower Museum, a wonderful walk through history with one route for Catholics and another for Protestants! There was a youth hostel in Magazine Street and a genealogy centre in Butcher Street, which seemed to be entirely populated by Dohertys even though Paddy claimed that most of them had been castrated by the British at one time or another. Glenn Barr's enterprise centre at Maydown/Ebrington grew and grew, while, out of a burntout supermarket, the Northside Development Trust built an impressive village centre for the people of Shantallow. Creggan soon followed. The Foyle campus of the University of Ulster at Magee gave the city a liveliness that only youth can bring. The years 1986–90 were exciting times for Derry/Londonderry and the industrial regeneration was still to come, as was the technology park.

22

SPRINGTIME OF HOPE

B Y EARLY 1990 BELFAST CITY CENTRE was 'doing rightly'. Shorts
and Harland and Wolff had been successfully sold off to the private sector. Laganside was attracting investors and Making
Belfast Work was having some impact in giving the most isolated and
deprived a greater chance to influence and improve their lot. But we still
did not have a vision for west Belfast. We were still faced with the drip-
drip monotone complaint from the president of Sinn Féin that millions,
if not billions, were being poured into east Belfast to keep unionists
sweet while little or nothing was being done for his constituents other
than to harass and deprive them.

His arguments were patently absurd to any outsider. If we were
spending hundreds of millions in east Belfast, why were the levels of
unemployment, deprivation, sickness, and home and car ownership
there so very little different from those in west Belfast? Closing down
the shipyard and the aircraft factory and putting nine thousand workers
on to the dole, and from there on to the streets, would be hardly likely
to ease sectarian tensions. But as most people in west Belfast had never
been to east Belfast, they would know little of how their fellow citizens
a mile or so away lived, like themselves, far from the lap of luxury.

It was true that no earlier government had nationalised or even
thought of nationalising the linen mills, the staple employers in
west Belfast. But they were hardly strategic industries, and while

government customers could be found for the output of Shorts or Harland and Wolff, there were few obvious state-owned outlets for linen. There had been no new investment in west Belfast because bright young men and women who had the ability to start their own businesses soon moved away through threats of extortion, difficulty in raising finance or finding trained staff, or just out of fear of violence. Only the Church and its redoubtable priests remained to create jobs and provide safe havens for those struggling to get themselves going. But the Church could only be a plaster on a gaping wound. To find a major private investor to put in a massive new factory was well-nigh impossible. The government could provide the building and land free, give grants for the machinery and help train the workers, but no one could be seduced to own and manage it. Even Chairman Kim of Daewoo, whose philosophy was to build factories in the most unlikely and dangerous places, shied away from west Belfast and chose Antrim. (His reasons for investing in outlandish sites were shrewd. Competitors were few and far between. Local inhabitants were therefore welcoming, while delighted host governments offered large tax breaks, often coupled with financial inducements. As other potential investors were frightened off, there was no shortage of loyal and inexpensive labour. Daewoo drew the line only if the safety of their business and their staff could not be reasonably protected. Despite Gerry Adams's public assurances, Chairman Kim was not persuaded.)

What state-owned and managed company could we set up in Belfast? What would it make? Who would run it? To whom would it sell? Mr Adams's policy was to kick the Brits out, not to entice them into long-term state-owned investments. The whole world was moving away from Soviet state planning to private ownership in a free market system. Nevertheless, because of their potent propaganda, Sinn Féin's demands could not be left unanswered. In any event something big had to be done to offer the decent people in the west of the city, who constituted the massive majority, a chance to pull themselves up.

The change of ownership in Mackies proved the key. If the government could not directly provide the jobs or the factories, at least we could produce a safe and attractive environment which might entice investors and employers. To do this we had to find ways of producing a massive redevelopment which would cut across the confines of both communities and act as a bridge between them. The east–west road systems had become boundaries rather than links. It was fortunate for us that the Forth River ran from north-west to south-east, smack through the most difficult areas of Belfast. The river valley was to be the link for the rebirth of the west of the city.

I launched the Springvale Project on 4 April 1990 in an article in the Northern Ireland edition of *Today*:

Today may prove to be one of the turning points in the war against terrorism and misery in West Belfast. Mackies, the most distinguished manufacturers of linen-making machinery, has agreed a buy-out by an American company and is moving over the road.

You may ask why such a mundane event has such far-reaching implications. The two communities in West Belfast have long been divided by roads and walls driven east–west from the centre of the city to its periphery. Each community jealously guards its territory, cross-fertilisation is almost non-existent. Moving Mackies gives an enormous chance for West Belfast Nationalists and Loyalists to save themselves from another dose of misery.

For it allows the redevelopment of a great industrial site in the heart of West Belfast. About 150 acres have become available for a major industrial and commercial zone which could offer thousands of jobs to both communities.

It also allows for the possibility of a development running north and south through both communities with a further 150–200 acres of developable land. At last it will be possible to offer investors a secure, well-designed, properly landscaped, grant-assisted prospectus that can bring work to thousands of decent people longing to be free of bomb and bullet, intimidation and harassment.

For twenty years government money has been used to try to mitigate and overcome the tribal tensions on which the IRA and the UDA feed. As anyone who has visited Belfast will know, there have been many successes: new public housing to the highest standards, the best equipped of leisure centres, new hospitals and health centres, schools and community halls which are a match for any inner city.

But that alone does not create wealth. The future of Belfast city centre and its adjoining deprived and strife-torn neighbourhoods depends on private investment which will bring manufacturing, commercial and retailing prosperity.

The city is currently enjoying one of its longest periods of sustained growth. In the last five years some £573 million of private money has been invested, is being invested or is pledged. New restaurants, hotels, office blocks, car parks and shopping centres open regularly.

205

56,000 people are now employed in the city centre and the number is rising. The population of outer Belfast is also growing again.

Yet the question remains, will the IRA and their political frontmen, Sinn Féin, allow growth and prosperity to come to the long-suffering people of Belfast? Jobs mean youngsters off the streets making money, not on the streets making petrol bombs.

If the disease of terrorism leads to deprivation, ignorance, morbidity and intimidation, a major antidote must be jobs and opportunity. In Northern Ireland these antidotes are beginning to work. Sinn Féin now finds the bomb and the ballot box are not compatible. Martin McGuinness, leader of Sinn Féin in Derry, has recently been musing in public about the need for some sort of dialogue, hardly surprising when his party receives less than 2 per cent of the popular vote in the South and according to opinion polls in the North it has slumped to around 5 per cent.

The alternatives now facing the IRA are even less inviting. Bombing economic targets destroys jobs – increasingly jobs on which the Nationalist people depend – while bombing the security forces will not stop the resurgence of economic growth. Now that the Iron Curtain has lifted, the problems of ethnic unrest in Ulster can be seen to be no different to those of the minorities of Eastern Europe. In fact the similarities are striking.

There is however one further crucial ingredient to overcoming intercommunity rivalry. That ingredient, wherever different nationalities live peaceably together, is prosperity in a free/private enterprise dominated economy.

This is the policy objective which the government has followed in Northern Ireland with increasing success over the last five years. Private money, entrepreneurs, self-employment, increasing self-confidence are returning Belfast to the glory that the city enjoyed as one of the great industrial giants at the end of the last century. The bell is tolling for the IRA not because of any sudden political or security solution but because relentlessly, the people of Northern Ireland are getting back to normal, making the best of the opportunities presented to them and improving their standards. Over the last eight years the economy of Northern Ireland is, for the first time this century, growing as fast as the rest of the UK. There is no reason why over the next ten years it should not do even better and that is bad news for the IRA and good news for the rest of us.

My objective was political. It was to undermine the authority of the IRA

206

and to try, through economic and social opportunity, to bring them into politics – politics alone.

Once again, it was Gerry Loughran who was the architect of both the detail and the tactics of selling our proposals as a community venture, not an NIO directive. It was clear that we would have to open a dialogue with Sinn Féin. The time had come to draw them into the net. We were confronting them with hard choices. Springvale could offer job prospects, new housing and a greener environment, but it would also require changes in road access and in land use which would draw local criticism from those who would suffer in the short term through disruption or dislocation. Choices would have to be made and for once the NIO could not be blamed. The difficulty was how to rope Sinn Féin in without breaching government guidelines banning meetings between them, ministers and senior officials.

We decided to open an information office in west Belfast where local groups and ordinary residents could see the plans, be briefed on the alternatives and have explained to them how their input would influence the decisions. We also announced that a senior official (Gerry Loughran) would be on hand to discuss alternatives with the most senior public representatives. If Gerry Adams did appear Gerry Loughran could hardly disappear. In due course they met. In this way Sinn Féin entered the partnership and became locked into the regeneration. Without their good will we would have found progress hard if not impossible. I also agreed to explain the government's strategy to an invited audience at a session on the eighteenth floor of the Europa Hotel overlooking west Belfast. My first face-to-face exchange with Sinn Féin representatives was enlightening and frightening. The distrust, the disbelief, the dislike were all so evident. To them there had to be another agenda. Why were the Brits trying to help? What was their game? The gulf was unbridgeable. British ministers have little opportunity to gauge the real mood of those whose support for violence is based on hate and distorted views of history.

But the bait caught the herring, for in June 1990 Gerry Adams sent his proposals to the Springvale development team and proposed a £60-million package for two hundred houses and two thousand manufacturing jobs (again). At the same time organisations 'sympathetic' to the republicans continued knocking. In August 1990 Obair organiser Eileen Duffy shrilled: 'We need sixteen thousand jobs. The British government claim they are interested in job creation but they are only interested in defeating Sinn Féin and use poverty and unemployment as pawns in their game.' She went on to promote the Conway Mill just off the Falls Road which, she insisted, could provide two hundred jobs if only the government would allow it money from the EC or the International Fund for Ireland. Two hundred jobs would hardly dent the sixteen thousand required. Furthermore some of the public money destined for the Conway Mill might well have found its way on the dusty road to Libya, and it was Sinn Féin and the IRA that used poverty and unemployment to hold control over their often fearful constituents. Despite the criticism, discussion grew, and with it commitment and involvement.

The Springvale Project has worked. F.G. Wilson and Fujitsu now have new factories in a part of the city that would have been 'never-go' only a decade ago. There are new housing developments and a state-of-the-art training facility. The environment has been transformed. There will be improved sports facilities, more industrial sites and a linear park. The most impressive plan for a University of Ulster campus which would cross communities and cater for three thousand students, together with an outreach programme to improve the skills and employment prospects for locals, took five years' 'consideration' before it gained NIO funding. A chance to entice hundreds of outside students into communities exhausted by fear and fury, students who would introduce new vitality, new perspectives and new hope, has gone a-begging for far too long through lack of political will and bureaucratic obstruction. Of course such a vision is not cheap, but neither are the costs of policing terrorism, patching up victims or paying benefits.

What Springvale proved was that at a very local level the government had no 'no-go' areas, that there was a role for republican political leaders to provide a better quality of life for their people, that guns and bombs added nothing to the process of improvement and reintegration. On its own, Springvale could not have solved the misery of west Belfast, but it pointed to another, a better, way, and Sinn Féin became part of that very different part-public, part-private partnership which was the essence of our long-term solution.

23
THE 'COW' AFFAIR

O NE OF THE NERVE ENDS THAT CAUSED NIGGLES between the
security side of the Northern Ireland Office and departmental
ministers was how best to handle the cancellation of a planned
engagement if there had been a breach of security. The rules were that in
the event of a 'leak', the private secretary would ring up the event organisers and tell them that unfortunately the minister had suddenly been
forced to change his schedule to undertake another engagement elsewhere. This tactic caused maximum annoyance, which was exactly
what the IRA most wanted.

I decided in the autumn of 1990 to turn the tables and to tell the
world that if a visit had to be aborted it was because a terrorist group
had uncovered our plans and that to go ahead would put at risk not only
the minister but also everyone else involved. I would then announce
that I was extremely sorry to have to cancel after so much effort and
time had been spent on planning such a high-profile launch, but the
blame lay not with me but with the men and women of violence.

The first occasion on which we 'owned up' was a long-scheduled
get-together with Joyce McCartan in her fish and chip shop, The Gaslight, on the Lower Ormeau Road. Joyce was one of the truly great
ladies of Northern Ireland. A Protestant married to a Catholic, she had
a large family and she lived and worked in one of the nastiest and most
difficult streets in the city. The Lower Ormeau Road is in a constant

state of tension and foreboding. It is the scene of countless Orange marches. There have been some sickening murders, not least the chilling shootings of five Catholics cut down in Sean Graham's bookie's shop in February 1992. As always, Joyce was first there to comfort and calm. One of her sons, Gary, had been assassinated by the UVF in her kitchen some years earlier. But she abjured bitterness or revenge and spent her life raising money to fund job-creation schemes and improve the drab, run-down streets or houses in her 'village' by the Lagan. There were hard and vicious men who did nothing to help her plans for returning to normality, but she was afraid of none of them and by the end of her life they were rightly scared of her.

Joyce had become a good friend to me and I tried whenever I could to help her efforts in cash or kind. I had persuaded Peter French, who had taken over some fast-food outlets in Belfast, to advise her on the best equipment for her fish and chip shop, which she also used as a drop-in centre for all those from the Lower Ormeau Road who wanted shelter, a chat and a bit of crack. When word of my planned visit to her shop seeped out, probably from some volunteer in the shop talking to a customer, the RUC became nervous, aware that there was an active IRA unit in the area. I told Joyce the truth and Joyce told the press and the Provos received a public roasting. Some in the NIO were not amused. This was another example of Needham breaking the rules of accepted procedure. The fact that the NIO knew that the IRA knew that I was going was of itself 'confidential'!

Such nonsense could be deployed as a reason for never venturing beyond the gates of Stormont Castle. Meanwhile, quite separately, a minute had been circulated warning ministers that mobile phones were not 'secure' and that under no circumstances should we, while using a mobile phone, divulge details of what we were doing or where we were going. Without my having sight of it, my private office quite rightly read it and shredded it, as there were some rules on security that after so many years were second nature to all of us. There was no mention in the minute that equipment could be bought for a few pounds which would enable anyone to tape with crystal clarity any phone call on an analogue mobile. Nor was there any plan to provide ministers' offices with secure phones; there was no budget for such items.

The background to the minute was that a small piece had appeared in one of the Ulster Sunday tabloids saying that a conversation between a minister's private secretary and his private office, allegedly mine, had been listened into by a paramilitary group. Then, a week or so later on Tuesday, 6 November, I was returning from the opening of the Clanrye Centre in Newry. It was early evening and as we entered the outskirts of Belfast I phoned home on my government-supplied mobile. As always, my day was full, fun and hectic, and keeping in touch with my family could only be done late at night or early in the morning. The arrival of the mobile was a godsend, or so I had thought.

The last week of October 1990 was a cataclysmic and traumatic one for the Tory Party. Margaret Thatcher was about to be challenged by Michael Heseltine for the leadership. I greatly respected the Prime Minister both personally and politically. She had made me a minister although she knew I was 'wet' on the unions and 'wet' on Europe, and even though, as Sir Charles Powell, her private secretary, later remarked, if we had still had the empire she would have found a post for me a long way further away than Northern Ireland. Her inability to do so was now to return to bite her.

During the course of my evening call I told Sissy that I thought it was time the 'cow resigned'. I have to say that, like most of my party and most of the country, I felt that, after ten years of being bossed about, we had had nearly enough. Had I known that a paramilitary group had the capacity to lock into my phone and tape my conversations with a CD-type quality, I would have phrased my suggestion somewhat differently.

Three days later and I had completely forgotten my phone call when at lunch-time on the Friday, while I was touring a chicken factory in Wiltshire, there was an urgent summons from Norma Sinclair, my private secretary. She had been called in by Andy Wood, the NIO press officer, a blunt and, as it turned out, not very supportive Yorkshireman. He told her and my own departmental press officer, Don McAleer, that there had been a call from the *Sunday Times*. The paper had received a tape of a conversation between my wife and myself, and before they printed their scoop, which they intended publishing along the lines of 'Security Leak Puts Minister at Risk', they would be grateful for a response. This would also include my reaction to the descriptive comment which appeared on the tape, a copy of which they very kindly provided him with.

Andy Wood's personal view was that my number was up. I phoned him and naturally enough I tried to wriggle. I did not remember making the comment. 'The tape is clear enough,' he replied. 'Could it not have been doctored?' I meekly suggested. 'Listen,' he said, and played it back; no, it could not have been doctored. There was no escape. 'Well, this is a party matter,' he intoned. 'I have told Bernard Ingham and No. 10 but there is no question of the *Sunday Times* not publishing.' Dry-mouthed, I drove home, telling Sissy on my car phone that something terrible had happened but I could not tell her what.

I rang Tim Renton, the Chief Whip, but he was unavailable. Everyone else appeared to be unavailable. After a panicky half-hour, I found his deputy, Alistair Goodlad. I explained. Alistair is not one for saying anything when words have no purpose, and so I stared at a noiseless handset for several seconds. 'Hard luck, old boy,' finally came the reply. 'You will have to say sorry.' And that was that. I rang Chris Patten who was then Secretary of State for the Environment and had the Poll Tax hanging round his neck like a dead chicken. What did I want, the imperious private secretary wanted to know. Secretaries of State do not usually talk to lowly parliamentary under-secretaries of state from other departments. It was private. He was very busy; could it not wait until Sunday evening? No it could not. Half an hour later, Chris rang and I explained. 'How did the *Sunday Times* get hold of the tape?' he asked. 'Apparently from a Belfast news agency.' 'And where did they find it?' 'On their doorstep with the compliments of some paramilitary organisation,' I told him. 'Well, she can't sack you because that would be a victory for terrorism and you can't resign because that also would be a victory for terrorism. So you better think of a form of words to get yourself through till next week, and by then anything might happen,' he wound up and hung up.

An hour or so later, a call came through from No. 11 Downing Street; the Chief Whip would like to talk to me later that evening. He rang around nine o'clock on his way home – using his car phone. I refrained from asking him whether he thought it wise to continue the conversation. 'I will arrange for you to ring the PM and apologise,' he said, 'and that will be the end of the matter.' Not if she survives, I thought. I would be happy to apologise for embarrassing her, I told him, but I could not be sorry for what I had said because that would make me a liar. 'I leave the exact words to you,' he ended. Another hour went by, and the phone rang again. It was No. 10. The Prime Minister was prepared to speak to me. 'I am sorry for embarrassing you, Prime Minister.' 'If "cow" was the worst I have been called by my friends or my enemies, I should not have got as far as I have. Both of us, Richard, have jobs to get on with, so let's do that.' Click. She had behaved magnanimously, and I wished I had said nothing.

On the Saturday afternoon a woman reporter appeared at our back gates and tried her best to stop me as I drove back after a constituency surgery. She had the persistency of a Far Eastern street hawker, banging on the gate and shouting that it was in my interest to answer her queries. This is a standard line taught to English journalists, along with 'we need your side of the story'. The opposite is, of course, the reality. All a newspaper is after is further indiscretions which can then be gilded by the editor. There is something disconcerting in the way national newspapers now expect their reporters to hound for news. Very few have career structures for their staff or give them the self-esteem and self-confidence they need for a long-term future in reporting the truth. Many young journalists seem to have succumbed to a jaundiced instinct that their 'quarry' inevitably has something to hide, is usually dissembling and is generally without morals or principles. As a result, too many reporters closely resemble the fictional character they are investigating. If a rival newspaper has a scoop, all the editor wants to know is why his hacks did not get there first. So out the window go decency, honesty, balance and manners, and in comes a rat pack jostling to pick at the carcass they have been sent to smell out.

As they had proposed, the *Sunday Times* ran their front-page lead under a headline 'Minister apologises to PM for telephone insult' and then stated that the call had been secretly recorded by a paramilitary group using a radio scanner. The implication throughout the piece was that the tape came from the IRA. The *Sunday Times* claimed that an agency had passed the tape on to them. The agency stated they had received it from the terrorists. But I doubt if they revealed all. Why should the agency 'give' the tape to the *Sunday Times*? Surely, having been lucky enough to obtain such 'Danegeld', any agency would have expected some reward or auctioned the story to the highest bidder?

If money changed hands, did any find its way back to the paramilitaries? None of the London media professionals in the BBC, ITN, the broadsheets, the tabloids or the weeklies sought to enquire. Nor did anyone seem to care that the *Sunday Times*'s lead was potentially an enormous victory for the terrorists, if indeed it was they who were responsible, for they had succeeded in further undermining a wounded Prime Minister and they had put in question the position of Northern Ireland's longest-serving minister. Well done *Sunday Times*. It was left to a correspondent in the *Spectator* a year or so later to point out that the invasion of privacy was perhaps one of the nastiest aspects of this self-serving, repulsive piece of journalism.

It was not to be the last time I was to clash with the *Sunday Times*'s editor, Andrew Neil. On the next occasion, when I had to defend Britain's trade interests after he had published a story accusing the Malaysian Prime Minister of corruption, I was on surer ground with ruthless allies. I had always been told that, after love, revenge was a man's most powerful motivator. Several years later I succumbed to it without regret.

The day of the *Sunday Times* 'cow article', 11 November, was Remembrance Sunday and I had agreed to be one of those taking the salute at the march past following the afternoon service at Malmesbury Abbey. The former chairman of the county council and high sheriff for the year, Nigel Anderson, was a redoubtable old Wiltshire soldier who had a profound dislike of Mrs Thatcher and kept muttering, 'Well done, keep it up,' in a loud whisper at every opportunity when there was a lull in the service. Outside the abbey, the press had gathered to ambush me on my way to tea in the town hall, but as I was part of the procession there was little they could do until I was inside the mayor's parlour, where the door was shut in their faces. It took them a few moments to find the back way in, but by then I had slipped away. On Monday all the papers waded in with varying degrees of abuse, most calling for my execution. Even though we refused to answer the phone or the doorbell, the tension was immense. Robert, my son, had gone back to our London flat to find himself besieged outside our front door on the seventh floor. So much for the supposed secrecy that was meant to surround the addresses of Northern Ireland ministers. Nor did the persistent lady at the back gate cease to shout over the wall that a comment to set the record straight would be in my own interest. She was joined by others.

Meanwhile another equally unpleasant side plot was developing. The security angle had not gone unnoticed by those in the NIO, not all of whom were my friends. Much of the *Sunday Times* article had dealt with the security lapse aspects, including a paragraph which read: 'This is the second time Needham has been intercepted in recent weeks. Security forces have confirmed that the opening of a community shop in south Belfast had to be cancelled last month when it became clear that terrorists were monitoring his movements.' The *Sunday Times* had neatly joined the earlier tabloid report on the first mobile phone 'leak' which had involved my secretary using the office hand phone and my visit to Joyce McCartan's Gaslight, which had absolutely nothing to do with phones of any description. A report by Chris Ryder appeared in Monday's *Daily Telegraph*, the gist of which was clear: Needham has always been a bit of a loud mouth. We have had to warn him on several occasions to keep quiet. Very dangerous these volatile ministers, you know. Some of us could not care less what happens to him but it's a bit rough on his escorts and his secretary if they get blown up because of his blatherings.

This was nasty and a step too far. Certainly I had tried to be open and to let some air into the musty private rooms of government where security could pass as a byword for cover-up or cock-up, but never had I ever been reprimanded or warned about anything I had said or done being a security breach. I had thought, wrongly, that the RUC might be looking for those who had criminally taped my conversation rather than having their reputation protected by anonymous briefers from within the NIO. I rang my solicitor, who confirmed that the article was libellous and damaging to my reputation and said I should sue. Then I discovered, as so often is the case, that nothing is quite as it seems.

I was advised that as a minister I needed the agreement of the Solicitor General, Sir Nicholas Lyell, and the Attorney General, Sir Patrick Mayhew. I explained to the NIO in London that this was a private matter, as indeed had been the telephone call. Nothing is private when you are a minister, I was informed. I rang Lyell, who was a friend of many years, and explained. 'Very difficult,' he replied. 'Could be awkward if the case ever came to court.' I was incredulous. 'Well,' he said, 'the *Daily Telegraph* might claim that your recent revelations about why you had cancelled a visit to the Lower Ormeau Road was an indiscretion. They might ask you how you had known that the IRA had known you were coming, and in those circumstances our security sources might be put at risk!' Never in my life had I heard such bunk. As I have already explained, the real source from the Lower Ormeau Road was almost certainly one of Joyce McCartan's helpers excitedly telling customers that some bigwig was coming to open their new kitchen, and the IRA had put two and two together.

'Well, you can always resign, if you feel so strongly,' Patrick Mayhew told me in the lobby. Perhaps I should have, but on balance I believed my going would have been another tick in the terrorists' ledger. Once again it proved how completely subservient and out of touch English politicians are when confronted with security advice. There were some who were of the opinion that the Attorney General remained in that position long after he had become Secretary of State for Northern Ireland.

A compromise was agreed. I could write a letter to the *Daily Telegraph* in which I could state, with the authority of the Secretary of State for Northern Ireland and his permanent secretary, that I had never been disciplined or spoken to about personal security lapses. The *Telegraph* lost the letter for a fortnight and I smelt another conspiracy, but after a phone call to Max Hastings, the editor, it appeared.

Meanwhile matters had rolled on. Sir Geoffrey Howe had delivered the most powerful speech of his life and the leadership race had begun. Michael Heseltine had left the blocks. I had become yesterday's news. Over the next weekend Kenneth Baker rang me. Ostensibly as chairman of the party, he was canvassing views. I told him that I thought the Prime Minister had run her course and that her endless confrontations with everyone and everything had alienated too many of the public to make her re-election possible. From a constituency perch, it appeared to me that there was no interest group, no profession, no section of society that was free from her revolutionary zeal. Furthermore she had so dominated her colleagues for so many years that they either were cowed by her or detested her. The mark of success in her Cabinet had become how effectively a minister could introduce a deeply unpopular measure without flinching or losing the confidence of his colleagues. However, as a wet, I told Ken Baker, he would hardly expect me to say otherwise.

I suspect, perhaps unkindly, that he had another agenda. I had told him a year previously, as had Jonathan Aitken and I have no doubt others, that I would support him in a leadership election. I respected his political style and although he was a bit of a smoothie, the Tory Party and the country needed a bit of smoothing. However, his rapid conversion from left to right had confused me, and I was no longer prepared to mark his card, so I said nothing about his chances if the Prime Minister fell. He must have found the same reticence in others.

Meanwhile the Prime Minister had made it clear to the world that she would carry on as if nothing was happening. She had long planned to visit a factory in Northern Ireland and then an army base, where there would be no end of photo opportunities. The trip was set for Friday, 16 November, and I was the minister designated to greet her as she stepped down from the helicopter. Mrs Thatcher's approach to Ireland was one of exasperated despair. She would have liked somehow to get rid of the problem. She did not like or trust the unionists and never forgave Enoch Powell, rightly in my view, for his highly personal, exaggerated attacks on her. She felt deeply about how 'her boys' were being maimed and murdered, and she had found that it was impossible to trust the Irish. She once told me that she had, in response to some request from Charlie Haughey, retorted, 'When are your boys going to stop killing mine?'

The rain was pouring down. I hid her under my umbrella as we greeted each other with exaggerated smiles. As always, her entourage was enormous, and so I stayed at the back with Sir Charles Powell and Bernard Ingham, both of whom were friends of mine even *in extremis*. 'You would be raving mad if you vote for that lunatic Heseltine,' Bernard growled as we stood next to one of the factory's sewing machines. I was not sure. I had run into Heseltine at the members' entrance at Westminster the previous day, and he had winked and I had winked back. To Margaret Thatcher and to her closest allies, the leadership election was the work of traitors and faint hearts. She, after all, had single-handedly driven through a successful revolution against all doubters, including myself. But one of the key decisions that any politician has to make sooner or later is when to go. She, like so many before her, was going to finish a magnificent career in tears and defeat.

At the end of the tour there was the usual reception at Hillsborough. Many of my friends and supporters were there and they kept up a constant and self-defeating stream of 'Please keep Needham in Ireland' comments as they were introduced to the PM. After an hour she must have wanted me strangled. She gave a speech studiously omitting me. Peter Brooke gave a speech pointedly stressing his love for and loyalty to his chief. Then she was bustled away from Ulster for the last time as

Prime Minister of the United Kingdom. There are those who blamed her parliamentary private secretary, Peter Morrison, for not keeping her in the tea-room of the House of Commons often enough during that week. But although he had some limitations, he was as shrewd a political tactician as I had encountered, and I would doubt that by November 1990 there was anything that could have been done to avoid the big drop.

The announcement of the first leadership vote was at 6 p.m. on Tuesday, 20 November. I had had a message from Chris Patten's secretary that he would like me to be in his office at 5.30 p.m. He was late as usual coming back from somewhere. There was me, minister of state, David Trippier, Chris's PPS, Robert Key, and others. Later we were joined by the permanent secretary, Terry Heiser – the moment was too exciting even to exclude an un-Tory Sir Humphrey – and David Heathcoat Amory, another minister. Mrs Thatcher narrowly defeated Heseltine by 195 votes to 164. Patten tried to call Douglas Hurd, who was in Paris with the PM. He was in the bath preparing to go to the opera and would ring back. William Waldegrave rang; Chris told him he thought the time had come for a visit by the men in grey suits. Chris rang John Major, who told him that he was under a lot of pressure to endorse Margaret Thatcher in the second round. Patten advised him to say as little as possible (which was easy, as he was recovering from an operation on his wisdom teeth). The phone calls kept coming in and I was clear that the Thatcher era was coming to a final bitter conclusion. I was better out of the way. I had long since arranged an Industrial Development Board inward-investment mission to Japan and Basil Feldman, one of the PM's closest supporters, had agreed to come selling with me. A friend of Margaret Thatcher's who had become a friend of mine, he was upset at what had happened between the PM and myself, but he also knew that for Mrs Thatcher the game was up. So I phoned him and we agreed to go as soon as possible.

But first I had to decide who to support in the next round battle between Major, Heseltine and Hurd. More than anything else, I wanted to keep Patten's chances alive of one day taking over the leadership of the party. I did not believe Heseltine could win – it would have been too divisive. If Major won, Patten's chance might have gone forever, so the politburo of the Blue Chips – Chris Patten, William Waldegrave, John Patten, Tristan Garel-Jones (for whom the decision was excruciating, as

218

he was one of Major's closest friends) and I – campaigned for Hurd. A Hurd victory was the only outcome that could have allowed for a Patten–Major run-off later. I do not think any of us, including Douglas, believed that he would win but I owed it to my best political friend to try to keep the chink of opportunity open. Sometimes in politics a choice has to be made between friendship and ambition.

Ten days later I was far away in Basil Feldman's hotel suite in Kumamoto on the island of Kyushu. Sissy rang and told me that Patten had been on to her. He was to be chairman of the party following Major's reshuffle. There were to be no changes in the NIO with the exception of Brian Mawhinney, who had been parliamentary under-secretary of state in Ulster since 1986 and was now to be promoted to Minister of State. Of all the ministers I served with, Brian Mawhinney was the most awkward colleague. Calculating and patient, he always appeared to be working to his own agenda. His responsibilities in the NIO gave him plenty of scope for his appetite for political manoeuvering. He was Minister of Education, which was demanding but not overly time consuming. He was also Minister of Political Development. This was the foundation of his power and success, for it allowed him to dip into the activities of his ministerial colleagues if he deemed there was a political dimension. He usually involved himself only if he smelt trouble. Much of his time was spent with his officials in a ceaseless round of political analysis. He was also charged with promoting cross-cultural relations, which he did with deep Christian fervour.

An Ulsterman himself, Brian was unpopular with many of those he worked with and distrusted by some in his own community. It was a hard assignment for the local boy who had crossed the water, made good and come back to rule them. He knew his faults and worked hard on his image and his presentation. He had an ability to make a pregnant pause appear the precursor to wise judgements, but too often he delivered banalities while others searched for a deeper meaning. He kept his own counsel and sought power with the narrow single-mindedness for which Ulster's religious tub-thumpers are renowned. God and John Major smiled upon him and he moved up in the world, although wherever he went, many soon hoped he would move on. I have often thought that in politics the tough guys win in the end. Brian has, but so did Cromwell.

Chris told Sissy to order me to under no circumstances resign. Basil

Feldman was equally adamant. In fact I never really considered resigning at any time, least of all during the 'cow' affair. I enjoyed my job, and the thought of a combination of terrorist snooping and *Sunday Times* opportunism leading to my leaving was too defeatist to contemplate. In retrospect perhaps I should have offered to go that first weekend, knowing it might have placated the right wing, who never forgave me, and Peter Brooke, who did.

Peter is something of an enigma. He comes from a long line of Anglo-Irish military and political strategists. To listen to one of his convoluted after-dinner cricketing stories is to wonder how he ever made it as far as he has. He often appeared careful, cautious and contradictory as he grappled with the ever-recurring political or security crises. He certainly gave no impression of wishing to challenge the management or orthodoxy of the NIO. Yet his carefulness was the largest contribution to his strength. He had an uncanny knack of working through what was happening on the other side of the hill, and as a result it was his insight into republican thinking that started the road to the Downing Street Declaration and the IRA ceasefire. He did as much as any British Secretary of State and more than most to set Northern Ireland down the road to peace.

His first wife had died tragically and his new wife, who came from within the ranks of the Tory organisation, gave him a powerful new political stimulus when he appeared close to exhaustion. In January 1992 Peter was a guest on Gay Byrne's *Late Late Show* on RTÉ just hours after an IRA bomb had killed seven Protestant workmen near Cookstown, County Tyrone. He agreed to sing a silly song, partly because Byrne was asking him about his first wife in the presence of his second; he later told me he would have sung 'Deutschland, Deutschland Über Alles' to avoid further interrogation. Immediately afterwards he offered his resignation and apologised, accepting full responsibility rather than reprimanding those who had advised him to participate in an entertainment show in such inappropriate circumstances. I do not believe Peter Brooke has ever done or thought of doing a dishonourable deed in his entire political career. There were many Tories like him, if less able, who after the 1997 election saw their careers ruined and their chances of finding a life outside politics wrecked by the wickedness of a few, and the hounding of a foreign-owned, incompetent and often malicious London media.

I had gone to Japan to try to whip up Japanese interest in investing in Northern Ireland. I also wished to visit Governor Morihiro Hosakawa of Kumamoto who had arrived in my Whitehall office one day to tell me about his plans for cities of the future. The 'technopolis' would be founded on science and would feature 'living buildings' in which the windows would close automatically to avoid annoying the neighbours if children turned up their CD players, and as the outside heat increased, so would the output of the thermostatically controlled air conditioning. Hosakawa came from one of the oldest and noblest of Japanese families and he was an enormously powerful governor who later became Prime Minister, only to be brought down by the endemic corruption that tainted even the richest and cleanest. I wanted to see if his schemes had any relevance for Northern Ireland. I also wanted to persuade him to join the Anglo-Japanese 2000 Group, which he did (a 'wise men's' group, of which I was a founder member, consisting of political, business and academic leaders drawn from both countries). The other attraction of the trip was that Kumamoto was as remote from London as Siberia, if rather more inviting.

Basil Feldman had spent his private life in business and his public life in the National Union of the Conservative Party. He had become the key player in an IDB plan to use Mr Yosi Okabe, chairman of the London subsidiary of the Sumitomo Bank, to act as Northern Ireland's promoter among Japan's fifty-thousand-strong UK community. His quick, wide-ranging, entrepreneurial, witty, Jewish mind was a powerful additional tool to the IDB's rather stuffier style. He was also great fun to travel with, and together we never failed to find a way through any door that was blocked to us – often to the annoyance of the Scottish or Welsh Secretaries of State who were chasing similar leads. Nor was he a shy man. My private secretary's feet iced up as we were visiting the Korean royal palace in temperatures of minus 20 degrees Celsius; without fuss, Brian found a street-seller hawking tins of boiling ginseng tea and he promptly rubbed some up and down her frozen toes until her feeling returned. He has kept his hair and his figure, and for a man of some years he has the energy and the enthusiasm of a twenty-five-year-old.

24

THE BEST OF BELFAST

Even the most optimistic citizen of Belfast has learned to
hope for the best but not to be disappointed by the worst
and yet in the midst of such hard-headed and sometimes
grim reality, the best of Belfast shines through.

Alf McCreary

THE PROGRESS WE WERE MAKING IN improving the quality of life
in Belfast for many if not most of the citizens was phenomenal,
but other than the odd good news story on BBC's *Business
Breakfast*, screened at six in the morning, the national media's misery
drip continued to flow. The strategy we were pursuing, with its multiple
layers of programmes designed to pull people together in the communities,
find them work and give them self-assurance, was not the
stuff of political punditry. There had built up over the years a dedicated
cadre of influential commentators who saw everything in terms of an
all-embracing political and security settlement. This would be agreed
upon by all and sundry and handed down with the blessing of the Pope,
the President, the Prime Minister and the Taoiseach. Although I
accepted that any settlement would require acceptance within and
without Northern Ireland, I did not and do not believe that 'peace' can
be secured without removing intercommunity fear and replacing it on
the streets with jobs and tolerance. What we needed was to find a way
of giving Belfast an opportunity of celebrating what the city was, is

and could be. We needed a celebration where everyone could enjoy themselves, learn more about one another and be proud of themselves and the city in which they lived. We wanted to show the world there was another side to Belfast. While I accept that there is a limit to what the state can do, the dreadful conditions in some of the cities of Europe and the United States are proof enough that more rather than less political effort should be concentrated on the poor. Much depends on the quality of leadership, the effectiveness of the organisational structure and the calibre of the management.

Political commitment sets the scene, allocates the resources, drives through the agenda and gives hope and support to the risk takers while encouraging the wary. That commitment must be intrusive and insistent, must be concerned with outputs and with results. There are those who found me intolerant and occasionally, as they saw it, disloyal to the reputation of the civil service, but the role of a minister is to represent the people. He is there to serve the community, not to defend the public servants who are the conduits of his authority and his policy. I did whatever I believed necessary to achieve the objectives laid out in the opening statement of Making Belfast Work, and I was determined to sweep aside anything that stood in the way of that. Because I was a minister for so long, I knew what had to be done and I knew I had the support of the public and my young teams on the ground. Others who came afterwards were not long enough in office either to understand where some of the most sensitive issues remained hidden or to have the authority to insist on their instructions being fulfilled to the letter. An inevitable consequence of a lack of political control is that any bureaucracy, however good – and the Northern Ireland civil service is by and large very good – will slip back into a cosy consensus, avoid trouble and prefer the easy to the difficult. Without the Belfast action team programme, I am sure the lives of the poorest in our community would have been worse, in many instances much worse.

Billy Pinkerton from the Belfast Development Office had told me soon after I had arrived that he and his colleagues were negotiating to bring the Tall Ships to Belfast. If we could persuade the organisers to sail to Belfast, then we had the 'anchor' for our year of celebration. Liverpool had had its Flower Festival, inspired by Michael Heseltine after the Toxteth riots. Dublin had celebrated its millennium in 1988, although no one seemed quite sure what had happened in 988. Glasgow was the European City of Culture in 1990. Why should Belfast not have a year to show off?

But if the venture was to succeed, we would have to include every aspect of the city's talents. We would have to attract international stars to play to the 'haves'. But the 'have nots' had also to be in the audience, and everyone had to work together to organise cultural, sporting, musical, commercial, historical, horticultural and religious spectacles. I wanted everyone to have a part. I also wanted there to be a party, not for a day, a weekend or a month, but for a year, and I told everybody from 1987 onwards that that was what was going to happen.

We decided that 1991 would be the year and that the event would be known as the Best of Belfast. Robin Dixon, who had an Olympic bobsleigh gold medal and ran Redland Brick in Northern Ireland, chaired our Tall Ships Council, while the chairman of the 'Belfast 1991' Committee was Ivor Oswald who was chief executive of the Alliance & Leicester Building Society. I persuaded the slightly reluctant DOE officials to chip in £1.1 million towards the cost on the understanding that for every public pound there would be a matching private donation. The magnificent Aileen Porter was secretary to the committee.

The Tall Ships Council ran marginally more smoothly than 'Belfast 1991'. The council spent £1.3 million and their focus was narrower and non-political. Over at the 'Belfast 1991' Committee Ivor Oswald had the advantages and disadvantages of being a Northern Irish implant: it gave him a belief and enthusiasm for the place which was sometimes missing in some of the locals, but it also made it less easy for him to master his disparate members. His deputy, Ronnie Dunn of Laing's, was also an outsider who had done much for the rebuilding of Belfast, particularly Castle Court. I had intended that as many characters as possible with quirky imaginations and strong views should be included. We had a Sports Committee with Mary Peters in charge, which was astonishingly successful in pulling in the Irish games contingent who had a historical nervousness about government-sponsored programmes. Bob Crane, managing director of the *Belfast Telegraph*, was in charge of finances, Robert Agnew, assistant director of the Belfast Festival at Queen's, dealt with the arts, Bob Jourdan, director of the Northern Ireland Chamber of Commerce and Industry, dealt with business and commerce, and Robin Dixon with PR and advertising. They were all solid and supportive. Beneath them was a seething mass of creative talent waiting to burst out with pet plans they had been incubating for years.

I had made two slight errors. First, with fifteen members, the board was too large for any chairman to handle. Second, we had established the organisation as a limited company. Many board members took this to mean an independent company, which, although presentationally helpful in explaining that 'Belfast 1991' was not run by the government, was unhelpful when the spending of the £1.1 million had to be determined by Treasury rules. This led to clashes between the Belfast Development Office and the members of the board, and occasionally to factionalism. I had hoped that the Marxist dictum of thesis and anti-thesis leading to synthesis would apply. Unfortunately I do not believe Marx had a deep insight into the Irish character, and sometimes the result of the meeting of these opposites was nearer to chaos than to resolution.

But because everyone was determined that the year was to succeed, succeed it did, way beyond our hopes and expectations. The different committees took under their wing every community happening and badged and advertised it with the Best of Belfast logo. In all there were over four hundred events, starting with a Mozart concert featuring the Belfast pianist, Barry Douglas, and ending with a 'Big Night Out'.

The highlights, apart from the Tall Ships and the annual spectacular of the Belfast Festival, were the large numbers of local festivals at Donegall Pass, Poleglass, Lenadoon, Ligoniel and Duncairn amongst others. There was no triumphalism, no abuse, just people having fun. It had taken perhaps too long to galvanise local groups to realise how 'Belfast 1991' could support and encourage them, but by the autumn of 1991 the requests were coming in too fast for everyone to be accommodated by the end of the year.

Northern Ireland has always been famous for its rose hybridisers. Dickson's of Newtownards remains one of the world's great rose-growers. The other, Sam McGredy, had unfortunately left for New Zealand. What is less well known is that Belfast has one of the finest rose-gardens in the world, the Sir Thomas and Lady Dixon Park. Acre upon acre of every variety of floribundas, climbers, musks and hybrid teas, from every country and every grower, thrive in a climate from which mildew, black spot and greenfly appear to have fled. The Rose Society of Northern Ireland had persuaded the Ninth World Rose

Convention to come to behold this marvel. The Newtownards Dicksons had asked me to name a rose for the festival, hoping I would choose a commercial and saleable floribunda. Instead, bored with the ubiquitous 'Chinatown' and seeing a magnificent yellow hybrid tea in the nursery which was almost vulgar in its intensity, I picked that and named it 'Belfast Belle'. Big, buxom and beautiful, just like Belfast, I declared to a glum-faced Mr Dickson and the accompanying press. I have never seen these roses in anyone else's garden, but they are surviving splendidly in mine.

I did however repay Dickson's with one good turn. During 1991 Tim McNeil, who was the Industrial Development Board's outstanding roving inward-investment procurer in Asia, rang me to ask a favour. There was a famous and successful Dickson floribunda called Princess Michiko. Now that Emperor Hirohito had died, the Princess had become Empress. Could I find a way of securing the approval of the Empress to having another rose named after her?

Luckily for me, there was a meeting of the Anglo-Japanese 2000 Group being held at Turnberry in Scotland. The discussions included culture and education as well as industry and trade. One of the Japanese members at the meeting was Akio Morita, creator of the Sony empire. I had tried many times to cajole him to place a factory in Northern Ireland, but he always refused on the grounds that if a small country could not live at peace with itself, he was not going to allow his staff to become entangled in an internal conflict about which they knew nothing. My constant pleas had however at least elicited sympathy for the difficulties we faced. He was very close to the Japanese royal family, so I delicately broached the question of the rose. He said he thought there would be practical difficulties, but he would do what he could.

Several weeks later he rang my home. No one, of course, knew who he was and I was out. I gave orders to the family that if he ever rang back, they should all show maximum deference and find me. The next time he called, I was mowing the lawn. He had spoken to the Empress. She could not, of course, give her formal approval to anything that bore her name as she was not in the business of advertising roses. If anyone knew that she had agreed to her name being associated with the rose, she would be enveloped by demands for products to be named after her. Nevertheless, she would be very pleased to receive two dozen specimens to place in her rose-garden next to the bushes which had done so well and were called The Princess Michiko. A nod is as good as a wink.

Some three years later I went to lunch at the Imperial Palace with the Prime Minister, John Major, after I had become Minister of Trade. I sat on the Emperor's left. On my left was Akio Morita. The Empress was opposite. Half-way through the meal, Morita gave me a nudge. I enquired of the Empress if she recollected a small Irish company having named two roses after her. 'Oh yes,' she said, turning round. 'There they are, just outside the dining-room window. I love them dearly and I can see them from many different parts of the palace.' We may not have obtained a factory from Sony, but Dickson's had won the heart of the Empress of Japan.

The diamond of our celebration year was the arrival of the Tall Ships. Billy Pinkerton and Basil Singleton, BDO's outside marketing adviser, inseparably known as the 'Pingletons', had twisted every arm and massaged every joint on the Tall Ships Committee to persuade them to come. There were several doubters who understandably worried about the safety of the crews and the image of their organisation, should anything turn sour. But we had a formidable Tall Ships Council of our own, and no one could doubt either the professionalism of our organisation or the enthusiasm of everyone in public life in Belfast to welcome the ships. Our united approach to them, from across the religious and political divide, impressed them. The chairman of the Tall Ships Committee was Lord Burnham. He was fortuitously a first cousin of my mother's and as children they used to spend Christmas together. So she was turned out to support. My mother, who had rejected the chance of an Irish estate when my father succeeded, more than made up for that strange decision in her entreaties to Henry Burnham.

There was another benefit which I had not foreseen. Belfast City Council became heavily involved, and through working together, the pointlessness and absurdity of the boycott against the Anglo-Irish Agreement became even more obvious. The wounds of 1985 were subsumed in a common endeavour.

The Tall Ships are an awe-inspiring sight – but what was even more unforgettable was to see the thousands upon thousands of people spilling out of the Falls, the Shankill, the Ardoyne, Tiger Bay and east Belfast, and all converging on the Pollock Dock. The weather turned in our favour and for four wonderful days the people of Belfast forgot their troubles and came together in a seething mass of young and old, orange and green, rich and poor, enjoying a unique family outing. The dock was open to all, and all were there. Some of the RUC deserted their flak jackets and danced an Irish jig to the flute and the whistle. Jimmy the Duke (of Abercorn) sailed off in the *Lord Nelson*, crewed by the handicapped, leaving Hugh O'Neill complaining that the fast-food outlets owed more to Kentucky than to Portaferry.

I had made only one request to the Tall Ships Council. I wanted the greatest fireworks display the city had ever seen. Hugh O'Neill had taken me to the 100th anniversary dinner of the Savoy Hotel, which was followed by thundering fireworks over the Thames. Now that he had become chairman of the Tourist Board, I told him he and Robin Dixon would have to do twice as well in Belfast. Robin needed no prompting and the last evening of the fireworks was only surpassed when the next day 500,000 people watched as the Tall Ships sailed away down Belfast Lough. I had invited Chris Patten and his family to come over and see for themselves what had changed since he had told me to apply my mind to the Lagan. We walked round the city centre on the Friday. Word had leaked out, and there was the nasty, frightening sound of a large grenade thrown at an RUC patrol in the Markets. No one was hurt, but the walkabout was aborted. On the Saturday we mused upon whether such an extraordinary congregation of the majority of Belfast people in one place mingling together as if they were on a day out in Disneyland held any long-term meaning. Instinctively our doubts overcame our optimism. What we did not know was that, at that moment, the IRA were already plotting a final campaign to bring the city to its knees.

25
BLOWING OUT THE LIGHTS

B Y THE AUTUMN OF 1991 the Best of Belfast celebrations were attracting a wider and wider audience both within and without the city. The resurgence of private investment was gaining wider and wider publicity. Investors were becoming a charging herd, scared of missing out on opportunities they had never before considered.

If matters were going well for the city, they were not going nearly so well for Sinn Féin and the IRA. The IRA had been waging a nasty, vicious incendiary campaign for over a year, burning out shops in city and town centres all across Northern Ireland. They employed women and girls as look-alike shoppers. Their mission was to slip hollowed-out cassettes, filled with half an ounce of Semtex, a timer and a detonator, into the pockets of dresses on racks, or stuff them under the seats of chairs and sofas in furniture stores. Late at night the tapes would explode, and by the time the fire brigade had been called and the key holder turned up, the building would be wrecked. A previous IRA campaign of throwing petrol bombs through windows had frightened most shopkeepers into fitting sliding metal shutters. These, the terrorists quickly realised, kept the fires burning inside while the firemen were marooned outside. For the next few weeks, if not months, while the assessors did their valuations, a blackened eyesore would remind all and sundry, particularly potential investors, that Northern Ireland remained far from normal.

As no insurance company would cover commercial properties in the province for damage caused by paramilitary activity, the government was left to pick up the bills for the stocks lost and for the refurbishment and the rebuilding. But the government did not pay out for any loss of profits while the shops were closed down and boarded up. The IRA were well aware of the knock-on effect that their campaign was having on jobs and confidence. This led them to redouble their endeavours. Store staff had to stay long after closing time to search every article in case a bomb had been secreted into some unlikely orifice.

The IRA's largest triumph in the incendiary war was when they succeeded in burning down half of Sprucefield, the massive out-of-town shopping centre near Hillsborough. The incendiaries detonated in the early hours, and with a force 8 south-westerly blowing, there was nothing that any fire-fighter could do other than watch. The cost ran into tens of millions of pounds.

But even these calamities had the occasional lighter moments. On a Monday morning in early January 1991, a week after the destruction at Sprucefield, I went into Marks & Spencer's in Belfast city centre at the request of my son Andrew. Two Christmases before, I had bought him a pair of black brogues there. He told me that they had now developed a fault. They looked to me as if he had been playing football with them for the previous twelve months. They certainly had never had any relationship with a shoe brush. 'I'm a poor student having to pay my Poll Tax, Dad, please get me a credit!' So feeling ever so slightly guilty, I stepped onto the escalator to the first floor. As I reached the top there was an enormous kerfuffle. Staff were running in every direction. In the centre of the sales floor was a cluster of people all in a huddle. I was creeping towards the customer relations counter when an unmistakable voice roared out: 'Dick, what are you doing here?' It was Sir Richard Greenbury. 'Look, Clinton,' he said, turning to Clinton Silver, his rather more diminutive deputy. 'Dick's come in to show solidarity with us after the fire at Sprucefield.' He came closer and pulled open my raincoat. 'He's got a Marks & Spencer mac on, Clinton,' and then, after further investigation, 'He's wearing one of our blazers!'

As this running commentary was conducted within hearing of the entire first floor, a small crowd had gathered. At that moment, Rick noticed the plastic carrier bag I was trying to conceal. 'What have you got in there, Dick?' he blared as he grabbed it out of my hand. He pulled out one of Andy's dilapidated shoes. 'Oh look at this, Clinton, Dick's come in for a return. What have you been doing with them? Do you live in a quarry? Have you never heard of shoe polish? You want your money back! You should be giving us money after what you've done to them, and what's more, you have the cheek to bring them in here in a Tesco bag!'

Meanwhile a small, short Belfast woman wearing a violet mohair cap pulled down over her ears had pushed herself in between us and was following the incident intently. She shoved a finger in my stomach and, pointing upwards, announced: 'Look at your big red nose, Mr Needham. The problem with you is that you drink too much!' 'That's right, Missis,' declared Rick, 'that's one problem. The other is that if every customer we had wanted his money back after he'd worn a pair of shoes every day for a year in a quarry we'd be broke!' With that I was dispatched with a push towards the customer relations counter, followed by a further stream of advice that I'd better not try the same trick with the mac or the blazer. Rick's presence in the store that day, together with his visits to their other outlets, restored the confidence and morale of all his staff. They were friends in both need and deed.

I mounted a press campaign against Sinn Féin, insisting they explain how such destruction could bring about a contented united Ireland. For once Mr Adams appeared relieved that there was a government-imposed broadcasting ban on reporting his public comments, for answer came there none.

The following November, the IRA decided the moment had arrived for even greater spectaculars. The city was thronging with shoppers, many of whom had only recently picked up the courage to come back into the city centre. November and December accounted for some 40 per cent of annual takings and late-night shopping was a big new attraction. The terrorists' tactic was to leave hoax bombs night after night on the main approach arteries into the city. They paralysed the traffic and they caused frustration and annoyance which they knew would turn the customers away. By showing up the failings of the RUC and the army to keep the roads open, the IRA planned to crush the morale and self-confidence of the shopkeepers. Interspersed with hoaxes was the odd real big fertiliser bomb, which caused enormous damage over a wide area as the blast curled round buildings, blowing in windows and doors and scattering rubbish and debris in every direction.

Instantly I sensed that the IRA had decided to assault the very foundations on which we had tried to construct the restoration of Belfast's prosperity, normality and pride. If they could close down the city centre, day and night, the government would sustain a dreadful defeat and our crusade to create an atmosphere where both communities could work, eat, drink, dance, and sleep, together would once more become a distant aspiration. The IRA had very clearly understood the dangers that our achievements posed for them. They now moved to restore the misery and confusion on which their power depended. Many in the NIO, the army and the RUC appeared to have little realisation of just how dire the position was or what outcome would follow from an IRA victory in shuttering up Belfast.

The Secretary of State, the chief constable and the general officer commanding had regular meetings to discuss security, but ministers with other responsibilities were never invited. The absolute priority of the security forces was to avoid deaths and mutilations, and so no corners could ever be cut. Any criticism of any existing procedure was met with irate disbelief that anybody unconnected with the army or the police could offer a plausible alternative that might not further endanger the lives of police officers and soldiers. The very life of Belfast was bleeding away. The angry shopkeepers, many of whose businesses had been reduced to charcoal, the local and outside investors whose new buildings had been blasted, those who had received no recompense for the months when they earned no income and the frustrated commuters – all turned to my departments and me for reassurance and explanation. But I was excluded from the security tunnel.

Fortunately for the people of Belfast, there was a lateral-thinking and fearless Brit who was deputy secretary for security in the NIO. During his time in the Ministry of Defence he had been nicknamed 'Deadly Ledlie' and his time had now come. John was one of the few officials from that side of the NIO who had taken a deep interest in the work we were doing and who understood the importance of our success in improving the chances for peace. I turned to him in rage and despair. We had to find ways of co-ordinating our response to the bombs and the hoaxes. We had to show that we could react quicker to reassure the public and that we could win.

Ledlie proposed a new, all-embracing security committee; such a body had not existed since direct rule. Chaired by me as Minister of the Environment, the Belfast Co-ordinating Committee included the assistant chief constable for Belfast or a senior deputy, a colonel on the staff of the GOC, the head of the Belfast Development Office, the assistant secretary at the DOE in charge of roads in the city and members of the Belfast business community. The army came more or less willingly, the RUC less so and even on occasions not at all. It soon became clear that there were ways of diverting traffic around hoaxes which would lead to less disruption, and that by bringing more bomb-disposal officers into the city centre we could deal with incidents much faster; it had been taking anything up to an hour for the bomb-disposal team to arrive on-site from their base outside Belfast. We instituted proper liaison between the traffic control centres in the city and the local RUC stations and army bases.

At the first meeting we made two startling discoveries. The immaculately uniformed RUC representative aloofly informed us that although he was well aware that the IRA were testing the city's defences and that bombs remained hidden and undetected in west Belfast, security cover was to be reduced because of restrictions on overtime and lack of manpower. We were also told that the police and army were considering closing off the city centre and searching everyone and everything that went into it. Such a double whammy would have produced cackles of delight from the IRA's Belfast active-service units. The overtime was restored, the manpower problems were resolved and searches were moved out to the west of the city. The flow of bombs diminished and the city started rumbling back to life.

Some bombs continued to explode with a deafening, jarring intensity. One lunch-time, my office windows shook in their frames when an enormous device blew away River House in High Street, over two miles from where I was sitting. Never have I seen a room full of faces suddenly turn ashen, the fear for loss of life, the fear of shattered dreams and damaged aspirations, and the stomach-turning fear for friends and family. After every explosion I would be down on the site as fast as I was able. The scenes were always horrible. Shards of glass everywhere, metal frames tilting out of windows, torn blinds blowing in the wind. A black hole five metres deep and twenty metres wide where a car and its load had been parked. Sometimes the engine block would be discovered embedded in a wall five stories up. Often there would be a crowd standing around, watching the glaziers moving in to sweep up and board up. Some would commiserate; others would irritably challenge me on why the government was so impotent in defending their city and their jobs.

Most roads into the city from the west and the south led to the same block around the Europa Hotel and the City Hall. There were a few buildings which seemed always to take the brunt of the car bombs: the Europa itself, the Opera House and Windsor House. I promised that we would rebuild whatever was bombed, and that in the case of ugly 1960s and 1970s buildings we would do so using modern designs and modern materials. In a perverse way the IRA, I proclaimed, were doing our demolition work for us. But I knew that the reality was different. Money that would otherwise have gone to other budgets would have to be found to pay for the reconstruction work, with the result that much-needed services would be curtailed. We could not tell the people of Ulster that, not only had they to endure the bombing, but they would be penalised by paying for the aftermath as well.

In fact, we did rebuild and much of what was done did include new materials and new designs. But if the security response was occasionally inept, the IRA capacity for perpetrating horror was limitless. In early November 1991 they placed a large bomb by the doors of the tunnel leading between the civilian departments and the military wing at Musgrave Park Hospital. The explosion killed two people who were in the canteen at the end of the corridor leading from the tunnel and wounded eighteen others, some dreadfully. I was the minister on duty that weekend and went straight to the scene. I was very, very angry. I told the television cameras that the men and women who had done this came from hell and as surely as night followed day they would return there. There was a huge public reaction. The IRA were condemned, not least in their own communities.

By the first week of December the worst was over, by the end of the third week the city was thriving, and by the end of the January sales, the shopkeepers had enjoyed one of their most lucrative seasons ever. The people of Belfast and its hinterland had not deserted their city. They had come back, day on day, night on night, to work and enjoy themselves despite the delays and the disruption. They were not of a mind to surrender to the IRA.

Within a month of my leaving the following April I learnt that the six-month-old Belfast Co-ordinating Committee was to be disbanded. Sometimes I wondered whether the Italians were not making a better fist of running Sicily than some sections of the NIO were achieving in Northern Ireland.

26

TAKING CALNE TO ULSTER

D URING 1984, WHEN I WAS PARLIAMENTARY private secretary
to Patrick Jenkin at the Department of the Environment, I
read an article in the *Evening Standard* about a remarkable project to restore and conserve a derelict little slate town in Derbyshire
called Wirksworth. Apparently the quarry had been the only main
employer, and once that had shut the wealth and self-esteem of the
town had evaporated. Those with vigour and youth had departed and
the once-fine Victorian and Georgian buildings had become grim and
grimy. The Wirksworth Trust had been founded under the direction of
an architect and planner named Gordon Michell, and his work had been
funded initially by a Sainsbury Charitable Trust. Gordon had detailed
how the town could be revived, but his genius lay in his capacity not
only to draw and sketch what might be done in every street and to
every building but to organise. He had organised the councils – county,
district and parish. He had encouraged the townspeople to form a civic
trust. He had, through will-power and determination, demonstrated
that the town could be restored in all its former finery and that it was
up to the local people, supported from outside, to achieve it. The
Evening Standard article chronicled the astonishing progress.

Calne, in my constituency, was in very similar circumstances. Surrounded by wealthy Wiltshire, by the early 1980s Calne had lost its soul
with the closure of Harris's, the pork-processing factory. The Harris

building would have been listed had it been in the centre of Bristol or Swindon, but its bulk and height so overpowered the remainder of the small town centre that it had become a monument to failure, the surrounding streets had become shabby and run-down. It had to go. The factory had employed several thousand low-paid workers, many from the local villages as well as Calne. Nothing much had really been done to upgrade or invest in the place since it had been built in the 1930s. The pork pie machine had been cooking flat out for fifty years. With Harris's closure, the town faced an uncertain and miserable future. There was already an escalating crime wave, a growing drug problem, low educational attainment levels, and unemployment way above the Wiltshire average.

Patrick Jenkin had also seen the article and he also knew about Calne's difficulties. He scribbled me a note saying he would contact Gordon and arrange an introduction. He did more. He came to Calne and persuaded the town council to establish the Calne Project. Gordon was recruited, and in no time he had done for Calne – not without controversy – what he had done for Wirksworth. By then I was Minister of the Environment in Northern Ireland, and the Mitchell principles were badly needed in the bombed-out, barricaded, barbed-wired, often deserted centres of Ulster's county towns.

In 1986 the Northern Ireland Town and Country Planning Institute held a conference to which they invited councillors and planners from all the county towns. I invited Gordon to give a presentation. By the time he had sat down, his enthusiasm and slides had won them over. Douglas McIldoon was placed in charge of restoring some of the UK's finest architectural gems across Northern Ireland to their former glory, using the principles that had done so much for Wirksworth and Calne.

His first task was to see for himself what Gordon had achieved. When he returned, he decided to begin with Carrickfergus. Carrickfergus shared two unfortunate experiences with Calne. In the 1960s, Transport Department engineers, oblivious to anything other than the needs of the car, had driven roads through both, in Calne's case cutting the town in half, and in Carrick's case separating the wonderful castle from the town centre and denying any visitor the chance of wandering from one to the other. The other depressing comparison was that Carrickfergus had also lost most of its employment. Douglas appointed one of his best young planners, Tom Clarke, as the project manager, and it was not long before he had produced the same degree of involvement and enthusiasm as had Gordon in England.

We were fortunate in that, with the help of Urban Development Grant, we could encourage landlords to improve their properties according to a master plan by aiding them financially. There was another major benefactor. Following the signing of the Anglo-Irish Agreement, the International Fund for Ireland was established. The IFI, supported by the European Union, Canada, Australia and the USA, was looking for projects, and the small towns of Ulster were an ideal vehicle.

Before long, the news of the Carrickfergus project began to spread. There was a clamour from other towns to be treated similarly. Armagh, Newry, Dungannon, Downpatrick, Strabane and Enniskillen, as well as smaller backwaters such as Coalisland and Keady, the most deprived of the deprived, joined the list for project status. In each instance, a formal proposal, which included cross-community support and local political agreement, had to be agreed with the DOE. I had, of course, a political agenda. The projects offered a subtle opportunity to bring power-sharing into local councils. Everyone from Sinn Féin to the DUP could agree on the need to improve their local environment and everyone wanted to be part of a success story that was reviving confidence and attracting investment.

Right from the start I involved the MPs. I encouraged them to arrange international twinnings which had begun in Londonderry with Derry Boston Ventures. Seamus Mallon in Newry chose Pittsburgh – not least because of Dan Rooney, a Newryman who owned the Pittsburgh Steelers; Eddie McGrady and Downpatrick went for Chicago; Ken Maginnis was involved with TEDDY, the Tyrone Economic Development Initiative, which linked with Kansas city. The combination of projects and initiatives, although limited in their ability to attract inward investment, set off a massive surge of interest and excitement. I toured council after council telling them what others were doing and why they could not afford to miss out. The relationships between the government and local authorities were as close as they had ever been, power-sharing flourished in most councils and the dark days of 1985 were long forgotten. I do not believe that we would have succeeded as we did without the enormous commitment of Seamus Mallon, Ken Maginnis and Eddie McGrady.

Seamus had two towns that needed attention, Newry and Armagh. Newry, large chunks of which my family had once owned, had fallen on very hard times. The lack of a by-pass led to a constant traffic jam of vehicles going north and south, clogging up and polluting the town centre without bringing trade or profit. Newry also had an unenviable reputation for violence. The entry to the town from the north passed a massive fortress of a police station, with a line of RUC armoured Land Rovers always stationed in front of the thirty-foot-high steel gates. The railway line was regularly blown up outside Newry station, and there had been a number of dreadful murders in and around Newry over the years. Although industrial land had been zoned and serviced by the Industrial Development Board, there were no takers. A new but not very high-standard shopping centre, Buttercrane, had taken business from shops in the centre, but the frontier town was not a place to shop unless the Irish punt was 20 per cent higher than sterling. What Newry needed was a shared cultural identity and purpose together with a Marks & Spencer and two or three new factories.

Before Seamus had been elected to parliament the local council had been run by a strange alliance of unionists and independents led by a delightful character called Eugene Markey. Eugene's long career in public service resulted in his having a deep knowledge of how best to get assistance from the state to help Newry. Eugene could talk anyone into giving him anything. I had inherited my great-grandfather's Knight of St Patrick robes. They are very fine and quite valuable and I was not sure what to do with them. Eugene said he would house them in a glass case in the Newry Museum along with my blue velvet slippers embroidered with N & M (Newry & Mourne) and a viscount's coronet. This, he said, would remind the local Catholics of their colonial past. So now in Newry Museum, in a splendid glass case, are my slippers and my great-grandfather's robes. I did all I could for Newry, not least because John McConnell, the NIO's political officer, had been the district officer in charge of Newry and he arranged a constant stream of visits for me to make and visitors for me to see.

Seamus's arrival added very considerable weight to those seeking solutions to Newry's problems. Seamus has presence. He is a big, good-looking man with a fine baritone voice and a finer mind to go with it. In some ways he resembles Ken Maginnis, both of them large, solid men, both well endowed with hair, both partial to a jar and both decent and committed to their communities. About six months after the signing of the Anglo-Irish Agreement I was sitting in the Kremlin bar in the House of Commons talking to Seamus when Ken came in. He was supposed to be boycotting me, but the offer of a large brandy soon broke the boycott if it did not settle the argument – for soon all hell broke loose as each of us berated the other. Then Seamus suddenly said that the row reminded him of those they had had when Ken managed a bar in Warrenpoint and Seamus was earning a bob or two on the side as one of his servers. So I took them both home. If the problems of Ireland were left to the two of them, there would be plenty of rows but plenty of solutions.

When I first met Seamus in the USA in 1983 he was a sour man with much to be sour about. He had tried for years to be elected to parliament. He lived amongst the most difficult republicans who threatened and insulted him, as did the security forces from time to time when he tried to air the grievances of those he hoped to represent. But once he was elected, he grew in stature and confidence. The bile seemed to drain away from him and he immediately became consumed in the interests of his constituency. I was happy to go anywhere with him, not only for his company which was always funny and astute, but because at any meeting he would give a gravitas and a support which I found invaluable. We ventured round Pittsburgh together, we went to see Marks & Spencer together (at last they are coming to Newry), we tried desperately to bring a Japanese factory to Newry and very nearly succeeded. We supported the Sean O'Casey training theatre in Newry at the Clanrye Centre. There was no initiative he was not involved with. The same was true of Armagh city, although as the seat of the cardinal and the archbishop, the Churches were also closely involved there. Many men would over the years have become bigots if they had gone through what he has been through, but Seamus was a pillar of anti-bigotry. Perhaps time will suggest that John Hume might have handed over the leadership of the SDLP to him a little earlier.

Eddie McGrady, the SDLP MP for South Down, was a very different character from Seamus, more of a businessman than a teacher, but also remarkable. He nursed his wife over many years at the same time as nursing his constituency. If Seamus had too much through traffic in Newry, Eddie had too much local traffic in Downpatrick. Eddie's point was that when new roads were built they were invariably in Protestant areas not Catholic ones. In the sense that John Whitlaw's DOE men put roads where the traffic was densest, he was right. The problem was that with bad roads it was very difficult to attract inward investment and larger numbers of visitors. So Eddie was right and the DOE wrong, but the DOE had the money. But Eddie was nothing if not a trier, and with Downpatrick, the burial place of St Patrick, and the Mountains of Mourne in his constituency, he bombarded me with delegations and letters to improve access to that most stunning part of the British Isles. Eddie is a sober, solid man in whom burns a real determination to see an end to the Troubles. In his smart grey suits he would remind you of a well-to-do Bavarian businessman, that is until you were on the other side of the table.

Ken Maginnis was elected for Fermanagh–South Tyrone in 1983. One of my first tasks as Prior's PPS was to befriend him and his four new colleagues – Roy Beggs, Clifford Forsythe, Jim Nicholson and Cecil Walker. They shared a suite of offices off the upper ministerial corridor in the House of Commons which was so remote that few Commons staff knew how to find them, while even fewer of my parliamentary colleagues knew their names or their constituencies. In the 1980s an Ulster member of parliament was not high on anyone's agenda. I tried to show them the parliamentary ropes and procedures, gain their confidence and win them over to support the government's overall economic and social policies. The day of the Conservative and Unionist Party was well over. Ulster Unionist MPs were not prepared to take risks by offending their constituents' wishes for ever more services and subsidies and ever lower taxes. So the members would invariably vote for more of one and less of the other.

Ken Maginnis soon became their spokesman on security matters. As time passed, he learnt the political trade and, for the most part, to control his temper and his mercurial spirits. He had been headmaster of a primary school. He is not a great academic but he makes up for intellectual rigour with common sense directness and a built-in knack of understanding the other person's point of view. Like every really good schoolmaster, he can spot the rogue and he is a fund of very funny and apposite stories. He has enormous charm and when he wants to be, he can be extraordinarily sensitive and sympathetic. A Tory MP colleague – which one I cannot recall – told me that once when he was touring Ken's constituency with him, Ken was called to the home of a recently widowed wife of a murdered RUC officer. He told me that the way Ken listened to, and then chatted to, the widow was incredible. The reassurance, the broader picture, the bravery of her husband, the necessity of his job, that he had not died in vain, were all put across with gentleness and authority that gave her and her family renewed strength. Not many UK MPs are faced with such circumstances. However, for Ken and his marvellous wife Joy, it was an all too regular occurrence.

The IRA have come for him at least twice and when they come to call they have spent months planning, researching and reconnoitring, but he is so widely liked and respected that not even their evil cunning has been sufficient to corner him.

Ken was the first Ulster Unionist MP to agree to join up with me in trying to bring inward investment from the United States. We twinned the Tyrone area with Kansas and spent as demanding a time as any promoting Ken's patch as *the* economic opportunity in the European Union for any Midwest company wishing to find a partner to manufacture or to sell in Europe. To Americans we met he was real Irish and real Irish he is. Not Scottish, not Welsh, and least of all not English. Nor do his views and beliefs reflect those of the South. He exemplifies all that is most durable, respectable and loveable about the Protestant Ulsterman. He also has the obstinacy, the distrust and occasionally the myopia that sets them apart. If I had ever found myself in a trench I would have wanted Major Ken Maginnis next to me, which I could not assert for all his colleagues.

By the end of the eighties most of the main towns had their projects and their plans, so with the IFI's backing we supported another umbrella programme, called the CRISP initiative (Community Regeneration Initiative – Special Projects), to see what we could do for the smaller towns. One of these was Coalisland. During the 1960s many out-of-the-way places had had dumped on them large numbers of Belfast city dwellers who were placed in soulless, East European-type estates with no hope of employment or enjoyment. Downpatrick had the Flying Horse estate, Antrim had Rathenraw, Craigavon was a whole conurbation made up of housing that was meant to replicate Milton Keynes but was in reality closer to Ferguslie Parks, Glasgow, and Coalisland had its River Park.

Coalisland had a proud industrial past; perhaps that is why the planners picked it as one of the locations for Belfast's overflow. There had been an iron ore mine, a smelter and a coal mine to fuel the smelter. There also had been some significant weaving mills, though these had long since disappeared by the time the migrants from Belfast had been railroaded down. Coalisland had become a notorious interface between the security forces and an IRA cell which had left the town neglected and impoverished. At the end of the eighties a real attempt was being made to bring the town round. Jim Canning, a Dungannon district councillor, supported by Father Denis Faul, headmaster of one of Dungannon's largest schools, the local council and Ken Maginnis the MP, put together a project to clean up the town and put it back to work. One of the most exciting renewals was an industrial museum which restored to working order the magnificent linen mill with its power loom. Even after years of disuse, the generator was still locked away, all shining brass surrounded with Minton tiling.

I was asked if I would help procure the funding and launch the programme. No government minister had ever visited Coalisland, a rural version of the Falls Road. The local councillor was Francie Molloy, a Sinn Féiner who deeply resented the British presence and was bound to make trouble. The day before we were due to go, the newspapers were full of a security leak that the IRA had received advance notification of my visit and would do what was necessary to stop it taking place. That night the RUC superintendent of the division that covered Coalisland phoned me to say that, after all the effort that had gone into making the trip possible, he was all for going ahead. His exact words were: 'I'll carry you in on my back, if necessary.' He had been involved with Jim Canning from the start and was one of the enlightened policemen who understood that what we were trying to do across the province would make his life easier and the lives of his men safer.

The NIO was, of course, doubtful and fearful of being blamed for any incident. The DOE civil servants were emphatic: there could be no no-go areas for their minister anywhere in Northern Ireland. So off we went. The event was uneventful, although there was a lot of media coverage. Some of the TV cameramen stupidly pointed their cameras at the faces of the young RUC officers, apparently unaware that if they appeared on television they would become recognisable to the terrorists in both communities. Mr Francie Molloy bawled and hollered, but my new police chief friend told him to shut up, and he did. A few backs were turned but there were as many friendly smiles, and the regeneration of

Coalisland began. Six months later I returned and the security presence was less evident, the atmosphere less tense and for the first time in twenty years the SDLP had won a council by-election on the River Park estate.

Soon after I ceased to be a minister in Northern Ireland, the Parachute Regiment paid a visit to the town but not with the same intent that I had had. In two hours of bashing heads and breaking bones, they successfully destroyed two years of intense effort. Ken Maginnis, the Ulster Unionists' security spokesman, demanded that disciplinary action be taken against those involved and it was. It was also true that a member of the regiment had been brutally maimed before they created mayhem. But there has grown up a cadre of hardened men in some regiments of the British army who see Northern Ireland as both a place for revenge and a place to try out tactics they might one day be called to use elsewhere in the world. Such behaviour, although isolated and infrequent, is absolutely disastrous for raising confidence in the impartiality of the security forces amongst the nationalist communities. My heart bled for my superintendent friend and all he had tried to do.

27
MINDING THE FORT

NORTHERN IRELAND IS LITTERED with archaeological sites, from Neolithic Navan in Armagh to raths in Antrim. There are also some magnificent Anglo-Irish houses: Mount Stewart on the Ards Peninsula; Castle Ward on the west bank of Strangford Lough, Baronscourt outside Omagh, home to the dukes of Abercorn; Shane's Castle near Antrim, the property of Lord O'Neill; and Castle Coole in Fermanagh, the seat of the earls of Belmore. Some of these great architectural masterpieces were still lived in and looked after by their prosperous owners, but many families had fallen on harder times and the Department of the Environment was under constant pressure to find ever larger sums of money to help out the National Trust who had been inadequately endowed to maintain them.

One problem was that Northern Ireland attracted so few tourists that there was not a sufficiently large pool of local visitors to make the properties pay their way. Yet Mount Stewart had to be protected. The marquesses of Londonderry had long since fled, and only Lady Pamela Berry, daughter of Edith, Lady Londonderry, remained. Yet this was home to one of Stubbs's greatest paintings, the *Hambletonian*. There were the chairs on which Metternich and Castlereagh had sat while redrawing the boundaries of Europe at the Congress of Vienna in 1815. Ribbentrop had presented Lord Londonderry with a biscuit model of a Nazi storm trooper when he weekended in 1938. Edith,

Lady Londonderry, had created one of the great gardens of the world. Whatever happened, as an Anglo-Irish earl and an NIO minister I could not allow my heritage to crumble as had happened, through government neglect, to so many historic houses in the Republic.

There was a strong conservation lobby and the National Trust, under Raymond O'Neill's chairmanship and Ian McQuiston as director, maintained a constant stream of correspondence in defence of their claims. I was told to lobby the National Heritage Memorial Fund to come up with several millions for restoring Castle Coole, perhaps Ulster's greatest jewel. Before giving us the money, they paid us a visit and expected a slap-up dinner at Stormont House. It turned out that the chairman, Lord Charteris, the Queen's former private secretary, used to visit a girlfriend who lived in the house in the thirties. He wanted to see how it had changed. They were a various group, including Clive Jenkins, former general secretary of ASTMS, all jollied along by Martin Charteris. Though not too keen to pass over the fund's millions, they paid up when they had seen the masterpiece. That is more than Clive Jenkins did: he bet me a case of claret that the Tories would lose the 1992 election, but by then he had departed for Australia.

When the work at Castle Coole was finished, the Queen Mother accepted an invitation to see the renovations. I was late arriving and the only snippet of information I gained from the rear of the Queen Mother's entourage was that when the house was built in the 1750s the stippling effect on the plaster pillars in the hall had been done by Italian craftsmen who had erected screens around their work to stop prying Irish eyes from stealing their secrets. The same difficulties had apparently arisen in the 1980s during the renovation work. After lunch we flew back to Hillsborough through driving rain and low cloud in an RAF Wessex helicopter. After a while I heard the Queen Mother's voice over the intercom: 'Please, pilot, take us lower so I can see my beloved Fermanagh!' How many cows aborted and how we missed so many power lines, I shall never know. I told Peter Brooke the story and he ordered me to retell it after the next sticky meeting of the Anglo-Irish Intergovernmental Conference. It was not long before I was called into supper in his Admiralty Building office in Whitehall, where I told the Irish Foreign Minister of our great Queen Mother's delight in part of her daughter's kingdom – we laughed, he did not.

The archaeological side of the DOE was run by a persistent, kind and enormously knowledgeable woman, Ann Hamlin. She was English but she knew more about what lurked beneath the soil and what looked like rubble on the surface in Northern Ireland than 99 per cent of the locals. She had me spellbound, as would any really good teacher, about the history of Ulster from the Táin to the Normans. Little did I know that John de Courcy came from Stogursey in Somerset or that he had conquered most of Ireland with a few hundred men until he was put to the sword by the jealous King John at Carrickfergus Castle in 1210. Her greatest and abiding efforts went into saving Navan Fort and restoring Carrickfergus Castle. She had me as a staunch supporter.

Chris Patten had left me difficult unfinished business over Navan Fort. Navan is the ancient capital of Ulster, the legendary meeting place of Cuchulainn and the Red Knights of Ulster. It is as important to the Irish as Stonehenge is to the English and yet the DOE had allowed a Mr Acheson to open up an enormous limestone quarry which over the years had been extended and extended to include a dirty noisy processing works. Chris had asked a distinguished Edinburgh academic, Dr Jean Balfour, to conduct an inquiry into conservation and wildlife in Northern Ireland, and some but not all her recommendations had been adopted by the time I arrived. A strengthened section with a new director, John Phillips, was put in place to cover not only the countryside and wildlife but also historic monuments and buildings. John Phillips was a dear man, capable of seeing both sides of every argument. The problem was that the DOE was full of engineers and transport men who were more interested in making holes to make roads than they were in some old prehistoric mound.

In May 1986, after a six-week inquiry and a six-month deliberation, where I have no doubt the planning commission informally asked the DOE Planning Service for a view, I was presented with a Planning Appeal Commission recommendation that limited extended quarrying at Navan Fort should be allowed. I had made clear from the day of my arrival that I was unhappy about the existing quarrying, let alone any new excavation. I had visited the site with the then local MP Jim Nicholson, who was for the quarry, and received a delegation led by Seamus Mallon, who was against.

This was my first big test as a minister confronted by the system. I knew that Ann Hamlin had argued at a meeting of top officials against her own under-secretary, Jim Beckett, but clearly she had been outgunned. I summoned a meeting of those involved and told them that I was not prepared to accept departmental advice on the matter. 'I am afraid you cannot do that, Minister,' came the reply. 'You are in a quasi-judicial role, and have to follow precedent. There has to be a presumption in favour of continuing the excavation. It has, after all, been there for many years and if we were to turn down this limited expansion, the owner could well take us to judicial review, and if we were to lose, as is probable, the cost would have to be borne by the Department as it could be shown that the Minister was not prepared to heed his senior officials' advice.' 'What the hell is the point in having a Minister,' I exploded. 'If that is the case, you take the consequences and I shall inform the world that I am no better than a eunuch at the court of the Chinese Emperor!'

'Let us see what we can do,' said Dan Barry, the permanent secretary, as he ruefully puffed on his pipe and gave me a signal as the others stomped from the room. A few days later, Dan told me that on reflection he thought there was a sufficient planning argument that the public interest would be best served by a refusal to grant permission to extend the quarry. When we announced the decision, the result was universally acclaimed by all but Mr Acheson, although it did not take long for him to acquire a new limestone site some five miles away. I received a letter of thanks from the then Irish opposition leader, Charles Haughey. I discovered later that close by was another site, even larger than Navan, called Haughey's Fort.

After that we established the Navan Research Group with the vice-chancellor of Queen's University, Sir Gordon Beveridge, in the chair, and the bickering between the DOE and the archaeologists at Queen's about how to develop the site came to an end. Ann Hamlin then really started beavering. The research group turned into an initiative group. Money was found from the International Fund for Ireland, the National Heritage Memorial Fund and the European Regional Development Fund. The Northern Ireland Tourist Board appointed a project manager, and a very cleverly and beautifully designed and landscaped visitors' centre was constructed. Stonehenge now seems abandoned by comparison.

The other great battle in which Ann and I were engaged was to change the use of Carrickfergus Castle. The castle had a record of drama, thuggery, bravery and sacrifice unrivalled on the island of

Ireland but in 1985 it was the site of a large number of inappropriate, static exhibits from several Irish regiments, including the Royal Inniskilling Fusiliers, who were unable to find another home for their mementoes. The Historic Monuments Branch of the DOE wanted the military museum moved out, not least because it cluttered the magnificent Upper Chamber and prevented the castle being developed for historical, cultural and educational events that would describe the great moments in which Carrickfergus had played such a crucial role, rather than playing host to what brave Irish regiments had done in Flanders or at El Alamein.

I was quick to support a change in use when I learnt that at Carrickfergus in February 1760 five officers and 230 men of the 62nd Regiment of Fort – mainly recruits under training – were attacked by eight hundred French troops, landed by Commodore Thurot. The battle was so intense that when the garrison ran out of ammunition the soldiers fired off the silver buttons on their tunics. When they were finally overwhelmed, Thurot allowed his prisoners to leave the castle, the officers with their swords and the men with their muskets. But the heroic defence had bought time, and before the French could capitalise on their victory, a boom was heard at the entrance of Belfast Lough – the Royal Navy had arrived and the tables were soon turned. The 62nd Regiment of Fort later became the Wiltshire Regiment and many of its men must have come from my constituency.

The old soldiers of the 'skins' were not, however, to have their museum removed without a fight. Colonels wrote, brigadiers protested, a general fulminated, a field marshal was recalled – all seeking to defend the artefacts at Carrickfergus Castle. I was summoned to see the minister of state at the Ministry of Defence. Even Tom King was becoming nervous and asked me to find a compromise if possible. The minister was Lord Trefgarne. I was fortunate that I confronted a peer, as Commons ministers have a crucial advantage over lordly ones – we are elected and self-confident, and generally they are neither. I told Lord Trefgarne I would be happy to find an alternative site, perhaps the stables at Castle Coole or some disused barracks at Enniskillen, but the museum would have to go from Carrickfergus and it would have to go soon, as our other innovative and more appropriate proposals were ready. David Trefgarne huffed and puffed, but in the end it was my decision, and I had made up my mind.

It was not long before the castle had become a new centre for the regeneration initiative in Carrickfergus. It is now the most popular and most visited of all the state care monuments in Ulster. Each year it hosts banquets, fairs, festivals, private parties, charity events and product launches, and most importantly it serves as a wonderful educational backdrop to the history of Northern Ireland. Teachers develop their primary-school history programmes there, the highlight of which is a medieval day at the castle. There are two larger-than-life, as realistic as life, model soldiers of the 62nd Regiment on the battlements.

At a time when Northern Ireland is so divided over its present, it appeared to me to be crucial that the state should continue to nurture and protect the historic monuments and buildings that make up Ireland's chequered history. To privatise and farm out that role – as many were arguing for at the time in Great Britain – would have been to trivialise and commercialise vital aspects of our past.

28
FOUNDING THE TORIES

THERE HAD LONG BEEN A SMALL, DISSENTING, mainly middle-class political movement which eccentrically believed that Northern Ireland was, in the Prime Minister's words, 'as British as Finchley'. This simplistic view, often advertised from comfortable nests in north Down, was based on the premise that if Ulster was governed like Surrey, sooner or later the province would behave like Surrey. The IRA would then give up or go away. It was claimed that this 'non-sectarian' approach was the only sensible way forward, even though it attracted as little support among Catholics as did any other unionist viewpoint. These dotty ideas on integration would not have mattered except for the unfortunate fact that they appeared to be supported privately by Margaret Thatcher and were vociferously propagated by a small group of influential right-wing MPs who had her ear.

The integrationists in Northern Ireland were always looking for a champion. They have found one with Robert McCartney, QC, who is now the UK Unionist MP for North Down. Bob is clever and rich and a socialist maverick. He has dipped in and out of Northern Ireland politics as his commitments have allowed him. It was during one of his 'out' phases that the clamour for founding a Conservative Party in Northern Ireland reached a crescendo. There were some advantages. Ministers in Northern Ireland had no political base and therefore no political constituency to fall back on for support. The Conservatives are unionists, and once the old unionist party had ceased to take the Conservative whip, there was no reason why the Tory Party should not organise in Ulster. The non-sectarian Alliance Party shadowed the Liberal Democrats on the mainland and had never broken through the 10 per cent barrier. Perhaps somewhere out there was a large number of disenchanted unionist and nationalist middle-class voters who yearned to join a party for its economic and social credo rather than its loyalty to one particular tradition.

The integrationists could also point to the failure of twenty years of effort to find some system of power-sharing which would return authority over local issues to local politicians. If we could mount an effective Conservative challenge and overtake the Alliance Party, we could also exert pressure on the unionists to be more supportive if and when the need arose. Finally there was strong support among mainland constituency party activists to allow their Northern Ireland cousins to be brought into the family. At every party conference in the eighties there was a growing lobby of Northern Ireland Conservatives demanding right of entry. Our supporters, watching them standing in the Blackpool or Bournemouth drizzle pathetically handing out their leaflets and waving their banners, understandably sympathised.

In the late eighties the matter was finally brought to a head by a number of Conservative businessmen, including Hugh O'Neill and Sir Desmond Lorimer, writing to Tom King to outline their disgust at their disenfranchisement and their preparedness to support financially, organisationally and vocally a Northern Ireland Conservative organisation. In the NIO Brian Mawhinney was sceptical, Tom King stood in the middle and I, after many doubts, had come round to trying to make a go of it. After a lot of to-ing and fro-ing with Conservative Central Office, we agreed to affiliate the embryonic Northern Ireland Conservative associations provided they followed the rules and procedures of the Conservative Party organisation. Unfortunately we could not force the new members to follow the policies of the Conservative government, and they did not.

In retrospect the decision was flawed from the start. It was inevitable that the integrationists would hijack the party with the support of the Tory right and so, instead of having a large number of Northern Ireland Tories supporting Conservative ministers, we were faced with a small number of additional and persistent critics from within our own ranks.

The leading critic was the Conservative leader in Northern Ireland, the saturnine Dr Laurence Kennedy. Laurence had all the attributes of the righteous and the aggrieved which led him to sniff conspiracy and treachery at every turn. This did nothing to improve his latent sense of humour. It seemed that, for Laurence, politics in the Northern Ireland Conservative Party was not intended to be fun, although occasionally we had some.

I was determined to make the Conservatives as successful as possible, as was Peter Bottomley, who for some inexplicable reason had been appointed an NIO minister after an explosive time in Transport. He took over some of my responsibilities at the Department of the Environment, including transport, and although on occasion he was somewhat strange, he was popular and competent. Equally inexplicably, a year later he was sacked. Occasionally in Northern Ireland his urge for eccentricity got the better of him. Every year in November there was a campaign to promote safe driving at Christmas organised by Ronnie Troughton who had been the DOE's assistant secretary in charge of road safety for years. He was bubbly, enthusiastic and very professional. His exuberance was catching and the November event was always very well publicised with large numbers of children and their mothers being invited to a reception to be given professional advice by the RUC on how to look after themselves on the roads. There was a message but there was also an hour off school, with balloons, cakes and police cars much in evidence. Peter decided this was far too cosy an arrangement and needed some drama. His private office were surprised when he asked for some eggs to be provided at the occasion. A few hours later, Ronnie Troughton stood horrified as children screamed and mothers swooned. Peter had cracked the raw eggs and, with hands dripping yolk, mucous and bits of shell, the importance of belting up needed no further elaboration.

The first test of the Northern Ireland Conservatives' strength came at the Upper Bann by-election in May 1990 caused by the death of Harold McCusker. David Trimble was the Ulster Unionist Party candidate in a unionist stronghold with substantial pockets of nationalist and republican support. The Alliance Party, which in the past had polled pitifully, was represented by a local doctor. Upper Bann was not an ideal area for us to launch ourselves, but we had an excellent candidate in Colette Jones, a Catholic, Welsh, former teacher who lived in the constituency and who was as loyal to the government as any Ulster Tory could be without incurring the wrath of Laurence Kennedy. We fought a spirited campaign. Chris Patten came over and we canvassed large estates with a formidable entourage. Ian Gow helped and insisted on canvassing the nationalist areas, where he was photographed from inside the Sinn Féin offices as he walked past. There seemed to be considerable support. 'Oh yes, Mr Needham,' I was told at a surprising number of houses, 'we have always been Conservative.'

But when they had counted the votes we had lost our deposit and polled less than Sinn Féin. The only tiny consolation was that we had done better than the Alliance. It was a humiliating result even though we had never claimed that we thought victory, or anything like it, was remotely possible. The reality was that those who told us they were Conservatives were, of course, those who still believed that unionism and Conservatism were the same thing. In places such as Lurgan, Portadown and Craigavon, which had suffered much at the hands of terrorism, there was no likelihood of the vast majority of decent unionists abandoning their political protectors to come over to us. In their minds it was the Conservatives who should rejoin unionism, not the other way round.

There were other revelations, both personal and political, that I drew from the campaign. On election day I had toured the constituency giving support to the tellers at the polling stations and trying to make last-minute conversions amongst the voters. As they hurried by, ignoring my entreaties, I knew in my bones the game was up. 'I'll not vote for anyone named "Colette",' one man snapped.

The situation at some of the polling stations was disgraceful. Outside one school which was being used for polling the UDA had parked a caravan packed with unpleasant, tough, angry, young thugs who hurled abuse and jostled one of our helpers, Margaret Redpath. Margaret is the wife of Alfie Redpath, who was a north Belfast Official Unionist city councillor, so they were both used to intimidation, but it was frightening to witness and although Margaret never flinched, she was frightened too. When I arrived they launched themselves on me. With menace in every gesture, they accused me of failing the Ulster people, surrendering to terrorism and denying the right of the majority to self-rule. If Fred, my police protection officer, had not been with me, I would have been seriously beaten. Inside the grounds of the school stood one young and rather scared-looking RUC constable. The position in some nationalist areas was just as sour and intimidating. The RUC did not appear, on that day, to see that the proper policing of elections was part of their duties.

Late in the evening, about half an hour before the booths closed, I visited a remote country polling station. There was a single Ulster Unionist 'teller' who as I approached bolted out of the polling station into which he should never have gone. I stayed chatting for some minutes and no one came to vote although when the votes were counted, apparently the turn-out for that ward approached 100 per cent. During that last half-hour I suspect the voting slips of non-voters were being torn out, stamped, crossed and stuffed into the ballot boxes. I had nearly burst in on one of Northern Ireland's oldest political swindles. Both sides do it and the law stands aside. It is impossible to estimate the degree of electoral fraud, but it is substantial and in some areas very substantial. That such an abuse continues election after election in our democracy is a monstrous affront. One of the main reasons that vote rigging goes unchallenged is because neither of the main British political parties have organised in Northern Ireland and so they are unaware of its proliferation. Senior Northern Ireland civil servants are rightly outside politics. In the areas in which they and their families live, electoral fraud is unlikely to be a problem because political sectarianism is minimal. Most British-born staff in the NIO are as ignorant of its widespread use as their ministers. Until the government organises a concerted campaign to stamp out intimidation and impersonation in elections, a black cloud will hang over our reputation for freedom and damage our democratic credentials.

If there was one benefit to ministers from the arrival of Northern Ireland's Conservatives it was to force us out of the ivory tower at Stormont and confront us with the nasty realities of politics on the streets of a divided community. There was little else positive to say about the development of the party. We won a few seats in local councils and we established associations of a few members in most constituencies, but Kennedy's puritanical determination to promote integration left us bickering and divided. It was a minor foretaste of what was to happen later nationally over Europe. There were some very good and sensible people who joined us and believed that our economic and social policies should have been encouraged and supported, but they soon became disillusioned with the endless constitutional controversy and faded away. It was not a happy story and so far it has not had a happy ending.

29
SECURITY AND ESCORTS

DURING MY TIME IN NORTHERN IRELAND I was a category 'B' risk. This involved blanket protection while I was in the province and a nonsensical mixture of some and none when I was on the mainland. Though I represented Wiltshire, I lived in Gloucestershire. To the chiefs of the Gloucestershire police I must have been a little-known and unnecessary additional burden on their limited resources. The Royals, who lived in abundance in the county, were protected by the Metropolitan Police. Gloucestershire had to provide me with a level of cover which required armed officers to be on hand in fast response. They had to have dogs regularly search our grounds for explosives and they had to justify the costs to the local Watch Committee as the crime wave in the county rose. When I infrequently attended a function on their patch, which was generally at a weekend, the armed officers had to accompany me at the appropriate rates of over-time pay.

We also had to work out complicated codes to ensure that if our alarm was activated, the police could differentiate between a false call and the real thing. The alarm company, approved by the Home Office, seemed to be forever changing ownership and name, and as a consequence so did their protocols. At one time the system was devised such that the original call was answered in Cardiff from where it was trans-ferred to Birmingham who then contacted Cheltenham police

257

headquarters who rang Cirencester police station who told the local area bobby who once told me that if he really believed that the call involved the IRA his bike would be pointing in the other direction. Pilcher (not his real name) always called on a Sunday morning at around noon to see if all was well. On one occasion when he knocked I answered, 'Who is there?' 'Pilcher,' he replied. 'How do I know you are Pilcher?' I asked. 'You might be the IRA.' 'Don't play daft buggers with me,' he said. Perhaps it was fortunate that the IRA never came to call.

It was inevitable that with changes of police personnel some of the agreed procedures would occasionally break down. Being locked behind electrically operated, fortress-style gates also had the occasional disadvantage. After one incident when we had a dangerous fire on our top floor, the power cut out. This meant the gates could not be opened until, fumbling about in panic in the dark, my wife found the key to let the firemen through with their hoses.

The reality is that in an open and free society it remains difficult to protect public figures for most of the time within a sensible budget and without using up too much police resources. Nor do I think that many county police officers, expert though they are at picking up over-the-limit drivers on Christmas Eve, have the experience to counter a real terrorist threat should it unexpectedly confront them. On one occasion a local inspector came to tell me that the Home Office had demanded closer co-ordination between the local police forces in combating terrorism. He asked me whether I could give him the names of any prominent local personalities who had Irish connections which he, an ordinary policeman, would be unaware of. I asked him whether he knew of Sir Crispin Tickell, recently our ambassador at the UN, now a master of an Oxford college, one of the world's leading experts on the environment, a confidant of Mrs Thatcher and a Dublin landlord. The inspector looked incredulous. 'What does this man do?' he asked. I repeated Crispin's shortened CV. 'Excuse me,' said the inspector, 'how can Mr Tickell do all this and run a pub in Dublin?'

In Wiltshire the position was different. I was a well-known local figure. Should anything have happened to me, there would have been a massive public reaction and the chief constable's job would have been very much on the line. I was given every assistance possible and the Wiltshire Special Branch became close and personal friends. However, their writ ran no further than the county border, a position which was probably not appreciated by the terrorists. The result was that after a widely publicised weekly advice centre in my constituency I would drive back home with a police escort which would peel off just before I reached home. After several weeks I pointed out that any sensible terrorist would wait for me to park in the unlit garage which was sixty or so yards from the house and then shoot me as I locked up. No one would hear and no one would be the wiser. Following high-level discussions, permission was given for me to be covered by Wiltshire policemen until I reached the front door.

The system of county police forces in England made the fight against terrorism more difficult. Collaboration between forces was often poor, procedures were frequently different, equipment was not always compatible, objectives not always the same. In Wiltshire, too, there were lighter moments. I once was invited by the bishop of Bristol to a village church 'wine and cheese' buffet only to find him grim-faced on my arrival. Apparently the sniffer dog had cocked his leg repeatedly against the trestle tables, snuffling at the sandwiches rather than sniffing out the explosives.

There were disturbing times. When Alistair McAlpine, a former Conservative Party Treasurer, had his house blown up, we were told that all openings into our home should be closed and bolted. We had a cat-flap in the washroom under our daughter's bedroom. It was the most likely place for the IRA to insert a bomb and it was only a few feet from our fuel tank. To move the cat-flap elsewhere was for a variety of reasons virtually impossible. In any event the advice was to block it up. Should we get rid of my daughter's cats or explain why she could no longer sleep in her beloved bedroom? On another occasion the IRA turned to shooting targets through their kitchen windows. Our kitchen was alongside the village road and easily accessible. Should we stop eating in the kitchen or draw the curtains in the summer months long before twilight? When Ian Gow was murdered in his car, we all wondered which of us would be next. I knew that our private addresses had been found on several captured IRA terrorists. It was likely that I was a secondary target, as Ian had been. They would come for me if they found their route to their prime target blocked. This had already nearly happened with Tom King, who lived only a few miles away, when two terrorists had been caught on his land by his daughter. After they were searched, one of them was found to have our address concealed on him (or rather in him).

The key was to be careful and sensible, to vary the times and routes to and fro (which was not always easy or practicable), and to remember the advice of the Home Office security adviser. With a little care, he confided, we had as much likelihood of being assassinated as of being run over. I do not think any of us under threat worried much, if at all, about ourselves, but we had to worry about what we were doing to our families, and our families worried deeply about us.

My RUC escorts came in every shape and size, most were in their thirties to mid-forties and with one or two exceptions they were Protestant. Their backgrounds were as varied as their physiques, although many sprang from the ranks of Ulster's small farmers and businessmen. They were articulate, intelligent, well informed, balanced and fun. Almost all became family friends, as a minister and his family spent more time with his escorts than with any other of his team except the private secretary. The vast majority had, I suspect, drifted into the RUC because of the lack of other job opportunities. Ulster's economy had become dominated by the public sector and the 30 per cent remaining in private hands could not provide the very considerable income package that the escorts could earn in pay and overtime with the RUC.

The job must have been excruciatingly boring. Sitting around in the outer office waiting for the minister to appear, reconnoitring his visits, occasionally arguing with the private secretary about what was acceptable and what was not, trying to keep fit while following an inevitably sedentary life and being forced to follow petty rules and regulations that are the hallmark of any police force. One of the ridiculous rules was that as soon as a minister and his men had established a rapport they would be moved on in case familiarity bred contempt. For some reason this did not apply to the chief constable. Anywhere else in the country the majority would have made superintendent or chief inspector. In Northern Ireland the very best of them could expect to become a sergeant.

Their job was neatly summarised by one of my first protectors who laconically remarked, 'I am the man who shoots the man who shoots you.' This piece of honesty frightened me at first until I realised the subtlety of its deterrence. At times we all found ourselves in comical if sometimes scary circumstances, particularly when confronted by 'Ulster Says No' protesters. The escorts were armed and trained to deal with terrorists – not demonstrators threatening their charges with

Union Jacks and verbal assault. I never doubted that in the final instance they would have put their lives before mine. Thank goodness none of us ever needed to find out.

30
'MINISTER OF THE ECONOMY'

B Y THE END OF THE SUMMER OF 1989 I had been Environment
Minister and Health Minister for almost four years and Tom
King had become the longest-serving Secretary of State for
Northern Ireland. Peter Viggers had struggled with the Department of
Economic Development for three years, while Brian Mawhinney
continued to develop his political contacts. The papers had incessantly
debated for months about who would be reshuffled where. The uncer-
tainty was doing nothing for good government.

There had been a series of minor shuffles since my arrival in Northern
Ireland. Rhodes Boyson (Chris Patten's 'Colossus of Rhodes') had left
in 1986. His appointment to the NIO was an aberration. Rhodes was a
mainland political animal. He had been an inventive if sometimes dog-
matic Minister of Education in London. He lived for the party and for
parliament – he enjoyed the House of Commons and he was effective in
debate. Sending him to Northern Ireland was like consigning a fish to
an oxygen-less backwater. It was unfair on him and unfair on Northern
Ireland. Nick Scott had also left, sidelined to Social Security. His
replacement, John Stanley, had also been and gone, stopping in Ulster
barely a year before being replaced by Ian Stewart.

John had been the Prime Minister's parliamentary private secretary in
opposition. He had been minister of state in charge of council house
sales under Michael Heseltine and had moved with Heseltine to

Defence, where he had been wounded in the Ponting affair. He came to Northern Ireland, many believed, as the last step to an honourable ministerial exit. He aroused strong emotions among both his colleagues and his civil servants. I have never understood why. There were all manner of apocryphal stories about him which I found hard to accept and even harder to verify. One which came via the escorts claimed that John had all the roads cleared and the junctions manned so that he could reach Aldergrove Airport without having to pull up for fear that a sniper might shoot him through his bulletproof windows. This, some claimed, put the lives of the RUC officers who manned the crossroads at a greater risk than his own and on one occasion kept the Secretary of State held up for ten minutes at a traffic light waiting for Stanley to pass. I did not believe a word of it. There were, however, too many stories of one sort or another not to come to the conclusion that on matters of personal security he must have had one tiny screw insufficiently tightened. I always found him open, honest and informative. Over the years we have become close friends on the Anglo-Korean Forum for the Future. The man I know has nothing in common with the abusive anecdotes that seem so unfairly to have dogged him.

The life of a parliamentary under-secretary is rarely much more than four or five years. After that it is up or out. For Peter Viggers it was unfortunately out. I had hopes of going up. So, no doubt, had Brian Mawhinney, although as I had served longer I believe my credentials (leaving aside our respective records) slightly favoured me. The reshuffle of '89 was being written up as a 'big one', so I had to make a big push. The problem was how. As I had been out of Westminster for four years I had had little or no chance to shine at the Dispatch Box or to make my mark in Cabinet subcommittees. I would have to rely on Tom King's reports to the whips and on those other friends I had in high places.

During the seven years that I held a government post under Margaret Thatcher there were only two occasions when I was summoned in attendance. The first was a general meeting of all parliamentary private secretaries in the Downing Street whip's office. Everyone fell over themselves to be ever more sycophantic in an often vain effort to impress on the Prime Minister, within the thirty seconds allotted, why they possessed more shining talents than their colleagues. The whips stood around the back of the room making mental notes and smirking.

The second happening was an invitation to lunch at No. 10 in early 1988 when I had been two and a bit years a minister. There were eight of us. The Prime Minister, Lord Young of Graffham (then Secretary of State for Trade and Industry), Willie Whitelaw who had come for the lunch, Ian Stewart (minister of state at the Ministry of Defence), Colin Moynihan (Minister of Sport), Edwina Currie (junior Health Minister), Ian Grist from the Welsh Office and me.

The PM immediately started to savage Ian Stewart. 'What are you doing to tighten up spending in the Defence Department?' she demanded. 'There are many too many top brass; endless duplication, no understanding of value for money, waste everywhere. You have to get a grip and quickly.' Poor Ian had only been in the post a few months and a few months later he was moved on to take over from John Stanley in Northern Ireland. His attempts at explanation were cut off in mid-sentence and after a miserable quarter of an hour, the guns turned on Edwina. The Prime Minister had long had her eye on the NHS. 'It needs a thorough-going overhaul. Doctors, like lawyers, are one of the last group of closed-shop professionals who always complain whenever radical changes need introducing. Some nurses are, if anything, worse. Their organisation has become infiltrated by militants who are undermining nursing values and turning them into whingeing trade unionists.' Edwina was made of stern stuff and fought her corner. She supported the government's reforms but she pointed out the political pitfalls of introducing a market philosophy into health care. 'They will have to learn like everyone else that no one owes them a living. If doctors and nurses do not perform, patients should have the chance to go somewhere else,' declared the Prime Minister.

She then turned on little Colin Moynihan, former Olympic rowing cox. 'Why do we need a Minister of Sport?' she demanded. 'To deal with drugs,' he replied. This nonplussed her. 'Explain,' she rasped. 'Well, as you know Prime Minister, drugs are endemic in sport. When there are governing bodies which need government money or subsidy we can insist on internal rules and procedures that can eliminate drug taking. We are being successful, particularly in sports such as athletics, but the biggest problem is snooker.' 'Snooker?' she asked incredulously. 'That dreadful game where everyone smokes and drinks and which Denis watches late at night in the flat? What drugs do they take?' 'Beta-blockers, Prime Minister!' 'What are they?' 'They are designed to control blood pressure but they also slow down the heartbeat so the snooker player does not jerk as he plays his shot, Prime Minister, and they are a widely abused drug amongst senior players.' 'I've never heard of them,' she reflected. 'Then none of us round this table would ever have any need of them, would we, Willie?' Willie blinked and as he pushed his little pillbox under his napkin, boomed out: 'Certainly not, Prime Minister!'

The first and only rule about reshuffles is that it is every man for himself. It helps to have a champion but he will only consider your position after he has secured his own and when he is seeking allies for future battles with his rivals that can raise him another rung on the ladder. Tom King was understandably concerned with his move from Ulster to Defence. Tristan Garel-Jones's influence in the whip's office could have helped but he did not, and my other friends had their own careers to further. Only Ken Baker put in a strong word on my behalf, or so he claimed.

One of the greatest disappointments in politics is to be passed over by those who are less than your equals. It is hard enough to be left behind by those you rate as your peers. In the 1989 reshuffle both the former and latter seemed to conspire. I heard later from the journalist Bruce Anderson that Charles Powell, the Prime Minister's private secretary, had told him that Tom King had given me some 'Betas' among the 'Alphas'. Whether or not this was true, I suspect that when my name appeared before the Prime Minister she would have found sufficient reason for marking me down without recourse to others. Fortunately the reshuffle turned out to be to my long-term advantage. With Peter Viggers gone, what I really wanted was to become Minster of Economic Development as well as Minister of the Environment. This would give me control over all the major levers that orchestrated the Northern Ireland economy. I would be in charge of housing, planning, local government, urban renewal, transport, energy, employment, trade and industry. I would be in a position to do what I had always dreamed of, to write an all-embracing strategy for the regeneration of Ulster's economy.

Tom King had been asked by Peter Brooke to come over to introduce his key officials. As the junior ministerial portfolios were in the hands of the Secretary of State, it would be Peter's decision whether my ambitions suited his intentions. Tom already knew of my wishes.

The two departments had never been put together before under one minister. The Northern Ireland civil service claimed the burden and diversity would be too heavy for a single minister and certainly the importance of the position would have merited minister of state status under any other regime. For some reason I received a very ambivalent reply from Sir Kenneth Bloomfield to my private lobbying. The Industrial Development Board had been his creation, and I think he worried that my intervening, questioning and direct style of ministering would rub up against the IDB's philosophy of holding itself at arm's length from government while being lightly supervised by a part-time board of the great and the good. He was, of course, right in his assumption, for I had seen from the nearby DOE that much more might be done with the IDB. Tom was resolute in his support and Peter took Tom's advice. Lord Skelmersdale took over from me at the DHSS. I asked Gerry Loughran what I should call my new and unique position. 'Minister of the Economy,' he responded. 'But I have nothing to do with finance,' I ventured. 'That's irrelevant, just do it,' he said. So I did.

The permanent secretary at the Department of Economic Development was David Fell, later head of the Northern Ireland civil service. Most of his previous three years had been taken up with the privatisation of Short Brothers and Harland and Wolff and the preparation of fair employment legislation. David Fell ran like a smooth Mercedes saloon and Peter Viggers often appeared content to be driven around with an occasional touch on the wheel. I wanted to drive the vehicle myself in new and different directions and at breakneck speed. David Fell was not to find me easy.

David was a copybook model of what the Civil Service Staff College is most designed to promote: a concise drafter, a clear mind, capable of an almost inexhaustible supply of both alternative strategies and alternative tactics, a gregarious mixer and able to devour, seemingly tirelessly, a mountain of work. If he had any personal views of his own, which I am sure he did, he kept them to himself. He could assimilate the daftest political commitment from his ministerial masters and regurgitate a perfectly logical and presentable plan. David was capable, as are the best of civil servants, of moving from one position to another depending on his last set of instructions. He always pointed out the pitfalls of any particular course of action but he never proffered an individual preference.

This sometimes put us at odds. I liked my civil servants to be protagonists, advocates and supporters of my proposals both professionally and individually. I wanted their commitment to what I was doing. This may be an entirely unreasonable constitutional demand from a minister, but I found it hard to work with someone who for the most professional of causes would, in my judgement, have supported the exact opposite of what I was advocating had a new minister or a new government so suggested.

AT LAST THE TIDE COMES IN

In the late eighties Northern Ireland's gross domestic product was over £8,000 million, and of this public expenditure accounted for some 65 per cent – the reverse of the position on the mainland. Much of the linen and engineering industries, which once formed the base of Ulster's industrial revolution, had long since deceased. Brian Faulkner's impressive success in replacing them with inward investment, particularly from the new man-made fibre divisions of the chemical and textile giants, had created a stopgap. But they also had closed in the seventies, and in the harsher climate created by the Troubles it had become harder still to find replacements. Indigenous industry was small and often lacked international competitiveness. Surveys carried out by the Northern Ireland Economic Research Centre showed that companies made poor use of their capital, employed very few graduates, paid insufficient attention to training and lacked core skills in marketing and design. It was inevitable that many of the brightest and best sought careers either in Great Britain or as part of the American Irish diaspora, or alternatively sought security and opportunity at home in the public service.

The government's response to these deep-seated weaknesses had been to establish parastatal organisations to subsidise investment and training and to encourage inward investment. The Local Enterprise Development Unit looked after small companies; every company was allocated an official civil service case officer. The IDB was responsible for larger businesses and promoted Northern Ireland overseas. The Training and Employment Agency ran a myriad of schemes designed to cover every need. All three were supervised by advisory boards which were properly balanced between men and women, Catholics and Protestants.

The banks were conservative and careful. They could afford to be. Whatever money was needed was abundantly provided from the government's coffers. The consequence was that capable civil servants played at being businessmen without having the experience of being in business. Businessmen had little incentive to employ their capital to maximum effect because much of the money came free. Too many were content to survive on the existing customer base and leave themselves sufficient time for their hobbies. The quality of life for many Northern Ireland executives was superb.

This was not the situation the workless were in, in 1988. Male unemployment was running at about twice the rate in Great Britain. Long-term unemployment accounted for a significantly larger proportion of the unemployed than in Great Britain and was concentrated more in Catholic than in Protestant communities. Many found themselves in a multiple bind. They had low levels of educational attainment (grammar schools were wonderful for the 35 per cent, secondary schools were not so wonderful for the remainder), they often lived on estates dominated by paramilitaries and as a consequence they could rarely find work. When they did, it was often temporary and the poverty trap denied any incentive to take it. Northern Ireland had the highest birth rate in the European Community. The only way out for many was migration. As earnings were generally 15 per cent higher in Great Britain, there was every reason to go, but lack of skills, housing cost differentials, and an insufficient supply of rented accommodation on the mainland all acted as brakes. Nevertheless without migration unemployment rates might have been twice their existing levels.

The Northern Ireland economy, against this background, had shown considerable resilience. The percentage of the population in employment had risen over thirty years to the average in Great Britain. GDP had risen at 3 per cent per year between 1981 and 1988, nearly double the norm in Great Britain. Public expenditure had increased by only 1.4 per cent per year over the same period. The private sector was therefore considerably more robust than many supposed. But in order to reduce migration the economy had to expand by some 5–6 per cent per year to absorb the ever-increasing influx of young people onto the labour market. This required an annual growth rate of at least 10 per cent from private sector companies. If Northern Ireland was to come to grips with unemployment, we would need to match the former output levels of Asian Tigers over a similarly sustained period. The strategy that governments had pursued up to then had been only partially successful. Assistance was based on the begging bowl, which was counterproductive. As many as 40 per cent of the jobs created and 50 per cent of the capital subsidised through grant or interest-free loans would have occurred anyway without public support. Failure and inertia were rewarded while success was ignored. Dead-weight and displacement were often the name of the game. Many of the jobs vociferously announced by LEDU and IDB executives in the end never materialised.

As the NIO could do nothing to influence UK fiscal policy, I saw my new job as making a greater success out of the successes we had rather than propping up failure. What was required was a strategy not to pick winners but to back them, and in backing them to make them tougher and leaner. We should give help where it was really needed rather than subsidising the inefficient and substituting the financial risk of the banks. Much if not all of this would have been anathema to the free marketeers who under Thatcherism had dominated the Treasury and decimated the Department of Trade and Industry. Since very few ministers or their officials had hands-on industrial and commercial knowledge, many could not differentiate between the complexities of market failure or corporate inefficiency. To them it was all the same. Discard what you have if it cannot compete, and when markets clear something will turn up. In Northern Ireland no one could tell me what that 'something' might be. I suspected the most likely beneficiaries would be the pockets of terrorist godfathers.

Had I been a mainland minister, Margaret Thatcher would never have let me near an economic portfolio, but Northern Ireland's economy did not much feature on her television screen. Ulster's entire industrial base employed about the same number of people as British Aerospace and the turnover was broadly similar. British Aerospace had to put a three-to-five-year strategic plan before its board and its shareholders. I was determined to introduce strategic planning through analysing our strengths, our weaknesses, our opportunities and the threats that confronted us in exactly the same way as any large corporation would do in plotting its future.

After some hesitation from Peter Brooke, who was worried that the Prime Minister might find my ideas somewhat un-Thatcherite, we published a report, *Northern Ireland Competing in the 1990s: The Key to Growth*. The Secretary of State endorsed all my plans. The Northern Ireland Economic Research Centre, the main independent and respected Northern Ireland think-tank, did not. The centre was headed up by Graham Gudgin, a tall, gangly, gloomy man whose outlook was dominated by the thunderclouds surrounding Ulster and who viewed a silver lining only as a prelude to more lightning. He forecast a continuing decline in manufacturing employment between 1990 and 1995. While he accepted there would be some increase in total employment because of the involvement of unregistered women moving into low-paid service jobs, he predicted that unemployment would remain stubbornly over 14 per cent, rising to nearly 20 per cent by the middle of the decade. He was, I am delightedly able to point out, spectacularly wrong.

For the first time in living memory, Northern Ireland's economy, instead of entering the recession first and recovering last, did the exact opposite. A glum official had told me on arrival that we were like the pebble furthest up the beach – the last to be covered by the incoming tide and the first to be stranded. Unemployment did rise but not as fast as other areas of the UK, partly due to the stability provided by public-sector employment but also because of the resilience and growing self-confidence of the private sector which was being boosted by massive increases in private investment, not least in Belfast and Londonderry. I had to be blunt to Northern Ireland's businesses about their management failings but I also had to encourage and cajole them. My job was to persuade anyone who would listen that Northern Ireland was the place to be in the early nineties. I fervently believed it was.

The keys to driving local and international competitiveness lay in the IDB, LEDU, the Training and Employment Agency and in the DOE's economic regeneration initiatives. I was already well down the line with the DOE programmes, so in September 1989 I decided to set about the IDB.

31

THE IDB

THE INDUSTRIAL DEVELOPMENT BOARD had two main divisions: one attempted to attract inward investment by offering generous grants, the other sponsored indigenous business, also through subsidy. In 1988/89 its budget was £126 million. The IDB's view of itself was encapsulated in an event within days of my arrival.

There was to be an announcement of a Hong Kong company taking over a deserted textile factory to manufacture electrical appliances, thereby protecting a hundred or so jobs. Frank Hewitt, the deputy chief executive in charge of inward investment, wrote my speech, which naturally gave his division all the credit, and handled the press conference as if he were the minister and I were his civil servant. 'The IDB are separate from the rest of government. It sees itself as being autonomous and independent. We are a different bunch from other civil servants. Businessmen with civil service briefcases, cut free from government red tape, reliant only on our Treasury colleagues for our budget,' Frank grandly informed me.

There followed two months of trench warfare as I tried to impose my presence on the IDB and the IDB resisted. I asked for an office in IDB House – request turned down. I wanted to change some members of the board — that was none of my business, I was told. I suggested that we should use politicians such as John Hume and Ken Maginnis and other MPs who volunteered to come along on IDB inward-investment missions. The IDB did not want to use politicians as they might reflect a particular community bias, I was stuffily informed.

As the rows grew, so did the ripples. The chairman, Sir Eric McDowell, even intimated that one of the staff had gone sick following an intimidating encounter with me. Finally the two permanent secretaries, Sir Kenneth Bloomfield and Sir John Blelloch, formed up to the Secretary of State and told him I should be called to order. Peter Brooke invited me into his Stormont Castle office for sandwiches and hock. I explained that if I could not get to grips with the IDB, my plans for an integrated strategy to make Ulster business competitive in the nineties would fall at the first hurdle. The Secretary of State was in a bind – he was new, I had been in post for four years, he did not want to have a row with me but even less did he want a row with his two top civil servants. He suggested gently that I might amend my style while pursuing my objectives.

What I needed was a success. Fortunately for me, one was not far away. North America, Asia and Europe, in that order, were the IDB's priority markets. In the US we had offices in New York, Chicago, Boston and San Francisco. I was asked to do a tour of the first three, one of the highlights of which was to sit at the top table at the annual dinner in Chicago of the Ireland Funds, a private-sector foundation set up in the seventies by Tony O'Reilly to provide assistance to Ireland. O'Reilly graciously gave permission that I could say a few words – a very few words, it was made clear, as the great man had plenty to say on his own account. The mayor of Chicago, Richard Daley, was also scheduled to attend at some stage.

I had a friend in Chicago, Dick Heise. His wife, Clare, was a Fogarty from County Roscommon and her brother had been one of the main republican fundraisers in the Midwest. This had caused considerable family tension. Clare was a touch wary when we first met and gave the British Colonial Ministerial Master quite a torrid time. I decided to stay with them during my visit rather than with Ray Mingay, the British consul general. Up to a few months previously the IDB representatives had worked as extensions of the Foreign Office, often out of British consular accommodation. The British connection was a very definite drawback in trying to persuade Irish-American businessmen to invest in the North, and Irish-American business was bound to be our most fruitful opportunity. When the split occurred and the IDB separated there was some minor friction, but as the Foreign Office posts had to deal with Scotland, Wales and the English regions, they were not too sad to see the back of us.

Dick Heise was one of the most successful property developers in America and he had rubbed up against those in Chicago who were big shots in the City Hall. Dick was involved in trying to promote young entrepreneurs in the worst ghettos and his son had become active in voluntary organisations supporting community schemes amongst the most deprived sections of Chicagoans. They therefore were interested in the work I was doing in Belfast and I was keen to see what I could learn from them. One of the sponsors of these programmes was the alderman of the First Ward in Chicago – Alderman Fred Roti, son of Bruno 'The Bomber' Roti.

When Ray Mingay learnt that I intended to undertake a tour with Fred as my guide, he advised strongly against it and sent me a *Chicago Tribune* article by Mike Royko which contained some allegations about Roti's notorious accomplices. In spite of the article Dick was insistent, so off we went in a blackened, stretch Cadillac around the roughest parts of town with the alderman giving me a potted history of Chicago's problems which had more to do with his view on racial failings than with the liberal philosophy that I had believed was a touchstone of American Democrats.

We ended the evening watching a football game in an Italian restaurant. Plaintiffs seeking favours sidled up to the alderman who held court at his accustomed table only to find themselves waved away as he was in deep discussion with a 'Limey' minister from Northern Ireland. Fred was an engaging rogue but time was ebbing fast, as a few months later he was to find himself behind bars on an extensive list of indictments which even his contacts could not conceal. At the end of our meal a waitress rushed round and dropped the bill in front of Fred, who looked amazed. The waitress grabbed it back, blurting her apologies. 'I'm so sorry, Mr Roti, of course, you never pay!' Dick, who has an engaging stutter, is six foot two and looks like Cary Grant, drawled: 'Come to think of it, Fred, I don't believe, I've – I've ever seen you pay for anything in Chicago!'

There was much to be learnt on how companies in Chicago had banded together to give practical management and financial support to young blacks and Hispanics trying to set up their own businesses. Most had found it nearly impossible to break into the exclusive world of American commerce. I learnt some important lessons which we could apply through our Business in the Community programme in Belfast and which proved yet again that Northern Ireland's problems were in most ways no different from those in many other places around the world.

The following night was the Ireland Fund's ball. I was nervous. There gathered together was the cream of the Irish community in the Midwest, mostly big, red-faced men brimming with dollars and self-confidence and supported by many a face-lifted, dazzling consort with necklaces that certainly were not paste.

I escorted Clare Heise as Dick was elsewhere. At our table was Bill Farley, one of the most charismatic of Chicago's successes, a potential Presidential candidate, and a master of junk bonds. He was owner of Fruit of the Loom, the world's largest manufacturer of T-shirts and sweatshirts, and his company employed thousands in Donegal but none in Londonderry. There also was the Irish ambassador, who knew everyone and whose main role, as with all Irish ambassadors, was to promote the interests of the Republic amongst Irish-Americans. This promotion did not run to giving any favours to that part of the island that remained under British jurisdiction.

Across the dining area hung an enormous screen. Half-way through the main course, silence was called for. The audience was introduced to a fifteen-minute film eulogising Mayor Daley on his recent summer tour of the South of Ireland. I found the film extravagant and patronising. I tore up my speech and decided to go for broke. The mayor was embraced by his audience as if he had just carried the Democratic Presidential nomination. He gave a short, rather lacklustre address on his time in the Old Country and departed for his next engagement. I was next. The only applause I was aware of following Tony O'Reilly's introduction was from the British consul general's table.

I told them that, despite my accent or my aristocratic pedigree, I was Irish – Anglo-Irish. We may once have been English and conquered Ireland but many of us had remained. We were the builders of Georgian Dublin and the founders of Ireland's magnificent eighteenth-century inheritance. We were and remain one of the three strands of Irishness. The third strand, the Scots-Irish, had produced more American Presidents than the Irish-Irish. We had produced finer field marshals for the British army than the English. We had fought for an Irish parliament, and if Benjamin Franklin and the marquis of Downshire had not fallen out over the port, we could well have joined with the American revolutionaries against England's German king. The impositions and tariffs that so infuriated the American settlers were as onerous and as damaging to the Anglo-Irish. They too were as Irish as the Irish-Irish. Yet to listen to Irish-Americans, an Anglo-Irishman such as myself would have difficulty in discovering that we existed except as lackeys of British colonialism.

I explained that all Irishmen had one thing in common: when England played anyone else, we all shouted for anyone else. Some in the audience laughed, but not many. I told them that the Prime Minister had sent me to Ireland as Australia was no longer an option. A few more laughed. Then I went for them. They were rich and they were successful. They were the descendants of the best that had left Ireland, for it was common currency that the weak, the old and the foolish had remained behind. They could dress up once a year, enjoy themselves at a grand dinner and watch films of their mayor dancing a jig with a comic figure outside a bothy playing a tin whistle and wearing a duncher. All their prejudices about Ireland would be confirmed and they could put their hands in their wallets to support their simple cousins who had stayed home because they were too timid to find their fortunes in America.

There was an Irish sport common to all traditions, I informed them – horse-racing. Everyone knew that you could not breed a thoroughbred from a mule. How was it, then, if the best left Ireland generation after generation, that those that remained continued to breed winners? It was not, I announced, the best that left: it was the best that stayed. They had not run away. Ireland's population had declined from eight million souls in 1840, when Great Britain's was sixteen million, to five million by the end of the 1980s, when Great Britain's was more than fifty million. We that remained behind wanted to stay behind. We had no wish to go anywhere else. Evelyn Waugh once asked Cyril Connolly the reality of Irish migration and he responded, 'Hell and the United States.' We needed no charity or condescending hand-outs from faraway cousins. If America wanted to help us, they could do so by understanding all elements of Irishness, by investing in us and becoming partners with us so that we could find answers to our divisions through economic success and social conciliation. Their aim should not be to make easy judgements from afar, to wash their consciences with a few easy dollars and the odd round of golf. We wanted their commitment to a cause. The cause was that no young man or woman should ever again have to leave the shores of Ireland through economic or social or political necessity. Our ambition was to build an Ireland at peace with its different traditions, glorying in the breadth of its cultural diversity. Then I stopped. Silence, then a clap, then a thunder, and I received a reception that only American generosity can deliver. I returned to my table and as I sat down Bill Farley leaned over and whispered: 'I will build you a factory in Derry.' I had my winner.

In substance, the truth was more complex. Farley had taken over the Fruit of the Loom on the back of junk bonds, a high-interest-bearing instrument that highly geared American companies used to raise money on the market. As interest rates had climbed, so had his debts. To succeed he had to expand, and to grow he had to find other people's money, either free of interest or preferably through grants. Northern Ireland offered him an escape route, as did the Republic. He had already bought out the Irish factories of the McCarters. With us in the frame, he could play one development authority off against another. He could use transfer pricing to minimise his tax liabilities in the South. We had a pool of cheap, English-speaking labour. Why had the IDB not found a way to him before?

Bill Farley told me to contact John Holland, his chief executive, when he next came through London and then to meet up with Willie McCarter, who, with his brother Andy, still ran the Fruit of the Loom factories in Donegal. I tried to persuade Willie to locate one of the plants in Warrenpoint or Newry and we spent a day seeking out sites. Although the IDB was tasked with providing industrial land and industrial units, to my surprise there was nothing immediately available to meet Fruit of the Loom's requirements. The concerns of the planners and the rights given to objectors under our planning legislation remain a disgraceful block on employment opportunities even in neighbourhoods blighted by unemployment. Willie McCarter and John Holland wanted their capital-intensive spinning mill near their cut, make and trim facilities in Buncrana. As the capital grant was very high, the IDB insisted that, to bring the cost per job within Treasury guidelines, Fruit of the Loom also sign up for a stitching unit. Both units were built in Derry.

Eighteen months later, when the works was due to open, Farley flew over and we all paraded in our Fruit of the Loom T-shirts. The L sizes which were served up for John Hume and me barely fitted the bill, and as we stood waiting for the press photographs Bill Farley's personal assistant whispered to Norma Sinclair, my private secretary, 'You've got to do something about the Minister's nose!' Norma looked startled. It was true that it was cold and my nose is large and red, but she had never been told before to do anything about it. 'Here,' he said, 'I always carry make-up for Bill. Put some of this on it.' She gingerly dabbed the great man's potion on my shining snout. Unfortunately for me, Bill Farley spent a considerable time in Florida and was heavily sun-tanned, so his creams were coloured accordingly. That night to the delight of all, I appeared on television with a large brown nose in place of my usual red one.

There were some lessons to be grasped from my American trip. Before arriving in the Midwest, I had stayed several nights with Philip Maclean, the British consul general in Boston. The city is one of the most sensitive Foreign Office postings. There the Irish-American caucus is at its greenest and its most vociferous. The Kennedys' home town is dominated by Irish-American sentiment, and political success demands obeisance to the Irish mythology of British wickedness. Boston was strong on the MacBride Principles, a hub for Noraid fund-raising and ever-vigilant for examples of British heavy-handedness against the nationalist community in Northern Ireland. For years British officials had attempted to defend their positions, though often in patrician English accents that only further alienated the Bostonian Irish. In Boston, confronted by Mayor Raymond Flynn, his assistant Frank Costello and a hostile press, the consul general was forever reacting to rather than leading events. Philip was in many ways ideally suited to his role. He was tall, bearded, open-faced, gentle and apologetic. For much of the time, he appeared to blink like a startled rabbit confronted by an army of stoats. To begin with, he had me firmly in the stoat category.

I had been to Boston to promote Belfast and Derry before. There was so much that we could learn from men like Steven Coyle, who had revolutionised the run-down naval dockyards in exactly the way we visualised for the Lagan. The O'Connells had given tremendous backing to the Foyleside project. John Hume's contacts with the city politicians were matchless, and given a chance most wanted to be involved in making things work rather than carping and cavilling about British injustices.

The missing link was Irish-American business. Many half-heartedly supported the MacBride Principles because they could see no other role for themselves. John did not have a business background and had little pull with most of them. The IDB, who had for years worked out of the British consulate offices, behaved as if Northern Irish politicians were incapable of serving any purpose other than opposing the MacBride Principles and giving a general impression of being willing lackeys of British imperialism. The Hume-supported Derry Boston Ventures initiative had been John's way of side-stepping the IDB's flawed perspective, but his requests for money had fallen on heedless ears. I could see that the key was to build on the existing links by using Irish-America as the base for our inward-investment drive. For far too long, the Republic had had it all its own way, even with Irish-American investors who had originated in the North.

The IDB had a small squad of quite exceptional quality. Two of them, Frank Duffy in Boston and Declan O'Hare in New York, had impeccable credentials. But by the time I arrived in Boston, Frank had been told to leave as the IDB had written the place off as incorrigible. Frank and Philip had already been warned by Belfast about the appalling difficulties they were having in managing their new minister. Soon after I arrived I used a phrase to Frank during a friendly banter which Irish earls had used for centuries to those beneath them, only to discover later that Philip had complained in writing to the consul general in New York about my racist comments. I am Irish and proud of it. I was determined we were going to sell the North of Ireland as a team and the British were clearly a hindrance. We would now go off on our own and work to our agenda. After the success in Chicago, I knew it could be done.

In the spring of 1990 I flew to New York. Declan O'Hare took me to a breakfast with Bill Flynn, president of the Ireland–US Council for Commerce and Industry. Bill had courteously offered to pay for the breakfast but had not appreciated that this included the minister's team as well as the minister. Declan had already told me that since Bill's family had emigrated from around Kilkeel, his forebears may well have been evicted by the Needhams. Preferring attack to retreat, I told Flynn as he stared at the bill at the end of the meal that as his family had been in arrears with the rent for the last one hundred years, it was only right that he should pay up now. He now repeats that story with some decoration whenever I see him.

Next we called on Niall O'Dowd, publisher of the *Irish Voice*. Niall had the reputation of being greener than green but we found him to be eager to bring American investment to the North. We decided to sponsor his list of the top hundred Irish-American businessmen. Both Bill and Niall soon became supporters. Both have played significant roles in the peace process and both have become enthusiastic advocates of economic and social progress in the North.

The next step was to arrange a tour with John Hume. The IDB had now accepted that ministerial and political assistance might after all be of some service. We decided that we would concentrate on the east coast, ending up in Washington. A whirlwind expedition followed, arranged by Declan who had known John for years. Hume had previously made offers to share his contacts, but until my arrival the IDB had spurned them.

Our circuit, which we covered in the spring of 1990, was co-ordinated by Senator Christopher Dodd's office and took in United Technologies (who already had a large investment in Londonderry), GTE, Digital, Raytheon, Pittsburgh Glass, Westinghouse Defence and Loctite. We covered five cities in as many days. Pat Hume had brought John some new selling shoes, but by the fifth day on the stomp his feet had swelled up and the laces had been discarded. An attempt to comb his hair ended in disaster when the comb disappeared half-way across his scalp. His only irritating habit was to snaffle all the cookies while I was giving my presentation. We had a wonderful interval away from the relentless struggle of Ulster politics. The way we supported each other and gave different but complementary versions of the opportunities available to American companies wishing to invest in the European market impressed the vast majority of our listeners.

There was one exception. The British consulate had arranged for us to call on Ken Butterworth, chief executive officer of the Loctite Corporation. Mr Butterworth turned out to be an Australian. After thirty seconds of John's opening comments, he started to stare at the ceiling and twiddle his thumbs. The same routine was followed as soon as Declan began. Mr Butterworth was evidently no friend of Northern

Ireland. He displayed the same uninterested remoteness after half a minute of my dissertation. It was obvious that he was seeking to repay some favour (it must have been a pretty small one) which he owed the consul general. I told him I was sorry to have wasted his time, said we had plenty of other equally important companies to call on, collected up my papers and walked out. Two yards beyond his door a thought struck me. As I burst back into the room, I bumped into Declan and John who tried to push me back out in front of them. But before the door closed, I managed to shout how delighted I was that there was a real live Crocodile Dundee living in Stanford, Connecticut. There followed the second complaint about my behaviour to the consul general in New York.

In Washington I was very firmly on Hume's coat-tails. He had erected an impressive reputation for himself among leading Democrats. He was completely at home with Ted Kennedy, Nancy Soderberg, Tip O'Neill and those who would in a few years be at the very heart of the Clinton Administration. I gained the view that if the Democrats returned to the White House, they would follow John Hume's agenda, not the British government's.

British ambassadors to Washington are grand fellows who do not have much time for lowly parliamentary under-secretaries, although as Sir Anthony Ackland used to shoot with my father in Devon I did on one occasion get invited to tea. Hume had a much greater influence in Washington than any Northern Ireland Secretary of State. This led, I suspect, to some tensions with the NIO, who found it hard to get to grips with John's complex ways, his twists and turns, his compromises and inconsistencies. His base in Washington gave him both the confidence and the platform to pursue his multifaceted agenda. We were at one in our belief that social and economic resurgence was integral to reducing violence and constructing political solutions.

Although nothing concrete was to come out of our first marketing venture, the IDB staff were able to secure contacts that, left to their own devices, they would never have managed. We therefore were able to design a strategy that in time grew to include cross-Atlantic links between towns and cities: Derry–Boston, Newry–Pittsburgh, Tyrone–Kansas and Downpatrick–Chicago. We worked up regeneration initiatives which were founded on American prescriptions; that established between Father Myles Kavanagh in Belfast and Governor

Hugh Carey of New York State was but one example of several. The IDB started new programmes for promoting Northern Irish exports. The Derry Boston annual exhibition in the World Trade Centre led to over £40 million of orders for Northern Ireland companies. Waterside schemes, shopping malls and pedestrianisation of town centres owed as much to American as to British ideas.

The Northern Ireland Tourist Board became intertwined with a general promotion plan for boosting our image. Maebeth Fenton was the Tourist Board's wise and imaginative public affairs adviser in North America. She considered joining up with the IDB for a common Northern Ireland Centre, but partly because she was trying to work with the Southern Tourist Board, Bord Fáilte, and partly because of existing arrangements with the British Tourist Authority, the idea came to nought. The British Tourist Authority were hardly helpful. When I visited them in New York, the manager explained that there were no Northern Ireland holiday brochures on display because they did not want to frighten the visitors.

Only two small clouds appeared to darken our prospects. Brian Mawhinney, whose political responsibilities included canvassing American opinion, took it upon himself, supported by the NIO press office, to produce an expensive, pictorial glossy which was to portray Northern Ireland as it really was. No one could explain who this piece of pricey propaganda was aimed at. When published, it managed to alienate or outrage many who saw it. The Bostonian Irish complained that those parts that dealt with security were unsubtle efforts to excuse the excesses of the RUC and the army. Whatever the publication's intention, from an economic or tourist perspective the outcome would have been fewer investors and fewer tourists. We agreed in the IDB not to distribute it.

The second thorn was partly of the IDB's own making. Because the officials in Belfast claimed they were outside the NIO, outside politics and did not wish to be tainted with any of the unattractive aspects of life in the province, they left a vacuum that Dr Mawhinney and his political team could not be constrained from filling. He canvassed successfully, but in my view unnecessarily, for installing in the Washington embassy a Northern Ireland bureau. Two tip-top civil servants were sent out from Belfast to reach those parts of American life that the IDB, the Tourist Board and others could not reach.

As soon as the whizz-kids arrived, they found they were treated as *personae non gratae* by most of the embassy staff who felt the bureau was a slight on their professionalism. So having bought themselves identical cars, they proceeded north-eastwards where they sought out those investment opportunities the IDB could not find by asking for help from the staff of Derry Boston Ventures who were manning the Boston Ireland Festival. Thereafter they began compiling a register of names and addresses of all those influential Americans that any of us might know and who could be updated regularly on Northern Ireland affairs. I failed to comply with their directive. I am sure the bureau did no harm. I have seen little or no evidence that it did any good.

The bureau certainly cost money which might have been wiser spent elsewhere. Perhaps the Public Accounts Committee will find time to investigate their affairs with the same zeal that that august committee has shown in some of its more recent reports on Belfast.

My American tours reached their climax during the Gulf War in January 1991. Sunquest Vacations, a major Canadian tour operator run by Eddie Carroll, were holding their winter agents' conference in Toronto at which they were to launch their 1991 summer holiday programme. Every year thousands of tourists from Northern Ireland flock to Canada. There is a weekly jumbo from Aldergrove Airport. Numbers the other way were scarce to come by. This, the Northern Ireland Tourist Board hoped, Eddie Carroll would address, although Mr Carroll hoped the Tourist Board would pay for most of his advertising expenses. The conference attracted hundreds of delegates from all over Canada and the minister was to deliver a rousing keynote address on the attractions of Northern Ireland.

I had known before we left Heathrow that I might be called back as the Prime Minister was demanding a full turn-out for the debate which would commit the government to war in the Gulf. The message to return duly arrived as I was touring the Bombardier factory in Montreal. I was intent on calling on the company both because I wanted to find out how they were integrating Shorts – which they had bought in June 1989 – into their business and because I wished to see some kind of arrangement between Belfast City Airport and Aldergrove Airport which would keep both out of the clutches of the British Airports Authority and perhaps lead to Bombardier selling out. The intriguing aspect of the Shorts take-over was that Bombardier, a French-Canadian

Catholic company from the minority community in Canada, had assumed control over a Protestant company from the majority community in Northern Ireland. They had brought fresh ideas, fresh money (mainly taxpayers'), a new management style and hope where before there had been stifling bureaucracy and a measure of despair. They were as delighted with their acquisition as the workers were with their new owners. Productivity and profitability were leaping upwards. Bombardier was the best possible advertisement for foreign investors to come to Belfast. It also proved that east Belfast workers were perfectly content to work for Catholic masters, albeit French-Canadian ones.

From Montreal I flew back to Toronto, gave the keynote address and then flew on to London. I voted at 10 p.m. and caught the early-morning Concorde flight back to New York, which ministerial guidelines did not allow but British Airways upgraded me. From there I resumed my tour. We flew to Detroit for a night and an early morning meeting and then off to Houston. We had half a day in Houston and caught a plane to Kentucky. A day in Kentucky and then a private jet to Chicago. Twenty-four hours later, we were in Washington. Two days there and then back to London. A weekend catching up in the constituency and back to Heathrow, from where I flew to Munich. From there to Bonn. Back to London, then Belfast, then London, then Dublin for a meeting of the Anglo-Irish Intergovernmental Conference. I returned exhausted and a week later was in hospital with bleeding bowels. A barium enema and a colonoscopy found nothing wrong. So on I went.

The launch of the Sunquest holiday package was half a success. Attracting overseas visitors to Northern Ireland continued to be a laborious struggle. Canada was too small a market in troubled times, so Hugh O'Neill, the chairman of the Tourist Board, turned his attention to the States. He worked up a strategy with his long-suffering chief executive, Ian Henderson, to target tour operators to bring package tours to Northern Ireland as part of a European holiday. Maebeth did the selling and in four years the numbers rose fivefold to 100,000 or so, and from one tour operator to twenty. Hugh and his team had to persuade Bord Fáilte to see the North as a complementary asset, not a competitor. For a brusque man, his negotiating skills were considerable and I was sent to Dublin to meet with their minister, Charlie McCreevy, to witness the new arrangements.

But promotional campaigns to attract visitors would only succeed in the long run if the product was right. With money from Brussels and the International Fund for Ireland, the Tourist Board arranged quality accommodation for their clients, from the cheapest to the most expensive. New international hotel groups were enticed to Northern Ireland. Hilton, Radisson, Stakis, Holiday Inns and Jury's now compete with the once complacent local operators. New and imaginative attractions catering for every age, sex and culture were added: the Navan Fort Interpretive Centre, the Tower Museum depicting the history of Londonderry, the Irish Linen Centre in Lisburn, the Palace stables and the Saint Patrick's Trian in Armagh. Existing jewels such as the Ulster Folk and Transport Museum, the Ulster-American Folk Park at Omagh, Castle Coole and Mount Stewart already offered an extraordinary variety of uncluttered enjoyment set in breathtaking countryside. By the end of O'Neill's time the numbers of tourists had risen from 930,000 to 1,436,000 and 99 per cent went home happy. Yet the fact remained that because of Northern Ireland's tortured image this was only a tenth of the number that visit Cornwall. Violence was denying tens of thousands of people employment in an industry that was capable of offering as varied a holiday as anywhere in the world.

Our stopover in New York, where we met John Hume and Governor Carey, was to look at opportunities for twinning smaller American companies with Irish ones. There were many businesses making relatively low-tech products in the US that had never considered exporting. Our concept was to find them a new partner who would begin either by importing and distributing their goods or by producing them on a franchise or licence arrangement. We wanted to use start-up units in Father Myles Kavanagh's Flax Trust as a trial. It turned out successful in more ways than one. Myles persuaded Carey to hold an annual Flax Trust ball in New York which has raised many thousands of dollars over the years.

Montupet, a French car components company who had taken over the old deLorean plant in Dunmurry, had asked me to find out whether there was any chance of their exporting cylinder heads to Fords of Detroit for their secret new world car (the Mondeo). Fords were their only customer and they had considerable spare capacity in their Belfast plant. I had a friend, John Hougham, who was human resources director of Ford Europe and he put me in touch with the purchasing manager of Ford America, who luckily for me was English. But there my luck ran out, for he told me that Fords were planning to regionalise their component suppliers. In the future, all of the American factories would be supplied out of the US, Mexico and Canada.

From Detroit we flew to Houston to see Hughes Tool. The company had bought a small engineering business in Belfast and made drill heads for North Sea oil rigs. The productivity of the plant was abysmal. When I first met the management I was reminded of the 1974 three-day week. A cowed manager, implanted from England, told me it was impossible to raise output because of the trade unions' intransigence over working practices. I met the senior union convenor, who railed against arrogant Americans and incompetent, secretive management.

From time to time a Texan vice-president would come over and bawl out the managers, lecture the workers and threaten them with closure. He would then return to the States and they would return to doing nothing. I had been told by the IDB that this time the Americans would carry out their threats. The IDB were partly to blame: they had attracted the investor and then, apart from a lowly case officer, left the company to its own devices. Texans had no more an idea of how to run Ulstermen than Ulstermen had of managing Texans. The consequence was mutual incomprehension. What the factory needed was a tough, locally based works director who had experience of Belfast engineering, could win the respect of his men and had the guts to sack the troublemakers. We had asked Harland and Wolff to help us out and they had given permission for their production director to find a replacement for the existing manager. I was to fly to Houston to persuade the Americans to give us one more chance. They did. The right man was appointed and the factory has never looked back. The IDB learnt the lesson that a hands-on after-service required more than a monthly visit from a junior civil servant.

Having avoided tornadoes, we arrived in Kentucky. John Holland was the man responsible for building Fruit of the Loom into a world business. He had never really forgiven Bill Farley and his junk bonds for taking him over. He remained very much the chief executive in day-to-day charge of investment, production and sales. He is considerate, yet tough, with a digital mind. He grumpily told me the price of building a factory in Derry was nearly twice of that in the Midwest. British building regulations required ridiculous over-engineering so that a Northern Ireland factory required steel twice the strength and weight of an American plant. I had long suspected that building inspectors, fire officers and health and safety staff worked to rules that avoided blame ever landing at the door of their superiors. The cost of this belt, braces and straight-jacket approach was unnecessary and damaging. Some of the cost advantages of coming to Northern Ireland were lost because of the self-serving tunnel vision and timidity of statutory agencies who added nothing to the national wealth and were determined to avoid risk at no cost to themselves and substantial cost to others. Fortunately for us, it did not deter Fruit of the Loom from coming to Derry, but many of their Irish factories must find it difficult to compete with the cost structures that exist in Morocco or Sri Lanka.

John Holland lent us the Farley jet to fly to Chicago. At 30,000 feet I asked the pilot if he did anything else for a living. He was a real estate agent for 98 per cent of his time, he replied, as we hit a particularly nasty piece of turbulence. My fear of flying was reinforced. We were in Chicago to follow up the Lindy Dufferin weekend with the Pritzkers. If we could build a Hyatt Hotel in Belfast, perhaps even Macey's might follow. There was no problem, I was told. All we had to do was to find a franchisee with the money and Hyatt would provide the name, the management, the advertising and the architecture. It was no different from opening a McDonald's, they told us. But the fees were exorbitant and the room charges would have put off the most intrepid of travellers, even allowing for the grants that we intended squeezing out of the Tourist Board. My American excursion was being followed from afar by the Northern Ireland press, so I sent back a message to say we were in serious discussions with Hyatt about a site on the Lagan. The discussions were seen as being serious enough to start the Hastings Group worrying about their future and serious enough to awaken the interests of others who had long confused Belfast with Beirut. Hugh O'Neill and his team used my hyperbole on others and the Hilton Hotel is now open for business on the site we had reserved for Hyatt.

The last leg was Washington to close a deal. The IDB's deputy chief executive, Frank Hewitt, had now accepted that politicians might after all be of some benefit to his selling endeavours. He had hired an American public affairs company run by a Londonderry man, Tony Culley-Foster, who had persuaded a military aircraft servicing company, Dyncorp, to consider building a maintenance centre at Aldergrove Airport. Military work had declined and Dyncorp were apparently keen to find other profitable outlets in the commercial sector. This was to be Frank Hewitt's answer to Fruit of the Loom.

From the start I had my doubts, although I dared not express them. The company was happy to come provided we paid – which was fair up to a point – but they also insisted that we provide them with guaranteed airline orders. I had suggested that was more up to Dyncorp than me, but Frank packed me off to see Colin Marshall, John King and David Burnside, respectively managing director, chairman and public relations director at British Airways. They informed us that they had just done a deal with General Electric, who in return for an engine order had taken over all their servicing facilities in south Wales. Michael Bishop of British Midland also gave me a no, no. I rang up Raymond Royer, who was president and chief operating officer of Bombardier, and sought his advice. Aircraft servicing is a difficult business, he told me. There is no proprietary product. Any company located anywhere can do it provided it has the skills, as an aircraft can fly almost anywhere in twelve hours. Whether the business is successful therefore depends on the labour cost. He pointed out that Cathay Pacific were in the process of moving all their maintenance work out of Hong Kong to Shenzhen in Guangdong Province, where engineers came at a fifth of the Hong Kong price and a third of what he was paying his employees in Belfast. After further inconclusive negotiations assisted by Mr Culley-Foster at a price, and after many tens of thousands of pounds were spent on airfares, hotels, meeting rooms, lunches and dinners, Dyncorp and the IDB parted company.

I had foreseen the result and I was cross. There was too little control and direction over the IDB's inward-investment strategy. My contention was that if civil servants tried to be businessmen when there was a lack of measurable financial output to evaluate their focus and effectiveness, long-term success was unlikely. One problem was that the IDB board was purely advisory and board members relied entirely on the papers placed before them by the officials. They had neither the time nor the authority to dig deeper. I had tried to strengthen the board's business acumen by bringing in outsiders such as Roger Aldridge, the property development director of Marks & Spencer. (With him I also had an ulterior motive. I wanted to suck him into the life of the province so he would persuade his colleagues to open up more stores in, and to buy more from, Northern Ireland. Likewise I appointed Andrew

Smith and Alan Lambert, both senior Marks & Spencer managers, to the Training and Employment Agency and the Tourist Board respectively. The scheme worked in every way. The number of Marks & Spencer stores quadrupled over the years, their purchasing of product quintupled and the advice we received for peanuts from their employees on our boards proved invaluable.)

I suggested to Tony Hopkins, the IDB's chief executive, that he take his board off for a weekend to find ways of bringing a greater degree of accountability and value-for-money criteria to the inward-investment effort. He returned disappointed – whether with the board, his own efforts or both I did not ask. For the IDB's overseas campaign to function properly, the board required political leadership over a sustained period, preferably with a minister who himself had business experience. I believed that this was a lesson learnt by the Conservatives in the 1990s, and so the New Labour administration's decision to combine the security portfolio with the economic brief seems a strange aberration. The key to selling opportunities in Ulster is to minimise the security risk and maximise the educational, skills and cost advantages of coming to the province.

As I flew to London from Washington, I was told that Kieran McBrien, the IDB's man in Germany, had turned up an opportunity in Munich with Audi. Apparently Audi were looking to outsource their component supplies to low-cost regions of the European Community as their supplier base in Germany was becoming too expensive to compete with Japanese implants. At that time the D-Mark was strong and the pound was weak. This could have been a real opportunity for west Belfast if we had pulled it off.

Two days after we returned from Washington I was on the plane again. We gave a presentation to Dr. Ferdinand Piech, head of Audi, and I explained that our labour costs were half Germany's at 17 DM an hour and we worked 20 per cent more hours a year. 'That's no good,' he replied, 'I am looking for two thousand hours per worker per year at 6 DM an hour.' So the interview ended. The only crumb of comfort we returned with was a cake, as with Teutonic thoroughness the company had discovered that it was my birthday.

We had confided to the press the purpose of our venture and I now was confronted with a rebuff from Audi that would need some explaining. Mr Gerry Adams jumped in before me. He telephoned and faxed

Piech's office with a series of questions about Audi's intentions and then issued a press statement accusing me of raising people's expectations when the company had never had an interest in coming to west Belfast. This episode showed Adams at his most tenacious and his most hypocritical. Setting aside how a man on social security could afford the administrative back-up to pursue his enquiries, the claim that we were perpetuating a confidence trick on his constituents was monstrous. Adams had done little enough to bring jobs to west Belfast other than to bleat for more government money. His whole career had been dedicated to destroying jobs or the opportunities of finding them. His intervention allowed me to ignore Dr Piech's brush-off.

We had better luck in Bonn where Pauline Neville-Jones was the minister in the Bonn embassy and where, following a dinner with Dr Erich Riedl who was a vice-minister in the Economics Ministry, we agreed to introduce an exchange system for business school students. Dr Riedl also agreed to bring a delegation of senior German industrialists to Northern Ireland to assess investment opportunities for themselves, which he duly did.

My visits to Asia were confined mainly to Japan and Korea. Hong Kong, Indonesia and Taiwan were our secondary targets. The 'Invest in Britain' bureau in Whitehall has the co-ordinating role in promoting Britain's advantages to overseas companies. Their charter states that Northern Ireland should be their priority area for assistance. In reality they try to hold the ring between the competing regional and territorial agencies. As Northern Ireland's Secretary of State was bogged down in security and political crises for most of his working week, his opposite numbers in Wales and Scotland gained a head start as their positions opened doors in Asia which a junior minister could not hope to pass through. My connections in Japan through the 2000 Group helped redress the balance.

We were also fortunate in having a quiet, shy but workaholic consultant. Tim McNeil was fluent in French, Cantonese and Japanese. During the seventies he was managing director of Guinness in Hong Kong and he was responsible for taking Guinness into China. As always loyal and honourable, he returned home to help out his father's faltering agricultural produce export company. The IDB were fortunate to sign him up in 1983. He looked a bit Asian with his gentle manner and inscrutable smile. There was nobody he did not know in the political or business corridors of power in Asia's capitals. He could write lucid minutes and well-phrased, draft ministerial speeches. He was as conversant with the geography of the night-life of Tokyo as he was with the location of important ministries. For twelve years he was the hinge of the IDB's Asian strategy, after which his contract was not renewed on some shabby pretext. He was not treated well by the IDB and as a result he suffered, but not as much as the IDB whose Far East results since his departure have been worse than disappointing. He died of brain cancer in the summer of 1998, horribly young and leaving a widow and four student children.

Tim quickly persuaded me that we were wasting our time trying to lure mega-companies such as Honda or Nissan. The violent image was just too great to overcome. But if we could entice some small fry who succeeded, then that could be used as a case history for others. Canyon's arrival was almost entirely Tim's doing, and Tetsuya Tada, their chairman whose grasp of European geography and politics was somewhat circumscribed, along with his general manager, Yukimafa Ishihara became two of our most outspoken promoters. The Japanese became considerable investors. Kyocera bought out AVX, an American electronics company. Takata took over the Fisher Body Plant which manufactured safety belts from General Motors, and Ryobi came to build aluminium components for the European car industry. Quite quickly we had a small but significant number of Japanese investments, which at one time employed as a percentage of our workforce a larger proportion than those employed by Japanese companies in Scotland.

In order to impress the Japanese we invested a sizeable effort in social and educational projects. By 1992 there were more schools teaching Japanese language and culture in the North than in Scotland, Wales and England combined. There must now be thousands of Northern Irish students who have come through the exam system qualified in Japanese studies. We were enthusiastic backers of the 1991 UK/Japan Festival, and after the glowing endorsement of Ambassador Kazuo Chiba (I always made a special point of asking Japanese ambassadors to tour Northern Ireland), the Crown Prince made a visit at which he opened a Japanese garden at Sir Thomas and Lady Dixon Park and launched our interschools e-mail link to Japan.

Visits did not always run so smoothly. The Bunraku group, Japan's traditional and world-famous puppet theatre, had accepted the Opera

House's request to perform as part of the Japan Festival programme. Great care had been taken to calm down the nerves of the players, particularly as there were two living 'national treasures' amongst them – both octogenarians. As they were about to leave their bus outside the Europa Hotel, they were suddenly surrounded by a platoon of soldiers, armed to the teeth and with blackened faces, screaming at them to get out of the way. There had been a bomb scare in a building opposite. They ever so nearly remounted the bus and went home. But when they played to an almost full house and to rapturous applause, all was forgotten and our image was rescued.

Daewoo was the first Korean factory in Northern Ireland and is now one of the province's largest manufacturers. We sold ourselves to them as the gateway to the UK and Europe and we argued that, by being part of British Ireland rather than Irish Ireland, they would receive considerable support from London both in the UK and in Brussels. We also played on the Korean belief that Ireland was to Britain as Korea was to Japan. Northern Ireland gave them the best of all possible worlds, we told them. There are now eight Korean companies, several of them subcontractors to Daewoo. Given the circumstances and the competition, the IDB's success under Tim McNeil's guidance was extraordinary, despite one of his former minister's occasional gaffes.

On my first visit to Korea, Daewoo had invited us to a special lunch at the Seoul Hilton to meet up with the most senior directors involved in their Antrim venture. We searched the hotel but could not trace them. We always ended up back in the lobby, where a Korean band was strumming out jarring and tuneless musical themes. At last someone appeared whom Tim recognised. Only then did we discover that behind the band was a small, private dining-room which Daewoo had reserved. I bowed deeply and apologised profusely. In a feeble attempt at wit, I suggested that the dreadful musicians somehow disoriented us. The troupe, a director explained politely, was one of the most famous groups playing traditional Korean melodies and had been hired in our honour to play both before and during our meal.

We engineered one other surprising investment from Asia. Indonesia's most successful textile magnate is Mr Marimutu Sinivasan of the Polysindo Group. He is an Indonesian Tamil whose father was a small-town tailor. Sinivasan had somehow come across the opportunity to buy redundant machinery from Courtauld's defunct polyester yarn plant in Antrim. He transported the equipment to Indonesia where, with Indian engineers and Indonesian labour, he managed to produce three times the yarn at a tenth of the labour cost. Very soon he became very successful. He developed a soft spot for Northern Ireland and had his son educated there. As the European market became more important to him, he decided to ship the machinery back to Antrim, reinstall and start all over again. Northern Ireland boasted Indonesia's largest overseas manufacturing investment. Norfil Ltd, the local subsidiary of Polysindo, was a powerful ingredient in the quite extraordinary rejuvenation of the province's textile and clothing industry.

The cost of our inward-investment drive was substantial and in strict value-for-money terms sometimes questionable. But we had no alternative other than to compete with the Irish Republic and the UK mainland. To have had no success would have sent a devastating message about our economic prospects. Most of the incoming companies have stayed the course longer than the previous wave of overseas investors in the sixties. The products are more sophisticated and more integrated into larger operations, which are themselves dedicated to the European Union market. The next stage should be for the IDB, LEDU and the Training and Employment Agency to concentrate on attracting research and development laboratories. Then, with product design and development taking place in Northern Ireland and with the help of the universities, there would be an even broader and more substantial foundation for overseas companies to build on.

There was another category of inward investment which was cheaper to promote and required less grant per job. The property boom had led to a prodigious rise in office accommodation. There was also a growing shortage of skilled, white-collar workers in the south of England. The poorer regions of the UK began an acerbic turf war to persuade government departments to relocate. I found myself in a personal bind. My constituency of North Wiltshire was full of defence bases, both operational and administrative. The Ministry of Defence was keen to ship many of these jobs north and west, but my voters were not keen to leave leafy Wiltshire for the attractions of Glasgow or Cardiff. Most Ministry of Defence professional staff had contracts which contained mobility clauses forcing them to move or resign, but the more menial occupations that serviced them did not and were made redundant. The problems of moving schools and the prospect of second earners in the household also losing their jobs made for a torrid political time. If the man moved, his wife and any working children might not be able to find the same opportunities in, say, Liverpool as were available around Bath. But the Treasury did not see that problem as their problem.

Although in Northern Ireland there was little opportunity of attracting Ministry of Defence back-office functions, there were many other government departments and privatised utilities that we could attract. We also spotlighted the City and the support functions of the banks and the building societies. The IDB's secret weapon in this interregional war was the small and bearded Ian Walters, whose Northern accent comforted our audiences and whose bubbling 'no-nonsense-you-cannot-afford-not-to' approach worked wonders. We cajoled John Hume to join in pitching for Londonderry to be a preferred choice for the City of London. We were greeted as long-lost brothers by the lord mayor and his corporation. Tactfully they seemed to have forgotten or been unaware of the vitriolic and historic campaign to rid Derry of its London connection. They even presented me with my great-grandfather's tie which he had worn when governor of the Honourable the Irish Society at the beginning of the century. The duke of Abercorn, who was chairman of the Building Societies Association, allowed Ian and me to make our sales pitch to their annual conference in Brighton. We went to Glasgow to lure members of the Confederation of British Industry at an 'Ulster Fry Breakfast' to bring us back-offices. We used the IDB office in the centre of London for evening receptions with videos and slide shows. The Northern Ireland Partnership, which comprised successful men and women who had crossed the water, were unpaid, unofficial back-office promoters.

By the beginning of the nineties Belfast was in the throes of a building boom. The Belfast Development Office's promotion campaigns about the 'Buzz in Belfast' had finally rammed the message home. All those who had kept their money a closely guarded secret now joined the herd in the stampede to expand office space in the city centre. As the economy slowed in 1991, so boom threatened to turn to bust and I was surrounded by anxious developers and their builders demanding that I find tenants for their properties. In vain did I argue that that was the role of their estate agents. I had produced the hype, I should produce the investors. Estate agents usually wait for customers to knock on their doors and in the past not many have been known for their creative marketing skills. There were some real characters among the Belfast agents. They had, after all, been trying to sell property for the previous twenty years against a background of bomb and blitz. We joined forces with Eric Cairns, Andrew Best and Colin Millhench, and with some creative advertising designed, with my encouragement, by Colin Anderson we redoubled our efforts.

The new offices were almost without exception filled. The DHSS moved their helpline agencies into the Plaza Buildings in Chichester Street. There was an anguished discussion about whether a west Belfast social security adviser would be able to help an unemployed Asian phoning in with a Family Credit quandary from a Southall telephone kiosk. My reaction was that a west Belfast accent was no more difficult to interpret than a Glaswegian, Mancunian or Cockney one. The Royal Mail's depot for deciphering and redirecting post went into Tomb Street. We gained work from the Inland Revenue, the Child Support Agency (where Nick Scott's influence as the responsible minister swung the decision) and the Passport Office (we proved that we could issue a passport in a fifth of the time it took at Petty France in London Victoria – although not all wanted Belfast stamped as the city of issue). British Airways opened a reservations back-up office in Fountain Lane. British Telecom call centres spread around the province. The Prudential came to Brook Street. In all, well over two thousand office jobs were created in a period of three years. It was a major triumph, given the image of Northern Ireland and the competition from other UK cities, and it was proof, if by now any was needed, of the importance of designing an interdepartmental plan and then calling out anyone and everyone with a lever and an interest to play a part.

32
MOVING THE GOAL POSTS

THE IDB, LEDU AND THE MULTIFACETED TRAINING AGENCIES were originally tasked with saving desperate situations. In the seventies and early eighties many companies, large and small, were on the verge of bankruptcy. Unemployment, particularly among the young, was becoming endemic. Almost anyone or anything that offered a job needed to be supported. The agencies were constantly confronted by crises. They were required to save the day rather than change it.

By 1989 this corrosive phase was coming to an end. *Northern Ireland Competing in the 1990s: The Key to Growth* had set the new agenda. But imposing the new imperatives was more difficult. In place of civil servants doling out support subject to the conditions laid down in departmental handbooks, we now had to find ways of actively encouraging companies to remedy their often very substantial management failings. Businessmen do not rate the advice of civil servants, particularly if it is critical of their performance. We had to uncover other ways to back success and penalise failure. Grants for buildings and machinery needed cutting; support for training, marketing and design needed reinforcing. How could government achieve this when public servants had little or no experience of these matters?

We had to bring in outside opinions and give their advice greater weight. The obvious candidates for such a role were the members of the advisory boards of the IDB, LEDU and the newly reorganised Training and Employment Agency. The difficulty was that the outside directors were all part-time and some of them symbolised that which we needed most to change. We were also challenged by those who continued to rely on the existing drip feed of government money or had, as in the case of training, built up organisations dispensing it.

Quality had to become the name of our game. The arrival of international standards gave us a rack on which we could hang financial support. BS 5750, later ISO 9000, was a benchmark of professionalism that companies large and small were encouraged to strive for. As Marks & Spencer, Shorts and other large enterprises became more active in the province, so they demanded ever higher standards from their suppliers and these suppliers demanded similar quality from their subcontractors. I tried every way to make the advisory boards less advisory and more managerial, but with limited results. The Department of Finance was horrified at losing control to outsiders, some of whom might also become beneficiaries of government grants. We did however provide, through LEDU, business mentors who could bring their management experience in support of small and growing businesses.

The largest area for reorganisation lay with the training agency. Before 1989 there had been a plethora of statutory training boards under the umbrella of the Northern Ireland Training Authority which reported to the Department of Economic Development, itself responsible for training centres, the job training programme and Action for Community Employment (ACE). Many of these programmes were 'make work', and most who came onto them from the unemployment register returned to it.

The department had decided before I arrived to amalgamate all the schemes and the managing bodies into a 'Next Steps' agency which could settle on a design that moved funding from a patchwork of low-quality programmes to one that financed advanced training provision for all with verifiable and tradeable qualifications. This was some order, and its success would depend on the degree of managerial and financial training the agency could wrest for itself from the Department of Finance. The British Treasury, as always, wanted it both ways. They were determined to keep control of the purse-strings, and that could only be guaranteed by insisting that the agency's management report to them for the money. In this they were supported by the NIO's

Department of Finance, who were if anything more supine in their interpretation of the rules than the Treasury.

Both their underlying interests appeared to be to preserve a common position across the UK. If the Training and Employment Agency managed to embark on new programmes that the Treasury had neither vetted nor fully evaluated, precedents could be set for others to take advantage of. The consequences of misplaced public spending followed by an appearance before the Public Accounts Committee could prove fatal for any senior official having to defend the actions of colleagues. As the wheels of select committees grind extraordinarily slowly, many years would elapse before any investigation reached the committee floor of the House of Commons. By then, those responsible would long since have been transferred elsewhere. To enable some future permanent secretary to defend positively the position of his predecessors required extreme diligence at all times. Delegating now might only lead to public humiliation later.

This was all bunkum to me. We had to cut away at 'make work' schemes such as ACE and concentrate on providing training that would improve the employability and competence of the workforce, particularly the young. To achieve this, the Training and Employment Agency needed flexibility between budgets and it needed a board with authority to encourage its chief executive to run with new ideas. How could this be achieved by asking the great and the good, carefully balanced between sexes and religions, to attend occasional meetings to rubber-stamp decisions already stitched up between cowed Training and Employment Agency officials and the Department of Finance?

A fight ensued. As usual in such contests, no one achieved victory. The Training and Employment Agency gained a degree of autonomy but not sufficient to stop them looking over their shoulders and requesting Treasury approval for any programme that was innovative or different. Perhaps the clearest example of continuing supervision was that the sponsoring department, the Department of Economic Development, reduced its personnel and finance branch from eighty-one to seventy-nine while the agency recruited thirty-one staff members for the department's finance and personnel functions! The levers of financial control were also supplemented in a delightful piece of *Yes Minister* bureaucratic draftsmanship. The agency's framework document stated that ministers 'will determine the policy and financial framework'. The framework document also highlighted ministerial responsibility for approving corporate and operational plans, including setting performance targets. Ministers were also to receive 'monitoring' reports on the agency's performance against its targets. Any minister who had either the time or the experience to fulfil such a role would have no shortage of head-hunters after leaving office. This role in reality was the prerogative of the Department of Finance working through its servants, the permanent secretary in the Department of Economic Development and the chief executive in the Training and Employment Agency.

Despite the handicaps, we started to make formidable progress. The chief executive of the agency, Julian Crozier, appeared an unlikely candidate to face up to the powerful vested interest which stood in the way of change. He resembled a rather unworldly, diffident university professor who often appeared uncertain where he was and where he was going. But a slightly chaotic appearance hid a dogged sense of purpose and an instinct for survival which saw him and his agency over jumps that others would have fallen at.

The new outsiders I brought in, John Hougham of Fords (later chairman of ACAS) and Andrew Smith, a personnel executive at Marks & Spencer, gave a clarity and direction to existing schemes and brought an originality to new proposals which shifted the balance. They were joined later by an exceptional man, Brian Carlin, human resources director of Shorts. As a Catholic he was somewhat unusual in Shorts, as a Catholic director perhaps unique. He has done as much as anyone to integrate the workforce. Shorts' investment in the Molins tobacco machinery plant outside Londonderry started the process of giving north-west engineering apprentices the chance to work in east Belfast. Brian has done more than most to make fair employment a reality in Northern Ireland. His voluntary work for the Training and Employment Agency was truly invaluable.

In the early nineties, ACE represented a significant portion of the agency's budget. In 1991/2 the scheme provided over ten thousand participants who had been unemployed for a year or more with up to one year of temporary employment on projects of community benefit. The aim was to prepare the participants to compete more effectively in the labour market. For around 70 per cent the aim remained an aspiration, as only about 30 per cent found other work at the end of their placement. ACE involved little or no training and required from the employer a most rudimentary plan to raise the employability of workers. A year was too short a time to introduce National Vocational Qualifications into the programme. Most voluntary organisations who relied heavily on ACE for filling posts did not have the managerial resources to help ACE workers improve their skills. The tasks required of them were often menial and tedious and many left as unmotivated as the day they started. We tried to extend the programme by a year and tighten the criteria to make jobs more demanding, but a doubling of the annual £50 million budget was a bridge too far for the Department of Finance to swallow.

Community workshops were another area for disagreement and controversy. The workshops had a dismal record of accomplishment in providing skills. They argued that many of the workshop entrants were school failures and that there was no realistic likelihood of most of their students ever locating work within their own communities. The community workshops openly admitted that they saw their first objective as preparing their charges for a lifetime on the dole.

Such pessimism was self-fulfilling. The French government had set themselves a target of 80 per cent of their school-leavers achieving either the Baccalauréat Académique or Vocationelle by the year 2000 – the equivalent of two A levels. We would be lucky to have 50 per cent making a similar grade unless we changed our ways. Julian Crozier persisted and the results improved. But our real mission required the Training and Employment Agency to shift its entire focus towards providing world-class training programmes that would improve the competitiveness of Northern Ireland companies. The agency created a business support division and over the years a plethora of clever and successful programmes have done much to advance the credibility of the agency. There is an Invest in People Programme, a Company Development Programme, a Sectoral Development Programme, a Strategic Leadership Programme, a Managerial Leadership Programme, a New Horizons Programme for redundant experienced managers and an Explorers Programme.

The last takes young graduates with a language degree and loans them to companies to assist them in their overseas marketing. The students spend six months in digs in either Asia, Europe or America. They travel by public transport and they soon learn whether their sponsor

299

companies have exportable products. They are carefully controlled and monitored by an outside agency. These young graduates have brought a youthful enthusiasm together with a knowledge of culture and language that has been almost totally absent from Northern Ireland business. The vast majority have very quickly added a new dimension of expert professionalism to the companies for which they have worked. The results that many have achieved have been truly amazing. Some 90 per cent either stay with their sponsor company or move on to jobs elsewhere within six months of completing their programme.

The Training and Employment Agency may have relied too heavily on the ubiquitous ACE to massage the unemployment figures for the benefit of their political masters, but the switch to quality that has occurred will do much to improve Northern Ireland's managerial standards. Many young people who would previously have left to find worthwhile careers outside will now be able to use their talents at home. As John Simpson, one of the province's best-known economic commentators, pointed out in the January 1998 edition of *Ulster Business*: in 1987 there were 605,000 people in jobs in Northern Ireland; now there are 666,000. In 1987 unemployment reached 120,000; now it is down to 60,000. In 1987 the private sector employed 400,000; now the number is 473,000.

A very considerable sea change has taken place in the Northern Ireland economy and some of that change must be due to the efforts of the Training and Employment Agency.

33
FAIR EMPLOYMENT

ANY TELEVISION COMMENTATOR WHO PUTS Martin McGuinness or Gerry Adams under pressure receives not an answer to the question but a standard mantra response, the main plank of which is that the nationalist community was discriminated against for over half a century by Protestants determined to keep what jobs were going in their own pockets. There is truth in the allegation. The industrial revolution was begun mainly by sons of the Scottish Manse. Belfast was predominantly a working-class, industrial, unionist city whose masters employed their own tribe, not least because that tribe was frightened that their wages would be undercut by cheap Catholic labour imported from west of the Bann or south of the border. It was also self-evident that any state whose government was chosen by tribal loyalty would show preference for its own supporters.

However, there were often factors which had some importance and were not easily accepted by the nationalist community. The emphasis on 'arts' subjects in Catholic education was one. The belief in collective support, which large families required for survival but which did little to encourage the entrepreneurial spirit, was another. The grinding poverty that so often dogged many Catholic families gave little opportunity for bright youngsters to find time or space to study or expand their outlook. Those that sought to get on found the best way was to get out. The causes were more complex than the sound-bite snarls of the apologists for the IRA would admit. Indeed, the terrorists had become more responsible for Catholic unemployment than anyone.

By the middle of the eighties an enormous security industry had developed but very few Catholics were engaged in it. Some were deterred by IRA intimidation and others through genuine peer pressure. Research we had commissioned showed that although the numbers in work as a percentage of the working population varied (91 per cent Protestant compared to 84 per cent Catholics), the numbers seeking work and out of work showed a much heavier bias against the nationalist community. The type of work done by Catholics was on average more menial, more temporary, less interesting and less rewarding. There was a problem and the nationalist community was right to demand the injustices be addressed. Many unionist leaders had refused to accept the problem's existence. A number of superficial and sometimes almost racist anecdotes were often trotted out in support of insupportable arguments.

Discrimination had stirred the Irish-American lobby. Many Irish-Americans had memories of how their fathers had suffered, although some who had gained the upper rung in America had caused others beneath them to suffer similar indignities. They made up a very powerful lobby on Capitol Hill, pressurising the American government to pressurise the British government to legislate for affirmative action. These demands were often grouped under an umbrella called the MacBride principles. Most were founded on the civil rights programmes drawn up by activists in the Deep South. With one exception they were statements of impeccable worthiness; that exception, however was ridiculous and dangerous. The 'principle' of positive discrimination via quotas was obnoxious. Although enshrined in the laws of many American states, such policies were lightly if ever enforced. To insist in Northern Ireland that those already in work should be sacked on the basis of their religion would have led to dreadful bitterness. The consequent refusal to comply would have made any such regulation impossible to enforce.

There was no doubt that the British government had to introduce legislation to show the world (or rather Irish-America and Dublin) that employment practices were unbiased. The very existence of new legislation showed the power that a combined Dublin–Washington alliance had over a British government. I would need persuading that the Prime

Minister instinctively supported such an interfering law that was alien to her free-market instincts. But the Bill was passed in 1989 because there was discrimination, and it was often widespread if often unintended. I remain an advocate of Northern Ireland's Fair Employment Act. I became responsible for the administration of the Act the year after it had been passed by parliament.

The reality was that recruitment practices in Northern Ireland followed custom and practice, and custom and practice were often influenced by tradition. The Act was administered by the Fair Employment Commission (FEC) under Sir Bob Cooper's direction. Bob had an unenviable job which he did with purpose and considerable tact. Business and the unionist community were hostile. They saw the requirements as an unnecessary, onerous, bureaucratic addition to their workload. They were scared by the criminal sanctions that underpinned the Act. They also believed – with some justification – that the British government had caved in to Dublin and Washington and they were particularly annoyed when they considered the non-secular nature of the Irish Republic. But two wrongs do not make a right.

Some of the woodworm that emerged from the timbers was highly revealing. Queen's University professors had waged a long and determined campaign against discrimination. Their self-righteousness tinged with occasional pomposity had often irked those, particularly in government, at whom their arrows were directed. There had grown up over the years a whole caste of academics who from the safety of their garrets criticised successive governments for their failings. These complaints usually involved lack of state funding and benefited from the advantage of hindsight. Their irksome certainties found space in publications such as *Fortnight* and were presented with all the virtuousness of those who have never known responsibility. Furthermore the critics often failed to take into account the limitations of a government's ability to change practices that came from a century or two of inter-community conflict. Why has the NIO failed to introduce this policy, right this wrong or change this law? the editorials of *Fortnight* would trumpet. Their constant whingeing and whining was an unsolicited bonus to the likes of Gerry Adams, who could call on their sometimes spurious arguments. It was far easier to find detailed faults with government programmes than to accept the limitations of what was possible. It therefore came as a bitter-sweet irony to discover that a number of the pontificating professors at Queen's had not addressed their own back-yard. A damning report from the FEC concluded that employment practices in some parts of the university were as bad as any to be found in Northern Ireland. Catholics were not even to be found serving the dons at their high tables.

Elsewhere, elements of discrimination bordered on intimidation. The flying of flags and emblems over factories or the festooning of Union Jacks on machines was clearly triumphalist, as well as being demeaning and occasionally frightening to Catholic workers. Many companies relied on local communities to provide their workers. Son often followed father, or sister joined sister. This led to an exclusion of opportunity for others, even if through historical practice rather than overt malice.

The publicity surrounding a critical report from the FEC was often seen by management as a damning indictment on their professionalism and many took the findings as a personal attack on their attitudes towards one community or the other. Northern Ireland Railways had been dominated by Protestants ever since the building of the first station. Family units were strongly embedded through tradition and training. Without outside legislative pressure the practices would probably have remained the same in perpetuity. The FEC's criticisms of these practices made a deep impression on the chairman, Sir Myles Humphreys, who took them to some extent to be a reflection on his perceived bigotry. Nothing could have been further from the truth, but many businessmen were genuinely frightened of the commission's intervention. This did lead to them taking action but it also led to resentment and to accusations by Ian Paisley and others of the FEC's alleged Catholic bias.

There was never any actual evidence that Paisley and his supporters could adduce in support of their claims. In return I was able to show that even if a majority of cases involved Catholic under-representation, there were a significant number of employers where the percentage of Protestant workers was far lower than the travel to work area warranted.

None of what we had done made any impact on the Irish National Caucus and its supporters in the US. They were determined to force American companies investing in Northern Ireland to sign up to the MacBride principles either by product boycotts or by direct shareholder action through forcing state or trade union pension funds to divest their holdings. Wherever possible, they made as much trouble as possible for a company's chairman at its annual general meeting. A successful assault resulted in catastrophe for those they claimed most needed their intervention. Any company in Northern Ireland invoking the MacBride principle on positive discrimination would have been in breach of the law and would itself have been subject to prosecution, because reverse discrimination was rightly illegal. Caught between these two pincers, American-owned companies had to either ignore the MacBride principles or close down.

Most rode the storm but the task of attracting new American investment was made much more difficult by the silly if not hypocritically damaging campaign. The one real winner was the Republic where the MacBride principles obviously did not apply. Their corporate tax regime was a further incentive and the threat of terrorist violence was less. Little wonder their Industrial Development Authority gained four US jobs for each one gained in the North. We spent a lot of time sending local Catholic politicians and civil servants around American state legislatures counteracting the republican propaganda which was clamouring for the principles to be adopted. They were effective and dedicated to the cause of saving jobs in Northern Ireland and promoting new ones. John Hume was also a staunch ally, and because he was held in high respect by Irish-American opinion his influence was always significant and sometimes crucial.

I despise discrimination, partly perhaps because of my mother's Jewish ancestry. It springs from either incompetence or bigotry. If Northern Ireland's people were ever to draw together, careers would have to be open to all the talents. The FEC insisted on best practice, and best practice brought transparency and confidence. The law required professionalism of a high standard from every employer bar the very smallest, who were excluded by the legislation. Once the new requirements were embedded in managerial procedures, business opposition started to die and good managers began to ask themselves whether other areas of their responsibility, such as training, marketing, design and overall competitiveness, were as professionally structured as their recruitment policies. Fair employment legislation has been a milestone on the road to fairer administration. It has already gone a long way to liberating the Catholic community's enormous talents and ingeniousness.

34

LIGHTING THE CANDLE AT BOTH ENDS

IN THE ULSTER WORKERS' COUNCIL STRIKE OF 1974, the employees of Northern Ireland Electricity (NIE), particularly those at Ballylumford power station, had proved themselves the special forces of militant unionism. By turning off the power for longer and longer, they had made Northern Ireland unworkable and ungovernable. Their illegal and intimidating actions destroyed the power-sharing executive, made fools of the British government and endorsed the convictions of the extremists: that might was right, and violence, or the threat of it, was the most potent way to achieve victory. Once again the management of the NIO was found wanting. Merlyn Rees in his book *Northern Ireland* wrote: 'There was a lack of co-ordination between the RUC, the Army and the Executive and in particular a lack of co-ordination with the Northern Ireland Electricity Service. It was part of an overall lack of planning and thought about the consequences of a political stoppage in Northern Ireland.'

In the years following this blatant abuse of industrial muscle, the NIO and its ministers kept well clear of NIE. As a nationalised utility, it behaved like a mini Central Electricity Generating Board. There was a government-appointed chairman and board of directors who agreed an annual performance plan with the Department of Economic Development. In reality NIE represented the worst of every aspect of a publicly owned monopoly. The system was expensive, badly planned, isolated, overmanned, oversubsidised, cautious, inefficient, unproductive, unimaginative and loss-making.

The major generating unit, Ballylumford, was locked away in a unionist enclave outside Larne and was controlled by its workforce rather than its managers. Because Ballylumford was the largest of the power stations, with a capacity of more than 1,000 megawatts, it dominated the supply of power. Maximum demand peaked at 1,400 megawatts, so if Ballylumford went down there were three other power stations – Kilroot at Carrickfergus, Belfast West and Coolkeeragh near Londonderry – that could be called upon to keep the grid running. The total combined generating capacity was over 2,200 megawatts, which allowed a spinning reserve of more than 800 megawatts that was hardly ever called upon. Hong Kong by comparison has 7,500 megawatts of capacity and a maximum demand of 6,000 megawatts.

The planners' incompetence had not ended with massive immediate overcapacity. They had budgeted on extending generating output still further. Kilroot had been designed as a four-set oil-burning station and the machinery for all sets was purchased. Too late NIE realised, as the equipment began to arrive, that Kilroot II was not required. For ten years, alongside Kilroot, stood a vast park of Henry Moore shapes made up of £80 million of the components for the two superfluous sets. Attempts to find overseas buyers were abortive and from time to time some of the pieces disappeared. Meanwhile NIE continued to argue that as soon as extra capacity was required, Kilroot II should provide it – regardless of gas, lignite or an interconnector and regardless of the cost of flue gas desulphurisation needed to clean up the sulphur emissions. In the middle of the 1984 coal strike the two installed sets were converted to burn coal as well as oil.

The woes did not end in Kilroot. There was a massive overdependence on oil. Lignite had been discovered around Ballymoney, but NIE could not be raised from their lethargy to consider it as a serious future option. The old coal/gas network in and around Belfast had been shut down. The interconnector with the South had been blown up by the IRA, not only destroying one small step towards Irish unity but increasing the price of power even further to their impoverished community. Power was expensive. For the larger industrial users it was 30 per cent higher than on the mainland, while for the domestic consumer an average subsidy of some £70 million a year was paid between 1981 and

1986 to keep Northern Ireland prices at the same level as those in the most expensive areas in Great Britain. Money which could have been spent on hospitals or schools was poured down the throats of a complacent, voracious electricity service.

The Department of Economic Development had been in lengthy discussions with NIE about attracting a gas supply into Ballylumford by converting the station from oil. The department had also been trying to push forward negotiations on an interconnector with Scotland, where there was a surfeit of generating capacity. An interconnector would have reduced the need for the spinning reserve and done away with the need to replace old existing stations as they became obsolete. The electricity management were defensive, were generally satisfied with their performance and blamed their failings on the annual constraints of the Treasury plan. Other than agreeing the capital expenditure programme, the government had no involvement in decision-making within NIE. Furthermore, officials had no way of knowing whether the business was well or badly run. Instead of being a publicly owned, accountable service providing efficient and competitive power to its customers, NIE was a self-perpetuating monopoly run by an oligarchy who were responsible mainly to themselves.

Something had to be done and the most obvious and immediate solution was privatisation. The Treasury were insistent that Northern Ireland should be no different from Scotland or Wales and for once they were right. The 1992 election was looming and the government wanted to leave as little unfinished business as possible. To begin with I was hesitant, not because I was opposed to the principle of privatisation, but because every single politician in Northern Ireland was vehemently against it. Was it right for a minister who had no personal political legitimacy in the province to impose legislation which affected one of the essentials of life against the wishes of elected politicians? There would have to be an overwhelming case for such a change – and there was.

Why therefore did we face such political opposition? Sinn Féin as Marxist revolutionaries were unlikely to want to see British Gas take over Ballylumford, even though the workers were of the brightest orange. The SDLP as a sister party to the Labour opposition were against, though as much out of loyalty as conviction. The DUP were working-class socialist unionists who instinctively supported public ownership, a belief that was reinforced by the number of their party members who worked in NIE. The Ulster Unionists were more half-hearted; their spokesman, Roy Beggs, had long been a supporter of bringing gas to Northern Ireland and he and some of his colleagues had been critical of NIE's inefficiencies. (He once remarked that both Northern Ireland industry and the public of Northern Ireland were being crucified by the existing arrangements.)

Middle-of-the-road parties in Ulster are always looking over their shoulders at the extremists behind them. The Alliance Party had an even stranger basis for opposing the sell-off. Northern Ireland people were different, they proclaimed. They were not like the money-grabbing English who would do anything for a quick profit. The populace were content to see the electricity service in public hands so long as it provided a professional service. They ignored the fact that eighty-eight thousand Ulster men and women had applied to invest in Scottish Power. The lack of support for privatisation in the public's mind was connected with job losses and the threat of higher prices. These were strong enough grounds for the Ulster Unionists and the Alliance Party to be in the 'No' lobby, but not strong enough for some unionist MPs not to be in the first wave of applicants for shares.

I decided that my strongest suit was to take them all on and attempt to convince the people of Northern Ireland, over the heads of their political leaders, that what we were doing was the only sensible way forward. It was time the people of Ulster had an opportunity to take a direct share in an undertaking that they all were forced to buy from. I relished the chance of debating the arguments on the floor of the House of Commons and in committee because I knew that in demolishing the present order, I had an unanswerable case.

But first I had to deal with the leadership of NIE. The chairman, Roelof Schierbeek, had stubbornly and misguidedly opposed our plans with the support of his board and his chief executive, Tony Hadfield (who left five months later, despite his criticisms of our privatisation plans, to become chief executive of Northern Electricity plc). Their arguments were pseudo-technical. Privatisation would not bring competition because the system was too isolated and too small. Splitting the service into different businesses would undermine the benefits of centralisation, leading to more administration and more layers of management. Outside regulation would institutionalise conflict and lead to

309

management spending much of its time fighting with the regulator rather than providing an efficient service to the customer. Finally we were accused by NIE of selling the family silver at less than its true worth.

In late 1989 I went to see Roelof Schierbeek and Tony Hadfield to see if I could bring them on-side, but after a patronising lecture from Hadfield on why everything was for the best in the best of all possible worlds, I knew that I had to make changes if there was to be any chance of persuading the staff of NIE to accept the sell-off. I was only too aware that if the workers decided to take industrial action, I could be back in the Merlyn Rees position of 1974. My instinct told me that was unlikely, for all the huffing and puffing, but I needed a new chairman and he would have to be good.

There was really only one candidate, Sir Desmond Lorimer. Desmond has presence. Very tall, silver-haired, square-chinned with shiny white teeth, broadly built, he breathes authority and immediately demands respect. His business acumen may be more balanced than his political prejudices, but it was his commercial shrewdness, which came from an accountancy background, and his industrial reputation, which he had established at Lamont Holdings, that I was after. Desmond was nearing the end of his career. (He had been chairman of the IDB, and he was at the time chairman of the Northern Bank as well as Lamonts.) He is a very good golfer and has lots of interests, and I could not see how he could be persuaded to take on the prickliest industrial problem in Ulster.

The two of us went out to dinner and I tried every trick. There was no one else who could do the job. The Northern Irish people deserved better than what they were getting from NIE. It was high time Ulster men and women could buy shares and make profits in their province rather than across the water. Industry needed lower energy prices and a plurality of energy sources. We could never hope to compete against the South for inward investment if we did not build an efficient and competitive power system. It was a last great challenge for him. His country needed him. He looked distinctly unimpressed but said he would think about it. Others must have been more persuasive, because a week later he said yes and I knew then that we would succeed.

The strategy for privatisation was led by a very clever Department of Economic Development official, David Gibson. He was an Englishman but no one thought the worse of him for that. Both he and his energetic assistant, David Thomson, were accountants and both had experience of rapacious merchant banks from their earlier roles in Northern Ireland privatisations. They took to the project like converts to religion. Occasionally I would drive David Gibson to distraction with my constant interrogations. On one occasion he burst into my bedroom in the Stormont complex and told me he would take early retirement (at fifty-one!) if I did not let him push on without endless questions. I backed off. The team was able to call on the extensive experience in both the Treasury and the Department of Finance and Personnel. But without the arrival of Sir Desmond Lorimer, who turned the NIE people from antis into pros, it would have been much stickier.

The first decision we had to agree on was the structure of privatisation. The old NIE's fall-back position was to sell the whole business as one unit and turn a public monopoly into a private one. That option was rejected out of hand. I had hoped that we might be able to package the generators into a single company and the transmission and distribution into another company and float them both. It quickly became evident that what we needed was new owners and new ideas about generation, and this could only come by attracting outside investors. We agreed to sell the generators separately in a trade sale and then float the remainder of the company on the stock market. At the same time we resolved to persuade Brussels to help fund an interconnector with Scotland (they eventually agreed to provide 35 per cent).

The largest challenge facing Rothschilds, our advisers, was to find enough potential purchasers to hold an auction for the power stations so that we could raise a respectable sum from the sale and also allow us to negotiate tough supply contracts with the new owners. The gem that we had to secure was British Gas. Their arrival would bring enormous advantages, principally a new source of clean, cheap energy that would avoid the need for flue gas desulphurisation. Kilroot and Ballylumford were the major causes of acid rain in parts of southern Scotland. Furthermore, once gas had been established for power generation, it could be reintroduced for domestic heating and cooking.

One very clear December night in 1991, Peter Brooke and I flew back from Brussels having lobbied Bruce Millan, the Energy Commissioner, for funds for the interconnector. We were in a Lear jet well above 40,000 feet. Over London we could see south to Brussels and

Paris and north to Manchester, Liverpool and even Newcastle. When we got over Birmingham we started to look for Belfast. We thought the city had disappeared until David Gibson pointed out that a dense haze of smoke hung over most of the city, caused by 70 per cent of households still burning coal. It was supposed to be smokeless but no one had heard of Department of the Environment inspectors hammering on doors on the Falls Road and the Shankill to confront those who were ignoring the regulations and resorting to cheaper, smokier, varieties.

I was sent off by the Secretary of State to persuade British Gas that Northern Ireland was the place to be. Luckily for me, the head of new projects was a delightfully sympathetic Ulsterman, Professor Ernie Shannon, who needed no convincing but could not be seen to be partisan because of his background. He put me together with the chairman, Bob Evans, who did need convincing. Over a period of weeks stretching into months British Gas saw for themselves how lucrative a market Northern Ireland was. Their original suspicion turned into a carefully concealed enthusiasm. They wanted the best and most profitable contract they could secure and they played the violence and political uncertainty card with considerable cunning.

It seemed as if, for the two old power stations at Belfast West and Coolkeeragh, a management buy-out might be the only option. Kilroot should have attracted much greater overseas curiosity, but once again the image of Northern Ireland frightened off most of the promising players, particularly the English. Privatisation is a costly and complicated business. Government had its bankers and lawyers – as did NIE, as did British Gas over Ballylumford, as did AES/Tractebel (the ultimate buyer of Kilroot and Belfast West), as did the management buy-out of Coolkeeragh. Often the advice was contradictory and confusing. Sometimes, if not often, I concluded we were in the business of boosting City fees rather than achieving the most rewarding settlement for both taxpayer and consumer.

Desmond and I divided the load between us. He handled the City, the potential investors and the workforce, and I tried to convert the public and the politicians. After a few months he told me it was time to visit the power stations and talk to the shop stewards. He also advised me to address the annual conference of NIE managers at the Slieve Donard Hotel. It would give me a unique chance to put over my case to two hundred and fifty doubters, most of whom already had been convinced by his predecessor that they might face the sack.

I started my tour with considerable unease. Was it going to be a return to the abusive, early days of the Anglo-Irish Agreement? To my amazement almost everyone wanted to be involved in the arguments; people were open-minded and inquisitive rather than defensive and querulous. I toured each station and then met with twenty or so representatives in the canteens, where we argued through the case. I gave no promises about lay-offs, that would be up to the new owners, but I told them I was convinced that the vast majority would have more worthwhile careers under future management than under the existing one. A fair number agreed. Desmond and his new team had worked wonders in putting over the arguments. Even the middle managers, many of whom understandably took the criticisms I had made of NIE to be criticisms of them personally, were prepared to debate the alternatives in a constructive and friendly exchange. I came away with the conviction that the privatisation would succeed. Those in the industry had placed sufficient trust in us that we could not let them down, and many saw the advantages and opportunities of either working for themselves in a management buy-out or working for British Gas and AES/Tractebel.

The outstanding question was whether the new arrangements would bring substantial, long-term benefits to the domestic and industrial consumer. This was the overriding issue that needed debating in parliament. Of course it did not get debated. The debates, both on the floor of the House of Commons and in committee, rambled everywhere except to the point. Ulster Unionist leader Jim Molyneaux had already gone on record as saying that service industries could benefit greatly from privatisation and then said in committee he would be happy to support our proposals if the general public could apply for shares. When I told him they could, he shut up, never said another word, but still voted against. His party colleague John Taylor was opposed to privatisation, although he was in favour of an interconnector. Unfortunately for him, Walter Crossley, who had been a high-ranking official within NIE on whom ministers had relied for advice, had publicly denounced the interconnector. Ian Paisley's main argument was, 'If it ain't broke, don't try to fix it!' If we followed that doctrine, I pointed out, we would never have replaced the horse with Stevenson's *Rocket*.

Roy Beggs, the official spokesman for the Ulster Unionists on industrial matters, explained that his party wanted to retain NIE in its existing form and structure; yet he accepted that if gas was to be considered for generation, which he advocated, then the gas could only be provided by the private sector. Seamus Mallon of the SDLP said that NIE should have been done away with or should have been restructured in such a way that the defects could have been dealt with. He did not dwell on remedies. Finally, Roger Stott, the Labour front-bench spokesman, told the House in January 1992 that 'if a general election occurs before the Order is fully commenced we shall put a hold on it and reverse it; that is a promise which we will make to the people of Northern Ireland'.

Behind the scenes, Sir Desmond Lorimer and I were locked into a very different debate. The only public undertaking I could give on the forecasts for electricity prices was that they would be no higher after privatisation than if we had done nothing. In reality I knew they would be lower, but once the link had been severed between the highest-cost Great Britain region and Northern Ireland, it was inevitable that the overall gap would grow as the subsidies needed to maintain the link were withdrawn.

There were two separate problems. The previous reliance on oil and coal made generation expensive in comparison with gas. Bringing in gas and the interconnector with Scotland were vital but they were expensive. Moreover the size of an isolated system inevitably added cost. The other big problem was persuading outside private generators to buy into the system. The wretched image of Ulster was always at our shoulders. Any bidder wanted better returns and longer contracts in order to be enticed. We knew that once the new companies bedded down, the savings that could be made on the significant inefficiencies would make the generators highly profitable. Our problem was how to translate that into a benefit for our consumers rather than for the shareholders in British Gas, AES/Tractebel or the management buy-out.

We wrote into the legislation inducements for NIE to reduce energy consumption, whereas the mainland provisions if anything encouraged higher usage. We gave as much power to the regulator as we could but the salient challenge of shorter contracts between the new NIE and the private generators we could not solve. I suggested we maintained the tariff link. The Treasury turned us down flat. If we wanted to keep a subsidy, it would have to be vired across from other budgets. I proposed charging domestic customers slightly more to support large industrial users. The Treasury insisted on transparency.

Within two months of the passing of the order I had gone, but the rows reverberate to this day. In Douglas McIldoon, the regulator, the Northern Ireland consumer has a worthy champion. For once the blame for the discrepancy in charges between Great Britain and the province cannot be laid at the government's door. Gas has now arrived, the interconnector is on the way. The operators are far more efficient and responsive. Old stations have proved to have a longer life than ever contemplated by the old NIE. The villains remain those who wrecked the interconnector with the South, those whose balaclava-ed faces adorned the evening news for decades. It is they who have raised the premium demanded by the prudent investor. It is the people of Northern Ireland who pay the price through their fuel bills.

EPILOGUE

IN APRIL 1992 JOHN MAJOR, to the surprise of many but not to himself, won the general election. Three days later I sat opposite him on the sofa in the upstairs drawing room in No. 10 Downing Street and he told me I was to be Michael Heseltine's deputy at the Department of Trade and Industry. After seventy-nine months in Ulster, my time was up. To be Minister of Trade under Michael Heseltine was a thrilling new opportunity and one that I had long hoped for.

A week into my new post and with my mind still filled with the kaleidoscope of experiences – the drama, the fun and occasionally the frustrations – of the previous six and half years, I wrote my valedictory report as Britain's longest-serving minister in Northern Ireland since the introduction of direct rule:

To the Prime Minister:

The Ulsterman

Far back the shouting Briton in foray,
the sullen Roman with his tramping host,
the fair beard plaited in the Saxon way,
the horned prow torching terror to the coast:

then the dark chaunting Kelt with cup and cross,
the red Scot flying from a brother slain,
the English trooper plowing whin and moss,
the gaunt Scot praying in the thin grey rain.

These stir and mingle, leaping in my blood,
and what I am is only what they were,
if good in much, in that where they were good –
a truculent and irritable heir.

Kelt, Briton, Roman, Saxon, Dane and Scot,
time and this island tied a crazy knot.

John Hewitt

ULSTER, A PERSONAL VIEW

The American quip 'the luck of the Irish' may have been true of those who fled the Famine. It certainly holds no truth for those who stayed behind. From Cromwell to Grattan, from Parnell to Paisley, at every turning-point in Irish history the luck turned sour, the hopes were dashed.

In 1969, it must have seemed that at last the conflict of centuries had petered out. More and more housing estates were integrated, more and more Catholics felt they belonged to the State. More and more mixed marriages, more and more pluralism, less and less sectarianism were the order of the day. A few short weeks in the summer of 1969 put paid to that. Civil rights marchers, Paisley's bullying fundamentalism, the 'B' Specials, soon found a good but weak Prime Minster at Stormont with the flames of insurrection licking around his feet. For twenty years since, the British Government have tried to find a way back to the hopes of early 1969. How close have we come?

Certainly the economic and social fabric of Northern Ireland has changed in recent years out of recognition. Any visitor to Belfast is astonished by the difference between TV image and personal perception. New leisure centres, new shopping centres, new housing, new restaurants, new factories give an air of prosperity to Belfast that it never had in its nineteenth-century heyday.

It is private sector money in the City that is making the running – £600 million either spent or programmed. Shorts have doubled their turnover two years after privatisation. Harland and Wolff's productivity is up 35 per cent in eighteen months. The hope is spreading to the most deprived, the most depressed and forlorn parts of the City. The Making Belfast Work initiative has involved the ordinary folk in the regeneration of their neighbourhoods and brought confidence to their communities.

The 1991 Festival and the Tall Ships race which attracted 500,000 visitors gave all the citizens of Belfast pride in their cultural and industrial history and belief in themselves for their future.

The same changes are taking place in Londonderry and the county towns of Ulster where for the first time councillors are sharing power and working as a team to overcome their social divisions and their economic isolation. Thirteen councils now share committee chairmanships across sectarian lines. Even Belfast City Council, the most disruptive and argumentative, have offered posts to the members of the non-Unionist minority.

Catholics are taking over many more vital economic and industrial levers of power. Gerry Loughran is Permanent Secretary at the Department of Economic Development – the first to hold the post. John B. McGuckian is Chairman of the IDB, the first Catholic big businessman in what has up to now been a Protestant preserve. Pat Dougan, former Managing Director of Powerscreen, has been brought in to save the oldest and most prestigious Protestant manufacturing business in West Belfast – Mackies. The Fair Employment Act has taken the sting out of American-Irish criticism of alleged job discrimination.

In a recent poll of the Nationalist community, 30 per cent voted against a united Ireland, 30 per cent voted for and 40 per cent didn't know. According to one highly respected Catholic priest the 40 per cent knew perfectly well but weren't saying!

Economic and social progress is making it easier for politicians to find ways of accommodating each other's different tribal prejudices. The Anglo-Irish Agreement was a deep shock to the Unionist population but it made them realise that always saying 'no' was not enough and that they could not take Britain's patience and Britain's pocket for granted for ever. Furthermore once it was realised the Irish Government was not pulling at the levers of the State and that it was British Ministers at Westminster who still determined the governance of the Province, doubts and fears eased.

For the Nationalists the Agreement offered a long stop for their criticisms on security policy, discrimination and cultural identity. It undoubtedly helped the credibility of the SDLP who have now four parliamentary seats compared to one in 1985.

The debate over the future of Europe has also focused the minds of Ulster people on their relations with one another. They can now see that their dispute is not unique, that Orthodox Serb hates Catholic Croat (Paisley is an ardent advocate of Serbian nationalism!), that Albanians, Romanians, Sorbs, Moldavians, Turks, Hungarians, Germans are all living as minorities in other people's countries and suffer much greater poverty and discrimination than do the communities in Ulster.

It is also clear that elsewhere in Europe, governments are looking to formularise the 'droit de regard' over the minorities in neighbouring countries which has operated informally for so long and for which the Anglo-Irish Agreement has provided form and machinery.

The Ulster question is a typical European ethnic conflict which will have to be settled under the same principles and policies which apply anywhere else in Europe and the ground rules for which are already laid down in CSCEI. [Conference on Security and Co-operation in Europe which agreed that boundaries of Europe established at the end of the Second World War could not be challenged.]

Those countries that have succeeded in bringing harmony and integration between cultures have only succeeded on the back of constitutional certainty and economic wealth. Switzerland, Karinthia (Alto Adige), the Flemings and Walloons and Schleswig Holstein are examples.

However, economic and social progress coupled with political reconciliation are fragile vessels when confronted by the most vicious and determined terrorist menace in Europe. The IRA raises between £7 and £10 million a year in Northern Ireland through rackets and had been virtually unchecked by the Police and the Government until the establishment of the anti-racket unit, three and a half years ago. Why was this allowed to go on for so long?

The IRA are not a set of 'mindless cowards' as Police, Northern Ireland Office and Government officials so often call them. They are a highly intelligent, well-motivated and an often brave group of national socialists. They are fascists. The IRA Army Council controls Sinn Féin, the political wing, and determines all policy whether social, economic or military. Many members of Sinn Féin are also *de facto* members of the IRA and take their orders from them. The organisation is racist in that it wants all those loyal to Britain out of Ulster, dead or alive. The IRA is heavily involved in racist murders against Protestants. Its power is built on intimidation and violence, kneecapping and kangaroo courts. Its murder threats on any Catholic involved in security work show its determination to ensure the continued alienation of the Catholic people from the Police and the Army.

It treads the same boards that Mussolini trod in Italy in the early 1920s and Hitler in Germany a decade later. It can never be negotiated with until it gives up arms and if it gives up the armed struggle it is finished (2 per cent of the vote of the South and 10 per cent and falling in the North).

The UVF and UDA are mirror images of PIRA and are also fascist. The difference however is they are reactive and would probably cease their attacks if PIRA were to do the same. They do not have the same ideological commitment as PIRA and when peace comes will find it impossible to maintain the same levels of support within their own community. They will still remain as a vicious mini-Mafia which will take patience and resources to stamp out.

The Irish Government is also reactive. It is largely a surrogate for the SDLP and what the SDLP wants it will in the end go along with. If John Hume is happy so is Dublin. Generally Irish Ministers are frightened of the North, ignorant of the North, and while they hanker in their constituencies after some mythical Irish unity, the real chance of integrating a million recalcitrant Protestants into a Catholic population of four million would send them rushing in panic from the table.

Our policy is built on three interlocking strategies: economic and social regeneration, political devolution and the eradication of terrorism.

Although the strategy may be clear it is far less certain that the mechanics for its delivery are in place. At a meeting last month, chaired by the Secretary of State and comprising his Minister, the Permanent Secretary of the Northern Ireland Office, his colleague the Permanent Secretary of the Northern Ireland Civil Service and other senior officials, David Fell, Head of the Northern Ireland Civil Service, made the point that while the three-legged strategy had been in place for several years there was *no* machinery for its co-ordination or delivery! It is interesting that since Direct Rule there has never been an Ulsterman as head of the Northern Ireland Office. Imagine if the English had so treated the Scots!

Attempts to establish a committee to bring together Ministers responsible for security, economic and social and political matters have been deadlocked for nearly two years. My own efforts before Christmas [1991] following the bombings and hoaxes that were destroying trade and confidence in Belfast, to set up a co-ordinating committee for the City involving a representative of the traders, the DOE Roads Division, the Belfast Development Office, the Army and the Police, came to little when the Police refused to attend after the first meeting.

When the RUC did finally return one month and several bombs later, it was for the Assistant Chief Constable in charge of Belfast to inform us that although the Police knew the IRA were testing the City's defences and the bombs had remained undetected, due to restrictions on overtime and manpower problems, cover had been reduced over the New Year and the City Centre devastated!

Lack of co-ordination largely derives from several separate causes:

1. The suffocating secrecy indulged in by the Northern Ireland Office makes open discussion of new ideas and alternatives almost impossible. Security policy is never debated with the Ministers and Permanent Secretaries of the Northern Ireland mainline spending Departments.

2. The Chief Constable is responsible for all operational duties and only receives and takes advice on policy matters from the Northern Ireland Office and from the Police Authority for Northern Ireland. It is not clear where 'operational' duties stop and policy matters begin. Nor is it clear how the responsibilities are divided between the Police Authority and the Northern Ireland Office.

3. Relationships between the Army and the Police vary between divisions, depending on personalities and their chemistry.

4. Because the Army and the Police are cut off from social, economic and political policy, they do not always appear to appreciate how destructive the results of their actions can be in undermining confidence in other Government policies and giving succour to the terrorists.

5. Which Army Units serve in Northern Ireland is a matter for the Secretary of State for Defence; until recently the Secretary of State for Northern Ireland was not even consulted as to which Regiments were sent to the Province. As can be imagined some Regiments' records are more variable than others and their very presence can act as a recruiting agent for the IRA. (This will become even more difficult with the reductions in our land forces.)

6. Seven Security Ministers in seven years has not made for continuity.

The dangers facing the RUC remain horrendous but sometimes they appear unable to think out different ways of looking at the undoubted horrors that daily confront them. Policing in West Belfast does not seem to have changed at all over the last twenty years and while 'no go' areas can never be permitted, there must be some ways of trying out new ideas and involving the ordinary constable more closely with the community in which he is stationed. (I do, of course, appreciate the dangers faced by the RUC. There are a great many very brave, very dedicated and clever men in the force who in my view are often stifled by those above them.) Too often when challenged the RUC come over as defensive, reactive and secretive.

The dilemma facing Government is as follows: the security forces maintain that at present they can only cap the level of terrorism, they cannot defeat it. This, they argue, can only come about through political settlement and economic and social regeneration. But the political and economic policies are frail plants when confronted by the destructive power of the Libyan-backed IRA.

Will it be possible to achieve lasting cross-party devolved Government if the IRA maintain their murderous offensive while the Marines and the Paras patrol the streets of West Belfast and the lanes of South Armagh? Will it be possible to find people jobs and increase investment in the ghettos if the IRA keep blowing up the cities and towns of Ulster? If the strategy is to work it has to succeed at every level and it requires fresh discussion within Government and a preparedness to take risks.

CONCLUSIONS

What needs to be done? Northern Ireland has to come top of the UK political agenda and stay there until the Troubles are over. A lot of the work which needs to be done is being done but it needs support and drive from the very top.

We have come a long way since 1985. I believe the IRA (Sinn Féin) now know they cannot win but they do not know how to lose. They are frightened of schism which has confronted them before. Frightened that if some lay down their arms others will not. Then all will have been in vain. Those who died will have died for nothing, those in the Maze will stay there to rot.

They are increasingly isolated into West Belfast and along the Border. In Derry they have been marginalised. In South Down virtually eliminated. In the last election their vote has continued to decline while the SDLP's is up a further 2 per cent. It will be a great prize to whoever brings peace to Northern Ireland.

It is a startlingly beautiful country of contrasts, populated by clever, hardworking, cultured, witty people. It was said of Irish migration that the best left home. That is not true, the best stayed behind. Many who left want to return. It is up to us to enable them to do so. It is quite unacceptable that parts of our country and our cities live under the constant threat of the bomb, that our people should be kneecapped, murdered and mutilated. We need to end it in order to call ourselves a properly civilised nation at ease with ourselves. We need to end it to show the people of Central Europe that there is a way out for them too. The time has come to end it.

April 1992
[signed] Richard Needham

Much has happened since the spring of 1992. The Prime Minister, John Major, did become much more concerned with Northern Ireland than did his predecessors. When I wrote the prologue to this book two and a half years ago, President Clinton's visit really did seem to be a new beginning. Everything appeared to be looking up, from Mackies' new factory on the Springfield Road to new political initiatives that promised a lasting peace.

Two and a half years later, the future of Mackies appeared as uncertain as the peace process. We once again lived through peaks and troughs of anticipation followed by anguish. After 1992 I was no longer politically responsible for Northern Ireland but it was impossible not to have feelings and opinions, even though I expressed them privately. On 13 February 1996, four days after the shocking explosion in Canary Wharf, I wrote to an Irish-American friend:

Last Friday's bomb has left a sense of desolation. Of course, we knew the IRA might go back to violence. Avoiding division matters more to them than making peace. But we had all experienced after eighteen months what peace delivered. Hope had given way to expectation. Expectation to reality. Reality to action. Now all seems lost. What is most awful was the lack of trust, even of good will, in the Republic.

The mood in Dublin is, I was told, one of anger and not with

Adams and Sinn Féin but with Britain. It is our fault that the IRA are bombing us. We are to blame for the breakdown because following our retreat over the decommissioning of arms we had suggested elections as a way of creating an opportunity for the Unionists also to back down and accept Sinn Féin representatives as negotiating partners.

Where are most of the bombs and explosions stored? Where do the terrorists take refuge? From where are most of the attacks in the North and the mainland planned? And yet it is our Government's mistakes, our desire for party political gain, our insensitivity which is why we are attacked, our people maimed and killed.

I sat in the chamber of the House listening to the East End Labour MPs tell of how their constituents had no windows, no water, no ceilings and no money, how one of those killed was a quiet, shy man respected by all, who stayed on to help an Asian friend in his news agency on a busy evening only for both to be found mutilated and dead two days later.

I saw Pat Dougan at a dinner for the Chinese Trade Minister, Madam Wu Yi. It was a Chinese order which had first saved Mackies. Did anyone in West Belfast, the IRA, know or care? Pat said he had cried when he had heard about the bomb, so had John Patten who was at the same dinner table, so had I. What future for our grandchildren? Maybe some thought it was time for the Brits to pack up and leave.

No, that could not be right. But what was? One usually sensible diner suggested that perhaps the Irish should be told, either stop this hypocrisy or we will stop you. No more free access into our country, every channel by sea or air blocked by endless searches, and endless queues. The Israelis had done it with the Palestinians in Gaza. Perhaps that would bring the Irish to face up. Did they really want a United Ireland? Did they want the responsibility of integrating a million determined British subjects who considered them a bigoted little backwater? Let them be responsible for once. After all in 1921, 18 per cent of the South had been Protestant, now it was less than 3 per cent. We could then blame them for harassing, imprisoning and discriminating against our people. Someone else asked him what would that achieve – nothing but more misery. Protestant Sinn Féin replacing Republican Sinn Féin.

So in the lyrics of the song there is nothing else to do but pick yourself up, dust yourself down and start all over again. The reality is that the Irish are incapable of finding much of the guns and explosives and too often are impotent to bring to justice the murderers that roam along their side of the border.

Stuart Bell, my opposite number both in Northern Ireland and Trade, told me if the Irish did not catch themselves on, the tolerance of the British might finally break and the Irish would for the first time have to abandon the ways of history and confront the dilemma for themselves. Thank goodness for John Major and John Bruton – everything rests with them. Brave and decent men with horrible internal political divisions and minuscule majorities, trying their damnedest to stop another tidal wave of violence and recrimination. Another bloody bomb and Heaven knows what we'd do.

But if Canary Wharf was bad, the July 1996 marching season reached a shambolic and calamitous climax at Drumcree. Two weeks later I wrote again to my American friend:

[Sir Hugh] Annesley and his staff officers must have foreseen the consequences of blocking the Portadown march on July 8th, knowing full well they had only four days to resolve the stand-off with the Orangemen before the Province exploded on the 12th. This was a catastrophe that had at least one year in gestation and one year for finding a solution. Yet nothing appears to have been done to bring in the Church Leaders and the Politicians until it was too late. Even then their advice appears to have been irrelevant, as the RUC U-turn was implemented at about the same time as they were told of the volte face.

Northern Ireland is a place where it is the UNEXPECTED that makes policing so difficult. The expected should never have been allowed to develop in ways which anyone experienced in Ulster's affairs could have foreseen. The aloofness of the Chief Constable was matched by his short-sightedness. If he wished to win at Drumcree he had to know how to win when the Orangemen tested his forces in every other part of Ulster. If he squeezed at Drumcree and the violence escalated elsewhere he must have known that either he would have to back off or face widespread violence.

If he could not win, which any intelligent observer could have told him, he should have invited the communities under his Deputy to find an alternative. But he did not. The NIO, instead of insisting that the political situation demanded a solution, seem to have stood on one side with the Secretary of State [Sir Patrick Mayhew] claiming that it was for the Chief Constable to adjudicate on operational grounds.

It is my view that the most serious failing lay with the Chief Constable after what proved to be a disastrous change of mind. The Secretary of State must also share some of the blame for failing to think through the political consequences of the course of action proposed by the Chief Constable. He must have been advised that what the Chief Constable proposed was unsustainable in the face of 100,000 angry Orangemen. Martin Smyth and Jim Molyneaux told me that they had told Annesley of their fears of violent escalation across the Province if he was determined to stop the Drumcree march. They had been told not to try to intimidate the RUC. It was their duty to control their community!

However as always, the real culprit in this catastrophe is the NIO. Why can they not organise and manage predictable confrontations in a way which brings all those with a part to play into the Office to work on a best way out? I bet that none of the senior NIO Civil Servants who deal with both communities on social and economic matters were ever consulted by the RUC. Yet they are the ones most trusted by community leaders. No attempts that I know of were made to find a solution that bound every part of the NIO into a common strategy to avert violence.

As always, secrecy prevailed. The tunnels in which each department of the NIO operates remained intact and the peace was lost.

In London, at about the same time in 1996, I had bumped into a former GOC whom I had disagreed with over the public relations handling following the contemptible bombings at the Musgrave Park Hospital in which two of his men had died. I asked him what he made of Drumcree. There were three legs to the strategy, he said. He had heard me expand on them often enough. Political development, security curtailment and social and economic advancement. Each one, he believed, was followed independently of the others. There was no cross-referencing of plans and insufficient sharing of information and intelligence. Each programme lived a life of its own.

He gave me an example. He recalled that I had once privately criticised him because, while taking a group of important potential Japanese investors around Castle Court, I had been met at the front door by an enormous soldier, fully armed and camouflaged. He would have frightened Rambo and he certainly scared the Japanese witless. The General explained that he had been asked by the RUC to place him there in case of trouble! 'From the shoppers?' I enquired. 'I don't know,' he replied, 'at that time I had never seen Castle Court.'

The first decision at Drumcree left the Catholic population frightened and unprotected, with their leaders powerless, watching support drift back to Sinn Féin as the Orangemen flexed their muscles. The second decision united the whole nationalist confederation North and South in outrage and disbelief. The Chief Constable's fig-leaf excuse that he did not wish to risk a life is the exact opposite of what had happened. Yet no one accepted any blame. David Trimble blamed the Chief Constable and the IRA. The Chief Constable blamed bad men in both communities. The government wrung its hands in despair, while the Secretary of State told the media not to exaggerate the horror of the situation. Dublin and the SDLP blamed the government. Sinn Féin blamed the Orangemen.

Tom King and Peter Brooke were as bothered as me, although none of us wanted to rock an already leaking boat. I went to see the Prime Minister and told him that what had happened had deeply compromised all his efforts. I had never witnessed such a loss of morale and confidence in either community. 'I'll talk to Patrick,' he responded as the Division Bells sounded for a vote. I did not see much point in talking to one of the problems about the problem. By then the Prime Minister was so circumscribed by both events and the rebels within his own party who were conspiring his downfall, and paradoxically their own, that I sensed there was nothing to be done.

But as so often is the case, the closeness of the edge of the cliff forced everyone backwards. Slowly the most important of all truths about Northern Ireland was beginning to sink in. Nothing of lasting importance could be achieved unless London and Dublin agreed on a common position and stuck to it as much in private as in public. Both strategy and tactics had to be seamless garments worn by both and applauded by Washington.

A change of government in the UK brought a change of mood. The ceasefire was restored and representatives of terror came to the conference room, even though their guns remained at the door. Men and women who had vowed never to exchange a word began talking at each other if not to each other. But it is far from easy to find common cause between undefeated enemies who have detested each other for decades if not centuries.

In February 1997 I gave my last speech in the chamber of the House

327

of Commons. I ended with the following statement:

> If the ceasefire proved anything, it proved that, without violence, the economic border disappears. Londonderry becomes the hub of the north-west. Elderly people move there from Donegal or County Londonderry because of the facilities available in the city. Hospitals in the north-west start to rationalise their differing and overlapping services. Planning, power generation and tourism have no boundaries. When the economic border disappears – there is no police, no army, no customs – social integration is bound to follow. After social and economic integration, political change is bound to come. I do not know what that political change will be, because it may take years. When that change comes, it will be built on mutual respect for the differing traditions and cultures of Ireland's communities, both North and South.

Drumcree '98 has seen the Orangemen faced down, although at the dreadful cost of the lives of three young children. The obscene Omagh massacre has brought security reactions from both governments that would previously have been politically impossible. The island of Ireland has now voted overwhelmingly for a new relationship between North and South. The two governments are working more closely than ever before. But it is finding a new relationship within the North that remains, as always, the key. I am now convinced that there is a far higher probability of achieving a lasting reconciliation between the vast majority of both communities than at any other time in the last thirty years. There is now a light at the end of the tunnel.

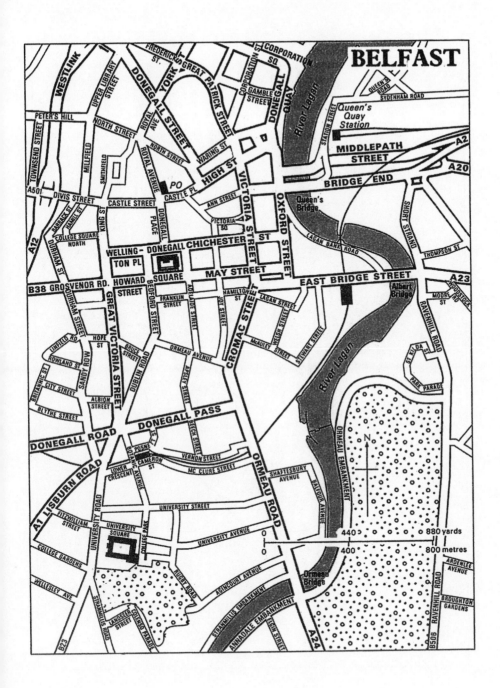

BELFAST

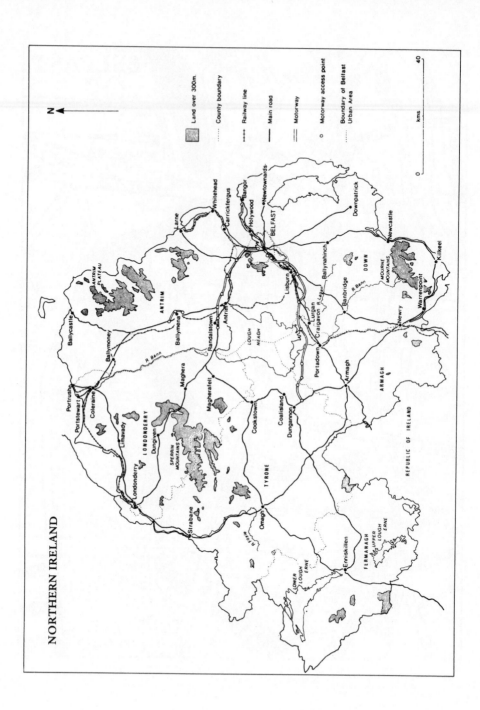

NORTHERN IRELAND

Land over 300m.

County boundary

Railway line

Main road

Motorway

Motorway access point

Boundary of Belfast
Urban Area

N

kms

0   40

Portrush
Portstewart
Coleraine
Ballycastle
Ballymoney
Limavady
Dungiven
Londonderry
LONDONDERRY
Strabane
SPERRIN
MOUNTAINS
R. Foyle
R. Bann
Maghera
Magherafelt
ANTRIM
PLATEAU
ANTRIM
Ballymena
Randalstown
Antrim
Larne
Whitehead
Carrickfergus
Bangor
Newtownards
Hollywood
BELFAST
Lisburn
LOUGH
NEAGH
Cookstown
Coalisland
Dungannon
TYRONE
Omagh
Enniskillen
LOWER
LOUGH
ERNE
UPPER
LOUGH
ERNE
FERMANAGH
Portadown
Craigavon
Lurgan
Ballynahinch
Banbridge
R. Lagan
R. Bann
Armagh
ARMAGH
Newry
Warrenpoint
MOURNE
MOUNTAINS
Newcastle
Kilkeel
DOWN
Downpatrick
REPUBLIC OF IRELAND

INDEX

338